Over the wall we never could see,

Over the wall and away,

Never could guess what a world there might be . . .

<small>Andrew Lang, "Over the Wall"</small>

A FIELD GUIDE TO

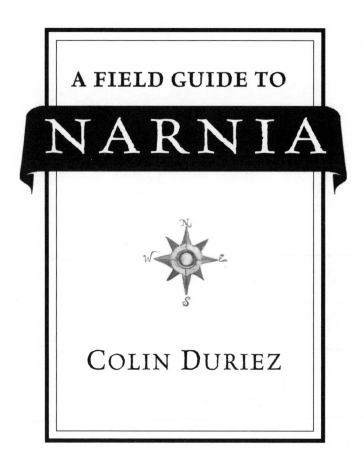

NARNIA

COLIN DURIEZ

InterVarsity Press
Downers Grove, Illinois

TO BEN DURIEZ

InterVarsity Press
P.O. Box 1400, Downers Grove, IL 60515-1426
World Wide Web: www.ivpress.com
E-mail: mail@ivpress.com

InterVarsity Press® is the book-publishing division of InterVarsity Christian Fellowship/USA®, a student movement
active on campus at hundreds of universities, colleges and schools of nursing in the United States of America,
and a member movement of the International Fellowship of Evangelical Students. For information about local
and regional activities, write Public Relations Dept., InterVarsity Christian Fellowship/USA, 6400 Schroeder Rd.,
P.O. Box 7895, Madison, WI 53707-7895, or visit the IVCF website at <www.intervarsity.org>.

Photos on pages 20 and 24 courtesy of Northern Ireland Tourist Board. Photos on pages 32, 33 and 35 courtesy of
the author. Illustration on page 31 courtesy of Kathy Martin.

Design: Cindy Kiple
Illustrations: Liita Forsythe
ISBN 0-8308-3207-6

Printed in the United States of America ∞

Library of Congress Cataloging-in-Publication Data

Duriez, Colin.
  A field guide to Narnia/Colin Duriez.
    p. cm.
  Includes bibliographical references and index.
  ISBN 0-8308-3207-6 (pbk.: alk. paper)
  1. Lewis, C. S. (Clive Staples), 1898-1963. Chronicles of Narnia. 2.
  Children's stories, English—History and criticism. 3. Christian
  fiction, English—History and criticism. 4. Fantasy fiction,
  English—History and criticism. 5. Narnia (Imaginary place) I.
  Title.
  PR6023.E926C5328 2004
  823'.912—dc22

                                                                                2004004355

| P | 20 | 21 | 19 | 18 | 17 | 16 | 15 | 14 | 13 | 12 | 11 | 10 | 9 | 8 | 7 | 6 | 5 | 4 |
| Y | 20 | 19 | 18 | 17 | 16 | 15 | 14 | 13 | 12 | 11 | 10 | 09 | 08 | 07 | 06 | 05 |

Contents

115118

The Wardrobe
Between the Worlds

"I once tried to get through the back of my parents' wardrobe!" It was an embarrassing confession! And the words had barely left my lips before I felt oddly foolish and vulnerable!

My confessor was the late Roger Lancelyn Green. I was in the library of his family home: a room lined with the many books he had written about children's authors, shelved cheek by jowl with books *by* many of those writers whose creations he had chronicled: Lewis Carroll, J. M. Barrie, Andrew Lang and Rudyard Kipling as well several who had been his friends, including J. R. R. Tolkien and C. S. Lewis.

The confession was prompted by reading Lewis's spidery inscription in a first edition of *The Lion, the Witch, and the Wardrobe,* acknowledging that without Roger's enthusiasm and encouragement (at a time when Lewis's closest friend, Tolkien, had proved an unsympathetic critic) Narnia might never have come into being.

Roger's silent response was to lead me into the drawing room and point to a large looking glass in a gilded frame above the mantelpiece. "One day," he said, "after reading *Through the Looking-glass,* I climbed up onto the mantelpiece and tried to follow Alice into Looking-glass House!"

I found this most reassuring! Since that day, I have met many others who have tried to find their way into Narnia either via a wardrobe or—just as I did when the wooden backboard proved unyielding—by simply squeezing their eyes tightly shut and hoping that Aslan would summon them into his world with a mighty roar!

So, what makes some forays into imaginary worlds so compelling that, when young, we are convinced we might also find a way there and, when older, we ache at the memory of that conviction?

It is surely their urgent, immediate and totally accidental nature. Alice, in pursuit of the White Rabbit, rushed headlong down the rabbit hole "never once considering how in the world she was to get out again." Lucy looked into the wardrobe out of little more than idle curiosity and soon found the fur coats transmogrifying into fir trees. One suspects that all those references to leaving the door open ("because she knew that it is very foolish to shut oneself into any wardrobe") were added later on at the insistence of an anxious publisher—perhaps wisely in view of my own experiences!

The choice of a wardrobe, more than any of the later routes from this world into that world, is compelling and unselfconscious: a door that, unlike other doors, leads neither in nor out of a room, but into a room *within* a room and, perhaps therefore, a world within a world . . .

In the more than half a century since the publication of *The Lion, the Witch, and the Wardrobe,* the book (along with the other six volumes of the Chronicles of Narnia) has become a "classic," but without gathering any of the dulling dust of respectability that tends to settle on books that have achieved classic status.

As fresh as the grass that springs up in the newborn Narnia at the bidding of Aslan's creation song, these books can be read (as they are daily read by many) without exposition or explanation—either of the curious alchemy that conjures up a host of disparate beings from myth, legend and folktale spanning half the world and several millennia, or of the mystical weft and warp of the canvas onto which this eclectic and exotic tapestry is woven.

However, since the books *are* now classics and since their creator has become one of the most pondered-over, written-about, analyzed and de-constructed authors of the twentieth century, the more curious reader will find it helpful and instructive to have a reliable guide on hand when exploring the lands that lie "between the lamp-post and the great castle of Cair Paravel on the eastern sea."

One could not wish for a better traveling companion than a preeminent commentator such as Colin Duriez, who combines a richly mined knowledge—sharply focused by wisdom and understanding—of both the world and the *worlds* of C. S. Lewis, and shares it with a passionate but clear-sighted enthusiasm that is as effortless as it is authoritative.

So, before you step into that wardrobe (and remember, "as every sensible person does, that you should never, never shut yourself in a wardrobe") pop *A Field Guide to Narnia* in your pocket and you will, undoubtedly, see that land with new eyes, perhaps even respond to it with a new heart . . .

Brian Sibley

PREFACE

I still remember first reading *The Lion, the Witch, and the Wardrobe.* The bracing air of the snowy wood intensified my exultant feeling of discovering another magical place as I followed Lucy. I already knew the riverbank and the Wild Wood in *The Wind in the Willows.* I had discovered the enchanting undersea cavern in *The Coral Island.* Later I was to discover the Shire, and the larger world of Rivendell and the Misty Mountains, in Tolkien.

The Chronicles of Narnia are classics of children's literature, along with *The Hobbit, Alice's Adventures in Wonderland, The Wind in the Willows,* the stories of E. Nesbit and George MacDonald, J. K. Rowling's tales of Hogwarts School and others. Humphrey Carpenter and Mari Prichard believe that the Chronicles "must be judged the most sustained achievement in fantasy for children by a 20th-cent[ury] author."

His seven stories of Narnia are already, forty years after his death, the most well known and widely read of C. S. Lewis's more than forty writings, and are as characteristic of his thought and imagination as his science-fiction books, his literary criticism and his popular theology, such as *The Screwtape Letters* and *Mere Christianity.*

The Chronicles have become part of the lives of generations of children since the stories first appeared between 1950 and 1956. Parents and teachers over the years also have read them to their children. In the 1980s the British Broadcasting Corporation adapted several of the books for television, and later for radio. *The Lion, the Witch, and the Wardrobe* is being made into a major film, directed by Andrew Adamson, with other Narnian stories to follow.

Some have supposed that Lewis turned to writing children's stories because he had lost confidence in writing books that argued, often philosophically, for the Christian faith. Nothing could be further from the truth. Writing for children is one of the most demanding of an author's tasks. The Narnian tales built on skills that Lewis had honed in writing earlier stories for grownups, such as his science-fiction trilogy. They also built on Lewis's exposure to the ideas and writings of his friend J. R. R. Tolkien, particularly the tales of the Silmarillion and his epic romance, *The Lord of the Rings,* though Tolkien was then unpublished except for *The Hobbit. Romance* for Lewis, as for Tolkien, meant literature that contains glimpses of other worlds, strangely stirring the spirit. Such stories hinted at realities beyond the "walls of the world."

In composing the Chronicles, Lewis found an integration of mind and imagination that allowed a free flow of creativity from his deepest self:

> The imaginative man in me is older, more continuously operative, and in that sense more basic than either the religious writer or the critic. It was he who made me first attempt (with little success) to be a poet. It was he who, in response to the poetry of others, made me a critic, and, in defence of that response, sometimes a critical controversialist. It was he who after my conversion led me to embody my religious belief in symbolical or mythopoeic forms, ranging from *Screwtape* to a kind of theological science-fiction. And it was, of course, he who has brought me, in the last few years to write a series of Narnian stories for children; not asking what chil-

dren want and then endeavouring to adapt myself (this was not needed) but because the fairy-tale was the genre best fitted for what I wanted to say.

Therefore, in reading the stories we are reading not an author who has lost his way but one who has become so convinced of the way that he can effectively point its direction to a very large readership that unself-consciously enjoys storytelling. Story in itself has extraordinary power to make concrete and real what is otherwise abstract and increasingly the domain of specialists. Literary critic Rachel Trickett, who knew Lewis, has observed, "He possessed to an extraordinary degree the freshness of a child's vision—obstinate, opinionated, but always open to new findings. He maintained on principle the importance of tradition and of wise habit in literature and in life, but he was always capable of being surprised and of surprising."

Even before the Narnian stories appeared, Lewis began receiving letters from children to which he always replied. Then, as the tales were published, the number of letters increased and began to include questions about Narnia. Though a bachelor until late in life, Lewis had some experience of children from his student days when he adopted Mrs. Janie Moore as his mother and thus became part of a family that included Maureen Moore, then a young teenager. In the Second World War years, he took in a succession of evacuees, who inspired the beginnings of *The Lion, the Witch, and the Wardrobe*. Later, when he became friends with and later married Joy Davidman, he took on her two young sons, David and Douglas.

Innumerable children in primary schools from New Zealand to Alaska have chewed their pens writing responses to the Narnian stories. Children's author Rosamund Bott remembers being caught up as a child in the world created by Lewis, having her own "Narnian animals." She used her model animals, including a toy lion, in Narnia play. She even carefully placed several bowls of water in her garden and jumped into them in reenactment of the scene in the Wood Between the Worlds in *MN*. The appeal of Narnia to children's imaginations is vividly captured in Katherine Paterson's *Bridge to Terabithia*. This story is about two children, Leslie and Jess, who are inspired to create their own magical kingdom:

> "We need a place," she said, "just for us. It would be so secret that we would never tell anyone in the whole world about it." Jess came swinging back and dragged his feet to stop. . . . "It might be a whole secret country," she continued, "and you and I would be the rulers of it."
>
> Leslie named their secret land Terabithia, and she loaned Jess all of her books about Narnia, so he would know how things went in a magic kingdom—how the animals and the trees must be protected and how a ruler must behave. That was the hard part.

Francis Spufford, in *The Child That Books Built*, evocatively recounts a childhood in which the world of reading takes him away from painful realities, as a drug but also sometimes as a revelation. There was one incident in which a sort of bridge was crossed from the story books into this world:

> I did experiment, sometimes, with bringing Narnia back over the line into this world. I imagined dryads in the woods at Keele, smoothing out their shining hair with birch-bark combs. My friend Bernard and I swapped Narnian trivia and called ourselves Narniologists. I scattered white rose petals in the bathtub, and took a Polaroid picture of the dinghy from my Airfix model of the *Golden Hind* floating among them, to recreate the lily sea. But I never felt I had connected to the live thing in Narnia which could send a jolt through my nerves, except once. I had the poster-map

of Narnia by Pauline Baynes up on the wall on the upstairs landing at home. In the top right-hand-corner, she'd painted Aslan's golden face in a rosette of mane. Once, when no one was around, I crept onto the landing and kissed Aslan's nose in experimental adoration—and then fled, quivering with excited shame, because I had brought something into the real world from story's realm of infinite deniability.

For Lewis, as for Tolkien, all storytelling points to a moment in this real world when "myth" became "fact," when events that normally can only be captured in the imaginative web of an invented story actually take place in the real world. His storytelling about Narnia is therefore firmly integrated into his deepest thinking about the nature of reality, where, in the words of his theologian friend Austin Farrer, Lewis presents "a world haunted by the supernatural, a conscience haunted by the moral absolute, a history haunted by the divine claim of Christ."

My book is based on the premise that the Chronicles of Narnia—and the secondary world of Narnia—represent C. S. Lewis as person and as author in a way unmatched by any of his other writings (which is not of course to diminish his other books). My purpose is to introduce, or remind readers of, the abundance that exists in Lewis's thought and imagination. The integration of these "right" and "left" mental faculties takes the themes Lewis explores in the stories into a whole new dimension. The book is made up of interweaving sections, relating to his life, thought and writing, but with the focus upon the Chronicles.

The debt I owe to others in writing this book is immeasurable, both those with whom I've talked Lewis and those who have written on Narnia. Particularly I am thankful for the late Kathryn Lindskoog's short but definitive *The Lion of Judah in Never-Never Land*, Paul F. Ford's *Companion to Narnia*, Walter Hooper's *Past Watchful Dragons*, Martha S. Sammons's *A Guide Through Narnia*, Clyde S. Kilby's *Images of Salvation in the Fiction of C. S. Lewis,* Brian Sibley's *The Land of Narnia* and Maria Kuteeva's superb unpublished thesis, "C. S. Lewis's Chronicles of Narnia: Their Origins in Mythology, Literature and Scholarship." My thanks also to the Leicester Writers Club, for support, stimulus and friendship, and for the encouragement of other friends, at Saint Luke's and elsewhere, particularly John Gillespie of the University of Ulster, with whom I revisited Dunluce Castle, and Andrea Deri, whose love of the natural world rivals Lewis's. I remember fondly, too, the unfettered delight of Ben and Emilia, when I read them the stories of Narnia as children. Thanks are also due to David C. Downing and Brian Sibley for reading the typescript and to Melanie McQuere for her attentive copyediting, though any errors are, painfully, my own. And of course I'm grateful to my editor, Cindy Bunch, for her inspired guidance and friendship. I have pleasant memories of exploring with her and her colleague Rebecca Vorwerk the Lewis places of Oxford such as Addison's Walk and the pond and woods nearby The Kilns, which almost could be part of Narnia.

Colin Duriez
Leicester, England
November 2003

Abbreviations and Symbols of Reference

Chronicles	The Chronicles of Narnia
HHB	*The Horse and His Boy*
LB	*The Last Battle*
LWW	*The Lion, the Witch, and the Wardrobe*
MN	*The Magician's Nephew*
N.T.	Narnian Time
PC	*Prince Caspian*
SC	*The Silver Chair*
VDT	*The Voyage of the "Dawn Treader"*

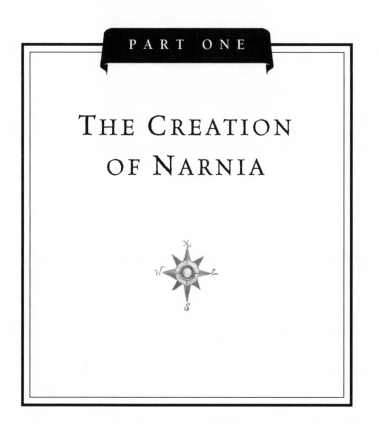

THE CREATION
OF NARNIA

The Life of C. S. Lewis

Dunluce Castle is an imposing ruin that juts out against its Atlantic backdrop. It is built on a basalt outcrop accessible today by a wooden bridge over a stone-built arch. The waves churn and smash a hundred feet below. Among its ruins are the remains of a great hall like the one in Cair Paravel, the seat of kings and queens of Narnia. To the east of Dunluce lies the Giant's Causeway, an apron of hexagonal columns formed when liquid rock spewed into the cold ocean long ago.

Portrush is a nearby coastal resort in the other direction, popular with families of a new middle class a century ago in the north of Ireland. Travelers at that time on the old tramline east from Portrush to the Giant's Causeway could not help but see the castle ruins on their left as they rattled and swayed on their way.

One summer a young boy called Jack or Jacksie Lewis (he had refused his christened name of Clive Staples) was brought with his older brother, Warren, by their mother to see Dunluce Castle. They were staying at an uncrowded resort further west than Portrush, just past the Bann estuary, called Castlerock, considered by C. S. Lewis in later life one of the most beautiful places he knew. Castlerock and the North Antrim coast helped

Dunlace Castle, on the Antrim Coast of Northern Ireland, with Portrush in the distance.

The White Rocks, County Antrim, between Portrush and Dunluce Castle. The Giant's Causeway lies in the distance.

to instill in him his lifelong love of northern lands. He stayed there in the summers of 1901, 1904 and 1906, between the ages of two and seven.

C. S. Lewis was born on November 29, 1898, on the prosperous edge of Belfast in the north of Ireland, the second son of a solicitor and a clergyman's daughter. His father, Albert, was the son of an evangelical Welshman and engineer who had settled in Ireland and had been a partner in a shipping company in the nearby docks. His mother Florence (Flora) was of cultured stock, from County Cork in the south of Ireland. As a growing and precocious child Lewis soon noticed the contrast of their temperaments—Albert was passionate and emotionally unpredictable, while Flora was analytical (she had a first-class degree in logic), sunny and stable; she was the young boy's dependable Atlantis (as Lewis later put it), a great island continent of tranquility soon to sink forever under the waves.

Belfast in 1898 and into the twentieth century was intensely alive as a burgeoning industrial city. At its heart was one of the world's largest shipyards. It had the biggest gantry in the British Isles and launched the largest ship, the *Oceanic* and later the short-lived *Titanic*. As the leading city economy in Ireland, Belfast's prosperity grew, and privileged families like the Lewises prospered with it. By 1905 they were able to move to a larger, untidily constructed house, Little Lea, "almost a major character in my story," Lewis later wrote. The house was bursting with books, lodged into every conceivable space, even the attic. The young Lewis explored

> **The castle of Cair Paravel on its little hill towered up above them; before them were the sands, with rocks and little pools of saltwater, and seaweed, and the smell of the sea and long miles of bluish-green waves breaking for ever and ever on the beach. And oh, the cry of the seagulls! Have you heard it? Can you remember?**

unhindered, savoring books that were (he later said) suitable and unsuitable, but discovering authors connected by a hidden thread, a thread that was to continue to run through his own many writings. From the moment he could read, he gave his allegiance, he tells us, to books in which the horns of elfland could be heard—stories and poetry of romance, that is, carrying tantalizing glimpses of other worlds.

This allegiance was reinforced by the tales told him by his nurse, Lizzie Endicott, rooted, he tells us, in "the peasantry of County Down," the fundamental source in fact of the later land of Narnia. As well as explaining during a snowstorm that "the old woman in the sky was plucking her goose," the nurse told him folk and fairy tales of Ireland. The boy sat enraptured as she recounted stories of leprechauns and pots of buried gold, the sagas of Cuchulain, the champion of Ulster, and of the Daoine Sidh, and stories of the faery people and their immortal worlds, the Isle of Apples and Tír-na-nÓg, the Land of Youth.

> **It flashed upon his mind that he now knew . . . that there really were other worlds and that he himself had been in one of them. At that rate there might be a real Land of Youth somewhere.**

The tale of the pot of gold at the end of the rainbow later was to get the young Lewis brothers into serious trouble with their more prosaic father. Seeing a rainbow while walking near Little Lea, the brothers became certain that its shining arch ended in their garden, precisely in the middle of the path from the gate to the house. Ever persuasive, Lewis convinced Warren that they had to dig there for the crock of gold. As darkness descended, the hole had become substantial, large enough for Albert later, wearing his smart office suit, to stumble into it in the gloom. He furiously accused the boys of creating a booby trap for him, dismissing as lies their explanation about the search for gold.

Into this imaginative world of Lizzie Endicott's storytelling came Lewis's discovery of the early Beatrix Potter books about talking animals, stories like *The Tale of Benjamin Bunny* and *The Tale of Squirrel Nutkin*—the latter the volume that gave him a clear experience of beauty and what he later described as "the Idea of Autumn." This was one of several qualities (like northernness, which he discovered in Scandinavian and Teutonic mythology) that enraptured the young Lewis and that connected with his growing sense of "sweet desire" or inconsolable longing so important in his writings as an adult.

The site on which Little Lea was built had been chosen by Albert and Flora because of its view—the north side of the house looked down over fields to Belfast Lough, with the "long mountain line of the Antrim shore" beyond, the south side to the Holywood Hills, "greener, lower, and nearer" than the Antrim slopes. As the boys grew, they were able to walk and cycle around those Holywood Hills. Here Lewis's lifelong devotion to the countryside of County Down was shaped. From the hills one could see Strangford Lough, gentle undulations of pasture land and woods, and, in the distance, the blue, majestic mountains of Mourne. Looking at these views afforded by the hills today, one seems to be looking southward across Narnia to the mountains of Archenland in the dim distance, the Eastern Ocean to one's left.

During this happy period Lewis, adept with pen and paintbrush, began writing and illustrating a cycle of junior stories about "chivalrous mice and rabbits who rode out in complete mail to kill not giants but cats." These stories, he later observed, were his attempt to bring together his two paramount literary pleasures, which were knights in armor and "dressed animals." In collaboration with Warren, Jack developed the stories into an "Animal-land" with a considerable history, known generically as Boxen. This land of talking animals is strikingly different from the later Narnian Chronicles, being full of a child's view of adult preoc-

County Down, Northern Ireland, with the Mourne Mountains in the distance. This landscape inspired Narnia, with the mountains of Archenland to the south.

cupations and being, in Lewis's words, "prosaic," lacking wonder rather than reflecting his emerging imaginative interests. In fact, in many features, the Boxen stories reflect the social history of early twentieth-century Belfast in its preoccupation with the issues of Home Rule versus Union (independence versus remaining in the United Kingdom) and financial affairs. Some of the dialogue is of interest in revealing Lewis's ear for the speech cadences around him, as in this extract from "The Sailor: A Study, Volume II," about events leading up to a railway strike.

> The foremost villain, who held a lamp, which revealed his fierce and bearded face, exclaimed, "Ah, have done with your talkin' an' pother! Come to something! Do you mean to strike or do you nut?"
>
> "We do," cried a chorus of hoarse voices.
>
> "Aye, an' its right ye are! In the old days, the raily men did what work they liked, & none more. Were they any better than we?"
>
> "No!!" came the chorus.
>
> "No," repeated the speaker, refreshing himself from a heavy jug. "A thousan' times—No! An' we will nut do it, either. This new stashun master, has a wrong noshun. He takes his men fer beasts of the field! An' will we stan' it?"
>
> "No!" thundered the others.
>
> "Then strike! Let him know he cant do without us! Do we mind work?"—the chorus seemed disposed to return an affirmative but the orator continued—"No! But we mind tyranny!!"

At one stage the youthful author made a list of his writings:

Building of the Promenade (a tale)
Man Against Man (a novel)
Town (an essay)
Relief of Murry (a history)
Bunny (a paper)

Home Rule (an essay)
My Life (a journal)

The frequent rain of Ireland's north was an important feature of Lewis's early life. Parental wisdom of the time, edged with fear of tuberculosis, was to keep children indoors during squalls and showers. Warren and his younger brother made good use of their confinements, reading, drawing and writing. A cousin, Claire Clapperton, was three years older than Lewis and a visitor to Little Lea. She recalled much later a significant activity of rainy days. In the house there stood, rocklike, a large oak wardrobe. It had been hand carved and built by their grandfather, Richard Lewis. The wardrobe made a den into which the children climbed. In the dark they would listen silently "while Jacks told us his tales of adventure." Colored by Lewis's later discovery of wardrobes as portals to other worlds in George MacDonald and E. Nesbit, this became the inspiration for Professor Kirke's wardrobe, which provided a gateway into Narnia.

> **"[Lucy's] not being silly at all," said Peter, "she's just making up a story for fun, aren't you, Lu? . . ."**
>
> **"No, Peter, I'm not," she said. "It's—it's a magic wardrobe. There's a wood inside it, and it's snowing, and there's a Faun and a Witch and it's called Narnia; come and see."**

The Lewis family was Church of Ireland (Anglican) and worshiped at nearby Saint Mark's, Dundela, where Lewis had been baptized as an infant. Flora Lewis's father, Thomas Hamilton, was rector of the church, and tears came easily to his eyes as he preached. He and his aristocratic, clever wife lived in a cat-ridden rectory, which was rank with feline stench. In contrast to her husband's shuttered views, Mary Hamilton happily employed Roman Catholic servants and supported Home Rule for Ireland. Albert and Flora had married in the church on August 29, 1894. Through the services, the young Lewis became familiar with the liturgy of *The Book of Common Prayer* and *Hymns Ancient and Modern.* When his mother became seriously ill with cancer, the boy found it natural to pray for her recovery. Even after she died he fervently hoped for a miracle, but the corpse he was forced to view removed this hope. The process of his mother's decline had filled him with fear, not eased by his father's uncontrolled emotions. Lewis's memories of this dark period are captured in Digory's story in *MN.*

Albert Lewis did not realize that, during Flora's decline, he was losing not only his wife but also his sons. In *Surprised by Joy* Lewis observed, "We were coming, my brother and I, to rely more and more exclusively on each other for all that made life bearable; to have confidence only in each other. . . . Everything that had made the house a home had failed us; everything except one another. We drew daily closer together (that was the good result)—two frightened urchins huddled for warmth in a bleak world."

With his mother's death, only sea and islands were left; Atlantis had sunk. Nearly fifty years later Lewis wrote: "All settled happiness, all that was tranquil and reliable, disappeared from my life."

Warren and his brother were together one September evening a matter of weeks after their mother's death as their four-wheeled cab rumbled its way to the quay. Together on the ferry in uncomfortable school clothes they watched the lights of Holy-

> **Digory . . . went softly into his Mother's room.**
> **And there she lay, as he had seen her lie so many other times, propped up on the pillows, with a thin, pale face that would make you cry to look at it. Digory took the Apple of life out of his pocket. . . . The brightness of the Apple threw strange lights on the ceiling. . . . And the smell of the Apple of Youth was as if there was a window in the room that opened on Heaven. . . .**
>
> **"You will eat it, won't you? Please," said Digory.**

wood and Bangor on the side of Belfast Lough slip away astern. Together they traveled the train journey from Fleetwood in Lancashire to Euston Station in London, getting a connection to Watford. Together they endured a regime run by a head teacher falling into insanity, in a school Lewis later dubbed "Belsen," after the infamous Nazi prison camp, an experience that haunted him through life almost as much as his war-time exposure to the trenches of World War One. Warren had already developed survival skills. Each morning the pupils had to declare how many sums they had done, with fearful consequences for lies. Warren announced with complete honesty that he had done five—the fact that they were the same five everyday was never noticed in that failure of a school.

In 1910, when the school was closed down, Lewis moved first to Campbell College, near Little Lea, for half a term, and then to Cherbourg House, a preparatory school in Malvern, Worcestershire. While a pupil at Cherbourg House he abandoned his childhood Christian faith in favor of a philosophical materialism—a view that ultimately was to empty reality for him of distinctive qualities like color, the appeal of a melody, and the particularity and moods of places. For many years thereafter he sought solace in his imaginative life instead. His memories, experiences and literary discoveries became a surrogate religion. It was just as if his materialism brought a spell of winter to his powerful intellectual life. Warren was close by his brother, studying at Malvern College. In an extreme winter during that time they were able to skate together on a frozen stream.

In September 1913 Lewis won a classical scholarship and entered the "Col." All this time he was writing avidly, composing, among other pieces, a poetic tragedy about his favorite Norse gods, entitled "Loki Bound." While back home in April 1914, he came to know a near neighbor who would become a soul mate. This was Arthur Greeves, with whom he carried on an extensive correspondence for the rest of his life. These letters to Arthur give rich insight into Lewis's life and into the development of his thought and imagination. In a sense they make up a more complete autobiography than anywhere else, even *Surprised by Joy: The Shape of My Early Life*. The foundation of the friendship of the two was a common insight into the joy, with its longing, that was the main and constant theme of Lewis's life and writings.

Lewis was never happy until he was finally sent to Great Bookham to study with a private tutor named William T. Kirkpatrick, dubbed by Lewis "The Great Knock" because of his intellectual rigor. Warren observed, "The fact is he should never have been sent to a public school at all. Already, at 14, his intelligence was

Susan ... had never dreamed that a grown-up would talk like the Professor and didn't know what to think.

"Logic!" said the Professor half to himself. "Why don't they teach logic at these schools? There are only three possibilities. Either your sister is telling lies, or she is mad, or she is telling the truth. You know she doesn't tell lies and it is obvious that she is not mad. For the moment then and unless any further evidence turns up, we must assume she is telling the truth."

such that he would have fitted in better among undergraduates than schoolboys; and by his temperament he was bound to be a misfit, a heretic, an object of suspicion within the collective-minded and standardising Public School system." Characteristically, Jack's first article for a school magazine was entitled "Are Athletes Better Than Scholars?"

His private schooling commenced in September 1914 and lasted until April 1917. This was one of the happiest periods of his life, and he later named Professor Digory Kirke of the Narnia stories after his mentor. There is something of the tutor's fierce logic in the Professor.

Not only did Lewis rapidly mature under the stringent rationality of this teacher, but he discovered the beauty of the English countryside. Hitherto England had always suffered in comparison to County Down in his opinion. He also encountered fantasy writers such as William Morris. Full of the discovery of George Macdonald's *Phantastes,* Lewis wrote about its power to Arthur Greeves in 1915: "Of course it is hopeless for me to try to describe it, but when you have followed the hero Anodos along the little stream of the faery wood, have heard about the terrible ash tree . . . and heard the episode of Cosmo, I know you will agree with me." In *Surprised by Joy,* Lewis describes the effect of reading *Phantastes* as "baptising his imagination." It would be several years before his intellect caught up.

The Great War had broken out, and its shadow loomed over Lewis's fervent intellectual curiosity and blissful imaginative discoveries. Warren was already on active duty. Lewis was not old enough to enlist until 1917. He spent his nineteenth birthday on or close by the front line. In spring 1918 Lewis was wounded in action by so-called friendly fire and was eventually discharged after a spell in hospital. During all this time he had been writing poetry and preparing a book of poems, *Spirits in Bondage,* for publication.

At the front he had lost an army friend named "Paddy" Moore, who was almost exactly his age. Before Paddy's death, Lewis had promised that, should anything happen to Paddy, he would take care of his mother and sister. Paddy had made a similar promise about Albert Lewis (presumably if Warren had not survived the war either). Lewis in fact looked after Mrs. Janie "Minto" Moore until her death in 1951, and it is possible that he had an intimate relationship with her up to his conversion to Christian faith, as argued by one biographer, A. N. Wilson. This is also deemed likely by the biographers George Sayer and Walter Hooper. Owen Barfield felt it to be unlikely. There is no conclusive evidence, however, and Lewis's moral beliefs and strong sense of duty make the explanatory story of Mrs. Moore being his adoptive mother plausible. In fact, she did much to heal the loss of Lewis's mother and his inner alienation from his father. Her troublesome personality was more a thorn in the flesh to Warren, particularly later, than it seemed to be to Lewis, who cheerfully washed up, solved domestic crises or ran errands, even when he had many pressing concerns, such as his writing and reading.

From January 1919 until June 1924, Lewis resumed his studies at University College, Oxford, where he received a First in Honour Moderations (Greek and Latin Literature) in 1920, a First in Greats (Philosophy and Ancient History) in 1922, and a First in English in 1923. During this time he was looking after Mrs. Moore and her household, and for a while was totally caught up in the terrifying ordeal of her brother Dr. John Askins's decline into madness and death.

Despite these outstanding academic successes, Lewis felt vulnerable about his future, entertaining nightmarish scenarios (for him) such as entering the civil service. He won a temporary lectureship in philosophy, however, at University College for one year. During this period Magdalen College appointed him, provisionally for five years, as a fellow and tutor in English literature. He was in fact to be a don at Magdalen for nearly thirty years.

Lewis wrote to his father in 1925 describing the rooms he had been given at the college: "My external surroundings are beautiful beyond compare. . . . My big sitting-room looks north and

Illustration of C. S. Lewis

31

The rear of the "New Building" of Magdalen College. From Lewis's rooms here—where he taught, and slept over during working days in term time—he could see over the deer park.

The front of the "New Building," Magdalen College, where C.S. Lewis had his rooms and tutored, and where the Inklings often met on Thursday evenings.

from it I see nothing, not even a gable or spire, to remind me that I am in a town. I look down on a stretch of level grass which passes into a grove of immemorial forest trees." Lewis could now divide his time between the rented house he shared with Mrs. Moore and her daughter, Maureen, and his rooms at the college. During term time he slept over at Magdalen. Lewis's pupils over the Magdalen years would include such figures as the critic Kenneth Tynan, the poet John Betjeman, the literary historian and novelist Harry Blamires, and novelist, academic and poet John Wain.

In the first year of Lewis's post at Magdalen he met Professor J. R. R. Tolkien, recently come to Oxford from Leeds University, who soon became a lifelong friend. They would criticize one another's poetry, drift into theology and philosophy, and pun or talk English department politics. Tolkien soon shared what had been a private world, early tales and poems of his invented mythology of Middle-earth. He also most likely

The grounds of Magdalen College, Oxford.

shared a beautiful verse translation of *Beowulf,* the Early English poem that inspired much of Tolkien's literary philosophy.

Tolkien's deep friendship with C. S. Lewis was of great significance to both men. Tolkien found in Lewis an appreciative audience for his burgeoning stories and poems of Middle-earth, a good deal of which was not published until after Tolkien's death. Without Lewis's encouragement over many years, *The Lord of the Rings* would have never appeared in print. Lewis equally had cause to appreciate Tolkien. His views on myth and imagination, and the relation of both to reality, helped to persuade Lewis (who had not long before been a convinced atheist) of the truth of Christianity. Seeing mind to mind on both imagination and the truth of Christianity was the foundation of their remarkable friendship. The Inklings, the group of literary friends that formed in 1933, grew out of this rapport between Lewis and Tolkien. A. N. Wilson, in his biography *C. S. Lewis,* remarks that, at the very beginning of the association between Lewis and Tolkien, "It must have seemed clear to him at once that Tolkien was a man of literary genius." Tolkien, who lost two of his closest friends in World War One, wrote in 1929: "Friendship with Lewis compensates for much."

Tolkien and Lewis first encountered each other at a meeting of Oxford University English School faculty, convened at Merton College on May 11, 1926. Lewis had been a tutor and lecturer in English for nearly an academic year. Tolkien, for the same period, had held the Chair of Anglo-Saxon—he had returned to Oxford after a stint as reader then professor of English language at Leeds University. Tolkien was slight of build, compared with the thickset and taller Lewis, and, in Lewis's view, rather opinionated. In his diary that night Lewis noted: "Nor harm in him: only needs a smack or so."

Tolkien was a Roman Catholic, with a deep emotional attachment to his faith, connected to the early death of his talented mother. Lewis was

Addison's Walk, in the grounds of Magdalen College, Oxford, where, one night in 1931, J.R.R. Tolkien and "Hugo" Dyson helped to persuade C. S. Lewis of the truth of the Christian Gospels.

Magdalen College, Oxford, from Addison's Walk. C. S. Lewis taught here for nearly thirty years.

still an atheist, committed to a materialist explanation of life and of the origins of human language, though there were some chinks in his armor, which Tolkien started to notice as the friendship developed.

Tolkien began trying to convince his friend of the truth of Christian faith, culminating in a long night of conversation in September 1931, when, aided by H. V. D. "Hugo" Dyson, he argued that the Gospels have a satisfying imaginative as well as intellectual appeal, demanding a response from the whole person. (Dyson was later to join the Inklings.) As they passed down Addison's Walk, in the grounds of Magdalen College, Tolkien accused Lewis of an imaginative failure in not accepting their reality. Warren Lewis portrayed Dyson as "a man who gives the impression of being made of quick silver: he pours himself into a room on a cataract of words and gestures, and you are caught up in the stream—but after the first plunge, it is exhilarating." Dyson undoubtedly gave emotional support to Tolkien's measured reasoning.

An enormously important factor in Lewis's conversion to Christianity was accepting Tolkien's argument that the biblical Gospels have all the best qualities of pagan myth, with the unique feature that the events actually happened in documented history. Lewis was fascinated that Tolkien, unlike modernist scholars like Sir James Frazer, did not divorce myth from history.

Lewis later recapitulated Tolkien's argument in his essay "Myth Became Fact":

The heart of Christianity is a myth which is also a fact. The old myth of the Dying God, *without ceasing to be myth,* comes down from the heaven of legend and imagination to the earth of history. It *happens*—at a particular date, in a particular place, followed by definable historical consequences. We pass from a Balder or an Osiris, dying nobly nobody knows when or where, to a historical Person crucified (it is all in order) *under Pontius Pilate.* By becoming

fact it does not cease to be myth: that is the miracle. . . . To be truly
Christian we must both assent to the historical fact and also receive
the myth (fact though it has become) with the same imaginative
embrace which we accord to all myths.

Tolkien argued that the very historical events of the Gospel narratives are
shaped by God, the master story-maker. They have a structure of a sudden turn from catastrophe to the most satisfying of all happy endings,
the "eucatastrophe" (literally, "good catastrophe")—a structure, Tolkien
believed, shared with many of the best human stories. The Gospels, in
their divine source, thus penetrate the seamless web of human storytelling, clarifying and perfecting the insights that God in his grace has allowed to the human imagination. In the Gospels, Tolkien concludes, "art
has been verified."

A few days after the long night of conversation, Lewis capitulated and
became a Christian believer. So there was, Lewis suddenly saw, a fully
historical story that contained the "Deeper Magic" of the stories he had
loved from childhood, yet a story like no other. His discovery resounds
in the beautiful story Lucy finds in the magician's book on the Island of
Voices in Narnia.

As she read Lucy came across a spell intended to refresh the spirit.
There were more words in this part than earlier in the book, but the pic-
tures were of great beauty. The spell in fact read more like a story, and
Lucy soon forgot that she was reading at all.

Lewis owed an enormous debt to Tolkien in pointing him to Christian
faith. The stabs of joy and haunting stories that had teased his attention
were now sharply focused on a definite person in an actual time and
place. After this, Lewis was an incorrigible realist, concerned with daily
choices and experiences that, he perceived, bring us slowly closer to
heaven, or hell. After his conversion, he gradually emerged as the unique
and perhaps unparalleled Christian communicator we know—writing

She was living in the story as if it was real, and all the pictures were real too. When she had ... come to the end, she said, "This is the loveliest story I've ever read or shall ever read in my whole life.... I did so want to read it again. Well, at least I must remember it. Let's see ... it was about ... about ... oh dear, it's all fading away again.... This is a very strange book. How can I have forgotten?

"It was about a cup and a sword and a tree and a green hill. I know that much. But I can't remember, and what shall I do?"

And she never could remember; and ever since that day, what Lucy means by a good story is a story which reminds her of the forgotten story in the Magician's Book.

fiction full of enduring images of God, our humanity, and reality transfigured by the light of heaven, and imaginative prose that has persuaded numerous people throughout the world of the truth of the Christian claims. His basic strategy for defending the faith to contemporary people was born in those persistent arguments of Tolkien, in which imagination and reason are reconciled, and in which storytelling is at the center.

The movement of Lewis's thinking at this time, as he gradually moved to belief in a God and then acceptance of the Christian faith, is vividly captured in his later book *Miracles* (1947). He confessed: "I never had the experience of looking for God. It was the other way round; He was the hunter (or so it seemed to me) and I was the deer. He stalked me like a redskin, took unerring aim, and fired. And I am very thankful that that is how the first (conscious) meeting occurred. It forearms one against subsequent fears that the whole thing was only wish fulfilment. Something one didn't wish for can hardly be that." In taking the initial step of accepting the existence of a God who was the person behind the creation of the universe, Lewis had the curious sensation of being presented, paradoxically, with the choice that he had to take—it was as if he were shedding uncomfortable clothes or passing through a door. He in fact later pictured it as the ripping off his very skin, in the story of how Eustace is "undragoned" by Aslan.

Recounting the event afterwards, Eustace confessed that, though he had become a dragon, he was afraid of the smaller animal. When the lion said that he would have to let himself be undressed, Eustace was fearful of his claws. But the boy who was now a dragon agreed out of desperation.

Not long after his conversion, Lewis brought out an allegory, echoing John Bunyan, called *The Pilgrim's Regress*. Though widened by the allegory, this set out Lewis's passage from atheism to Christian faith. It is also a brilliant satire on and map of the intellectual life of his day. The book reflects Lewis's scholarly interest in allegory.

> **"The very first tear he made was so deep that I thought it had gone right into my heart. And when he began pulling the skin off, it hurt worse than anything I've ever felt. The only thing that made me able to bear it was just the pleasure of feeling the stuff peel off.... Then he caught hold of me—I didn't like that much for I was very tender underneath now that I'd no skin on—and threw me in the water. It smarted like anything but only for a moment. After that it became perfectly delicious and ... I started swimming and splashing.... I'd turned into a boy again."**

During this conversion crisis that entirely changed the direction of Lewis's life, he was working on a book about the tradition of love in medieval and renaissance English literature. *The Allegory of Love* was not published until 1936. Lewis's studies for his book on the tradition of courtly love also greatly influenced his life. This mainly happened in two ways. First of all, through them Lewis came to believe that the idea of romantic love in literature only begins around the eleventh century. Before that, literature is preoccupied with such ideals as friendship and brotherhood, courage in war, loyalty, generosity, and being prepared for heaven. Thus Lewis's own ideal of masculine friendship was reinforced. Second, his studies in allegory gave him a deep insight—a key—into the whole medieval view of reality.

His growing knowledge of medieval reality spilled over into a series of brilliant lectures that he continued to develop. These were eventually published after Lewis's death as *The Discarded Image*. This insight inspired the technical framework of his popular science-fiction trilogy. In later years it was to give body to the enchanted world of Narnia.

The first volume of this trilogy, *Out of the Silent Planet* (1938), imaginatively recreates the medieval cosmos. In Deep Heaven, the planets are guided by intelligences, or Oyarsa, who, with the exception of the one concerned with Earth, are obedient to Maleldil. Our planet is the Silent Planet, *Thulcandra,* because it is cut off from the courtesy and harmony of Deep Heaven. Lewis was dismayed with the science fiction of his time, which usually portrayed extraterrestrial beings as evil and as the enemies of humanity.

Might it not be, reasoned Lewis, that humankind would inflict its wickedness on good creatures in space? This happens in Lewis's science fiction. In Lewis's trilogy, as in the medieval cosmos, only Earth is "bent" and ruled by a dark Oyarsa, the Bent One. Half-humorously, Lewis complained to a correspondent, his friend Sister Penelope, an Anglican nun, in 1939: "You will be both grieved and amused to hear that out of about 60 reviews [of *Out of the Silent Planet*] only 2 showed any knowledge that my idea of the fall of the Bent One was anything but an invention of my own. . . . Any amount of theology can now be smuggled into people's minds under cover of romance without their knowing it." Lewis had learned a valuable lesson, which he would later apply to writing the Narnia stories. Then, as with the science-fiction stories, his prime concerns were fidelity to the genre (in this case, children's literature) and keeping the story as the focus. The theology came naturally, as it had affinity with genres that dwelled on other worlds and with storytelling in general, just as Tolkien had shown him. This is beautifully illustrated in Lucy's recognition that Aslan is more important even than Narnia.

Lucy, Edmund and Eustace have arrived at the World's End, near Aslan's Country, where they encounter Aslan first as a lamb and then in his familiar shape. Aslan gently breaks the news to Lucy and her brother that they can never again return to Narnia, as they are now too old. In the future the way into his Country lies from their world, not from Narnia.

Several years before the first science-fiction story was written, a remarkable group of friends began to meet. On almost any Tuesday morning for thirty years this group of writers and friends, many of them Oxford dons, could be observed congregating in a snug room in the Eagle and Child public house, near the city center, or sometimes in other pubs. Among thick tobacco smoke, tables laden with beer or cider mugs, they discussed subjects (often loudly, and always wittily) that would include theology and books, poetry and stories, and issues as diverse as whether or not dogs have souls or the perils of transferring stories to film. Two of the group's members, Lewis and Tolkien, were honing ideas that were in later years to capture a vast audience across the globe. Like them, most in the group were Christians, committed to an orthodox expression of faith owing much to a cloud of witnesses that

> **"It isn't Narnia, you know,"** sobbed Lucy. **"It's *you*. We shan't meet you there. And how can we live, never meeting you?"**
>
> **"But you shall meet me, dear one,"** said Aslan.
>
> **"Are—are you there too, Sir?"** said Edmund.
>
> **"I am,"** said Aslan. **"But there I have another name. You must learn to know me by that name."**

The Inn sign that C. S. Lewis and the Inklings knew from The Eagle and Child Pub, St. Giles, Oxford. The Inklings often met here on Tuesday mornings, and later, on Mondays. This old sign now hangs in The Kilns, C. S. Lewis's Oxford home near Headington, which has been restored.

included G. K. Chesterton, John Bunyan, Saint Augustine, George Herbert, Arthur Balfour and John Henry Newman.

The same group also met once a week each term for over fifteen years in Lewis's rooms in Magdalen College, and occasionally in Tolkien's rooms at Exeter, with a specifically literary purpose. They read to each other for pleasure and criticism pieces they were writing, and usually enjoyed a good Thursday evening of "the cut and parry of prolonged, fierce, masculine argument." The Inklings embodied Lewis's ideals of life and pleasure. The literary group of friends orbited around his zest and enthusiasm. Tolkien, also a central figure in the Inklings, cast them fictionally in his unfinished "The Notion Club Papers." Their important years as a literary group were from around 1933 to about 1949. Charles Williams, another member, wrote poetry, novels, plays, literary criticism and imaginative theology. He powerfully influenced Lewis, though Tolkien was not so taken with him. When Williams suddenly died in 1945 undergoing routine surgery, it became obvious to all that the Inklings could never be the same again. Warren Lewis recalled "his thin form in his blue suit, opening his cigarette box with trembling hands." His death felt to Warren horribly unfair.

Other key members of the informal group making up the Inklings included Lewis's brother Warren, Owen Barfield (a brilliant thinker, follower of Rudolf Steiner's mystical anthroposophy, and author of *Poetic Diction,* a key book in Lewis's and Tolkien's thinking), Hugo Dyson and others. It is generally agreed by scholars that the four key members were Lewis, Tolkien, Williams and Barfield. Williams began regularly attending meetings when he was evacuated to Oxford from the London office of the Oxford University Press at the outbreak of World War Two. But there were other evacuees that also made an enormous impact on Lewis.

Days before the outbreak of war, one and a half million city children were dispersed around the country. The evacuation began at 5:30 a.m. on August 30, 1939. There were no illusions about Hitler's intentions. A first group of evacuees was assigned to The Kilns, the house shared by Lewis, his brother, Mrs. Moore and her daughter Maureen. Many more would stay there over the war years, including a six-month-old baby. Lewis was impressed by the children, though baffled by their inability to amuse themselves. They gave him an idea for a book for children, writing

This book is about four children whose names were Ann, Martin, Rose and Peter. But it is most about Peter who was the youngest. They all had to go away from London suddenly because of Air

Raids, and because Father, who was in the Army, had gone off to the War and Mother was doing some kind of war work. They were sent to stay with a kind of relation of Mother's who was a very old Professor who lived all by himself in the country.

The story was soon abandoned and, as often happened with abortive stories, was slipped by Lewis into a drawer and forgotten. It was not until almost ten years later, in 1949, that Lewis took up the idea again, and *The Lion, the Witch, and the Wardrobe* was born. In this, the first of the Narnia stories, four evacuees staying with a bachelor professor in the country enter a magical world of talking animals through an old wardrobe.

The war years established C. S. Lewis as a household name for communicating Christian faith in a popular style. He made righteousness readable, as one reviewer put it, with his *The Screwtape Letters, The Problem of Pain, The Great Divorce, Miracles* and slim booklets of his enormously successful broadcast talks on BBC radio (gathered together later as *Mere Christianity*). Lewis knew that his close friend, Tolkien, disapproved of his lay theologizing—he thought it should be left to the experts. Lewis also sensed that the deepest person within him—what he dubbed "the imaginative man"—was only partly engaged. When he began writing his first Narnian story, that deeper self took over, as it had when writing the science-fiction stories. "Sometimes," he wrote many years later, "fairy stories may say best what's to be said."

Some people think that I began by asking myself how I could say something about Christianity to children; then fixed on the fairy tale as an instrument; then collected information about child psychology and decided what age-group I'd write for; then drew up a list of basic Christian truths and hammered out "allegories" to embody them. This is all pure moonshine. I couldn't write in that way at all. Everything began with images; a faun carrying an umbrella, a queen on a sledge, a magnificent lion. At first there wasn't even anything Christian about them; that element pushed itself in of its own accord.

A professional theologian made an astute observation about Lewis's popular theology before the Narnia stories were born, an observation that now appears prophetic. On June 28, 1946, Lewis was awarded an honorary doctorate in divinity at the University of Saint Andrews. At the ceremony his promoter, Professor D. M. Bailley, pronounced: "With his pen and with his voice on the radio Mr. Lewis has succeeded in capturing the attention of many who will not readily listen to professional theologians, and has taught them many lessons concerning the deep things of God. . . . In recent years Mr. Lewis has arranged a new kind of marriage between theological reflection and poetic imagination, and this fruitful union is now producing works which are difficult to classify in any literary genre."

In 1949 Lewis began to read aloud to Tolkien from his manuscript of *The Lion, the Witch, and the Wardrobe* (the friends often read to each other from their work outside of the Inklings meetings). Later Lewis read part of it to Roger Lancelyn Green, whom Lewis had befriended not long before as a postgraduate and drawn into the Inklings. He told Green about how Tolkien had disliked the Narnia story intensely and asked his own opinion of the work. Green was resoundingly positive. Indeed a story of his (never published) had influenced elements of the story. Tolkien retorted later to Green, on discovering he was reading the manuscript, "It really won't do, you know! I mean to say: 'Nymphs and their Ways, the Love-Life of a Faun.' Doesn't he know what he's talking about?" Tolkien wrote in 1964, after Lewis's death, "It is sad that 'Narnia' and all that part of C. S. L.'s work should remain outside the range of my sympathy." Tolkien's reaction was complex, reflecting a differing approach to his art, a dislike of allegory, and perhaps a strong feeling that fairy tales should be written for grownups, not children. For too long, such stories had wrongly been associated with children. Unlike Tolkien, Green continued to encourage Lewis with his writing about Narnia, reading and commenting on most of Lewis's handwritten scripts. In fact, while listening to Lewis reading from the early chapters of *The Lion, the Witch, and the Wardrobe,* a feeling of awe had stolen over him. Green, who had recently published a study of children's literature, felt that he was listening to one of the great children's stories of the world—it was as if he were listening to Kenneth Grahame reading an unpublished *The Wind in the Willows.*

Lewis had been liberated to write the first story when suddenly "Aslan came bounding into it. . . . Once He was there He pulled the whole story together, and soon He pulled the six other Narnian stories in after Him."

The "prequel" to that first book, eventually titled *The Magician's Nephew,* didn't come easily. Lewis needed to explore and to some extent explain his "supposal" of a land of talking animals, ruled by a divine king of beasts, into which humans (Sons of Adam and Daughters of Eve) could come through portals or be called from their world. What was the origin of Narnia? How come there was a lantern in the woods to the far west? *The Magician's Nephew* was in fact eventually to be the sixth, not the second, Narnian tale that he wrote. He did start an immediate predecessor to *LWW,* "The LeFay Fragment," but soon abandoned it, one reason being that the magic was in this rather than in another world. It is an intriguing fragment, hauntingly evoking the original fall of humanity. Digory has the gift of understanding the speech of trees and animals but loses it forever when he cuts off a branch of his favorite oak tree to impress Polly. Digory is bereft when he discovers the truth: "The only life he had ever known was a life in which you could talk to animals and trees. If that was to come to an end the world would be so different for him that he would be a complete stranger in it."

The Lion, the Witch, and the Wardrobe appeared in 1950. Lewis had completed *Prince Caspian* by the end of 1949, *The Voyage of the "Dawn Treader"* soon after, and *The Horse and His Boy* by summer the next year. Within a few months he had written most of *The Silver Chair.* He then returned to the origins of Narnia, completing about three quarters of *The Magician's Nephew.* Roger Lancelyn Green, to whom Lewis was showing all the writing, pointed out a structural problem, and Lewis left the writing for a while. In the meantime he was taken up with work on his huge volume *English Literature in the Sixteenth Century,* a period that he particularly loved and that he drew upon in creating the world of Narnia. He then turned to writing *The Last Battle,* leaving aside the problems of *The Magician's Nephew* for the time being, finishing it in the spring of 1953. After this, Lewis completed *The Magician's Nephew,* which Green heartily endorsed in February 1954, noting in his diary: "It seems the best of the lot. . . . It's a single unity now, and irresistibly gripping and compelling." *The Last Battle* was scheduled as the last book to be published, appearing in 1956. It won the prestigious literary award, the Carnegie Medal, in recognition of the whole series. Lewis appears not to have read to the Inklings from any of the manuscripts, perhaps because of Tolkien's sharply negative reaction and, in any case, the Inklings ceased to function as a reading club from October 1949. This meant that the series failed to benefit from the comments of its members, unlike *The Lord of the Rings,* much of which was read to the Inklings as it was being written. Green took over the role that Tolkien and the Inklings might have provided.

In 1954 Lewis accepted the newly created Chair of Medieval and Renaissance Literature at Cambridge University, after heavy persuasion by Tolkien, who was one of the electors. In his colorful inaugural lecture, Lewis expounded a theme central to their friendship and affinity—that the rise of modernism, socially and culturally expressed in the creation of "the Age of the Machine," was an unprecedented fracture in Western civilization. Both friends sought in their work, particularly in *The Lord of the Rings* and the Chronicles, to rehabilitate the "Old Western" values that Lewis spoke of in this lecture. In the Chronicles it is the values of Old Narnia that are in danger of being lost.

The move meant that Lewis lived a few days a week in Cambridge during the term, commuting from The Kilns. This necessitated the Inklings meeting Monday rather than Tuesday mornings at The Eagle and Child.

An even more important change than the move to Cambridge was taking shape in Lewis's life. On January 10, 1950, Lewis had received a letter from a thirty-four-year-old American writer, Joy Davidman Gresham. This in itself was not unusual. Lewis had a large daily postbag, many of his letters from women, and he conscientiously replied to letters, generating even more mail. But Joy Davidman's correspondence stood out.

> **"Hush!" said Doctor Cornelius ... "Not a word more. Don't you know your Nurse was sent away for telling you about Old Narnia? The King doesn't like it. If he found me telling you secrets, you'd be whipped and I should have my head cut off."**

Joy Davidman was a poet and novelist, and also later published a theological study of the Ten Commandments, *Smoke on the Mountain*. Lewis's attraction to the New Yorker was at first merely intellectual, that of friendship. She was a brilliant Jew about to divorce, with two young sons, David and Douglas. Joy had been converted from Marxism to Christianity partly through reading Lewis.

A short time after meeting Lewis, Joy Davidman came to live in Oxford with her sons. Douglas Gresham's initial impression of meeting the maker of Narnia was one of disappointment. He seemed an old man to the boy, with a slight stoop and a receding hairline, though he soon grew to appreciate the man who had befriended his mother. Joy and Lewis gradually grew quite close. In retrospect Lewis wrote, "Her mind was lithe and quick and muscular as a leopard. Passion, tenderness, and pain were all equally unable to disarm it. It scented the first whiff of cant or slush; then sprang, and knocked you over before you knew what was happening." They married in a civil ceremony to give her British nationality in April 1956 so that she could stay in England.

In the autumn of 1956 they learned that Joy had terminal cancer. It was sudden, unexpected news, and Lewis was deeply shocked. Cancer was an old acquaintance. Her two boys were about the same age as the Lewis brothers were when their mother died; the parallels were uncomfortable. A bedside Christian wedding ceremony took place on March 21, 1957. Joy came home to The Kilns to die.

After prayer for healing, she had an unexpected reprieve. By July she was well enough to get out and about. She started smartening up The Kilns, known to friends as "The Midden," and also turned her attention to Lewis's attire. As The Kilns became more tidy, Lewis became neater in dress. Warren, who expected to move out of The Kilns, found himself made fully welcome by Joy, whom he held in deep affection. The next year Joy and Lewis had a fortnight's holiday in Ireland. The remission was the beginning of the happiest few years of both their lives. Lewis confessed to his Inkling friend Nevill Coghill: "I never expected to have, in my sixties, the happiness that passed me by in my twenties."

Lewis's brother, Warren, observed that the marriage fulfilled "a whole dimension to his nature that had previously been starved and thwarted." It also demolished a bachelor's doubt that God was an invented substitute for love. "For those few years H[elen Joy] and I feasted on love," he recalled in *A Grief Observed,* "every mode of it—solemn and merry, romantic and realistic, sometimes as dramatic as a thunderstorm, sometimes as comfortable and unemphatic as putting on your soft slippers."

Then Aslan turned to them and said ... "All of you are—as you used to call it in the Shadowlands—dead.
The term is over: the holidays have begun. The dream is ended: this is the morning." ...

For us this is the end of all the stories, and we can truly say that they all lived happily ever after. But for them it was only the beginning of the real story. All their life in this world and all their adventures in Narnia had only been the cover and the title page: now at last they were beginning Chapter One of the Great Story which no one on earth has read: which goes on for ever: in which every chapter is better than the one before.

In the summer of 1959 they returned to Ireland for a holiday in County Down, the area of earth that Lewis regarded as closest to heaven and that he embodied in the land of Narnia. But in October Lewis wrote to a correspondent: "The wonderful recovery Joy made in 1957 was only a reprieve, not a pardon. The last X-ray check reveals cancerous spots returning in many of her bones. . . . We are in retreat. The tide has turned." They decided, however, not to postpone a holiday planned for the next year.

The Lewises were able to have a trip to Greece in the spring of the year of her death, a journey much desired by both of them. They holidayed with Roger Lancelyn Green and his wife, June. The happiness that had come to Lewis so late in life, and subsequent bitter bereavement, has been made into two successful films and a play based on a similar script by William Nicolson and entitled *Shadowlands*. The earliest, for the BBC, is the closest to reality. The dramatic license used in all versions has created much debate, but they each are extraordinarily poignant. Many in their audiences have been inspired to read Lewis for the first time.

When Joy died in July 1960 at the age of forty-five, Lewis never really got over the loss, and his grief was combined with constant worry about his unassuming brother's alcoholism. The last book Lewis saw to press, *Letters to Malcolm: Chiefly on Prayer* (1964), affirmed his hope in heaven, now a place he associated with Joy. After a sustained alcoholic bout, during which his brother's near-fatal heart attack went unnoticed, Warren returned to The Kilns in September 1963, and thus the two brothers were together once again during Lewis's final weeks, throughout which he remained lucid, despite his bodily system gradually failing, his bloodstream filling with toxins. It was like the old days long ago when, as boys, they skillfully savored the holidays after the school term had ended. Lewis died on November 22, a week before what would have been his sixty-fifth birthday.

Lewis's grave is in the yard of Holy Trinity Church in Headington Quarry, Oxford. Warren Lewis died nearly ten years later on April 9, 1973, and was interred with his brother and friend. Their names are on a single stone bearing the inscription "Men must endure their going hence." Warnie had recorded the significance of that saying in his diary: "There was a Shakespearean calendar hanging on the wall of the room where she [our mother] died, and my father preserved for the rest of his life the leaf for that day, with its quotation."

The Background to
the Chronicles of Narnia

In Narnia children escaping a modern European war encounter a faun, a dwarf, a Snow Queen who is not even of that world, centaurs, a big bad wolf, talking beavers, a giant, dryads, naiads, a unicorn, a huge lion who made the land, and even Father Christmas, complete with gifts.

The Chronicles of Narnia have as their background an older world that is not dominated by machines and modern weapons. In C. S. Lewis's view, this is in fact a vast period, from classical times, through the rise of Christianity and the christianizing of the West, up to early in the nineteenth century. The Chronicles in particular draw inspiration from the Middle Ages and the Renaissance, most especially the sixteenth century. This is why Narnia is inhabited by imagined creatures from throughout this vast period—from Roman Bacchus to European Father Christmas. Classical naiads and dryads hobnob with chivalrous talking mice.

C. S. Lewis believed that we live today in a world that is fractured from this older world by what he called a Great Divide, which ushered in the Age of the Machine. Our new age is dominated by a persistent idea of progress, in which the past is superseded. The newer (even if this is a new moral attitude) is automatically, no question, superior to the older. By a singular inversion, we now place God in the dock, and find him wanting, instead of seeing ourselves as under God's judgment.

Lewis was particularly inspired by the literature, particularly the stories, of this older world. He was one of the most widely read people of his generation, so it would be an enormous task to trace even the most significant stories and books that provide a background to Narnia. Consequently, a select few are mentioned below to give a taste of this rich universe of discourse. Lewis hoped, however, that a love for his Narnian tales would encourage a recognition and exploration of the books, stories and attitudes of this older world.

It was not that Lewis was advocating a return to the social ways of the past, such as rule by monarch or emperor rather than government by democracy. He also was not against modern science, which in fact had its birth in a period still shaped by a century he loved, the sixteenth. Rather, he felt that this vast older world embodies a remarkably consistent wisdom about the nature of our very humanity. He used the ancient term, the *Tao* (borrowed from Eastern thought), to name the way of life of these values.

Lewis was concerned that the dominant worldviews of his twentieth century propagated values that would lead inevitably to the "abolition of man" (the title of a philosophical tract that he wrote on modern education). His disquiet was reinforced, as it was for many other thinkers, by the unprecedented savagery of the new world, in which unimaginable millions died under ideologies of the Right and Left. He even mapped the perils of contemporary thought in his *"Mappa Mundi,"* the geography of which featured in his allegory, *The Pilgrim's Regress* (1933).

Like his close friend J. R. R. Tolkien and with the backing of their informal literary club, the Inklings, Lewis wrote his stories, including the Chronicles, as part of a strategy to rehabilitate these essential human values. It was natural for him to draw on the imaginative resources and symbolic languages of this earlier, premodernist period. The stories and symbols of this vast and coherent period of history, he believed, articulated these values and attitudes in a splendid way, from Plato and Homer to Jane Austen and William Wordsworth. Lewis and his friends saw the future of the contemporary Western world as exceedingly bleak without these values.

Lewis's approach was eclectic (a characteristic of an older poet he loved, Edmund Spenser); he drew willy-nilly on the images and stories of the whole of the "Old West." His friend and fellow strategist, Tolkien, had interests that were more focused on the Early English period of literature and northern mythology, but his aims were similar—to encourage contemporary people to appropriate this important older history for themselves, taking it into their contemporary lives instead of simply absorbing the narrow myths and presuppositions of modernism. Lewis (and Tolkien) wished to open a door that would awaken desires and allow the experience of sensations yet unknown, pointing to a reality beyond "the walls of the world."

Lewis saw this older period of the West as having a feature rejected by many modern poets and critics—that of stock responses, a kind of decorum of the imagination. This feature was true of literature and art from earliest antiquity until quite recently (he saw the watershed of change as sometime in the nineteenth century, his "Great Divide"). Goodness and truth are light; evil and falsehood are shadow. Deity and worship are associated with height. Virtue is linked with loveliness. Love is sweet and constant, death bitter, and endurance praiseworthy. "In my opinion," Lewis wrote, "such deliberate organization is one of the first necessities of human life, and one of the main functions of art is to assist it. All that we describe as constancy in love or friendship, as loyalty in political life, or, in general, as perseverance—all solid virtue and stable pleasure—depends on organising chosen attitudes and maintaining them against the eternal flux." These are the virtues that are championed in Narnia. The virtues are reflected in the titles given to the Pevensie children when kings and queens in Narnia—Peter the Magnificent, Susan the Gentle, Edmund the Just and Lucy the Valiant.

These cultivated responses, likely enough, are closely related to mental patterns deep within us—to archetypes. Archetypes are universal and primal elements of ordinary human experience, belonging to the tacit dimension of our lives. Archetypes can be images or symbols, or the motif of a narrative plot (such as the quest, or the removal of injustice), or a character type (such as the swaggering tyrant, like Rabadash, or the noble warrior, like Emeth). They are captured in the iconography of literature and art of the "Old Western" period. Preeminent in Western literature in its embodiment of such primal and elemental archetypes is the Bible, reflected in Paul's injunction, "Whatever is true, whatever is honorable, whatever is just, whatever is pure, whatever is lovely, whatever is commendable, if there is any excellence, if there is anything worthy of praise, think about these things" (Philippians 4:8 ESV).

Archetypes are either positive or negative in implication. For instance, the rendering of landscape in literature and art can indicate the ideal and its contrary. Goodness is conveyed in landscape by a garden, grove or park; the mountaintop or hill; the fertile plain or valley; pastoral settings or farms; the safe pathway or easily traveled road; and places of natural refuge or defense (such as a rock, hill or hiding place). The sinister is rendered in landscape as the dark forest; the wilderness or wasteland (which is either too hot or too cold); the dark and dangerous valley; the tomb; the labyrinth; the dangerous or evil pathway; and the cave (associated with barbarism) or pit (as a place of confinement or imprisonment).

Lewis deliberately used such stock symbolism in his construction of the stories and world to which Narnia belongs. Particularly the lush valley world of Narnia is an indicator of its spiritual health. In contrast the northern and southern lands are largely barren.

Here then follows a very brief taste of books and authors that were important to Lewis's makeup as the creator of Narnia and that provided the intellectual and imaginative background to the kind of world that the land of Aslan is.

THE PERIOD OF THE CLASSICS

The books of this period that are significant to the background of Narnia are pretty much those that were fundamental to the Middle Ages and Renaissance. (Many were rediscovered during this vast period, for example, during the slow recovery from the collapse of Rome.) In thought, Plato's and Aristotle's writings predominant, though of course they built on the work of earlier thinkers. The emphasis of Plato (c. 427-348 B.C.)—an ideal world of forms upon which the visible shapes of nature are indefinite copies—is the imaginative background to the Chronicles, most clearly pictured in *LB*. It is signaled in Professor Kirke's comment, "It's all in Plato." The virtues identified by Aristotle (384-322 B.C.) are championed in Lewis's stories, just as they were in his great sixteenth-century model, Edmund Spenser's *The Faerie Queene*. Lewis was as well read in classical poetry as he was familiar with its philosophers, but two writers particularly form a background to the Narnian tales, as they do for the medieval and Renaissance period. These are Homer (c. ninth century B.C.) and Virgil (70-19 B.C.), though many others are important. Lewis's *VDT* is in part a homage to Homer's *The Odyssey,* telling of a sea journey with numerous adventures, many of them full of fairy-tale wonders, that test the courage and skill of Odysseus. Virgil, revered in the Middle Ages as a virtuous pagan who anticipated the coming of Christ, spun a great myth, *The Aeneid,* which was appropriated as the epic of Western civilization, embodying virtues that Lewis prizes in Narnia, epitomized in its Golden Age when the Pevensie children are kings and queens. Even today, Western ideals of civilization draw on Virgil's momentous story of the founding of Rome.

THE RISE OF CHRISTIANITY

The primary documents of Christianity, the Judeo-Christian Scriptures, extensively impact the Chronicles. (*See* chapter three, "Aslan, Narnia and Orthodoxy.") Like Tolkien, Lewis uses the gospel as the model for the fairy story; a pattern of what Tolkien calls the *eucatastrophe*. The gospel marks the reversal of tragedy and catastrophe—a remarkable and sudden turn in a story that signals the presence of grace. The gospel is also, for Lewis (and Tolkien), the fulfillment of human storytelling, bringing the imaginative insights of this storytelling into the nature of reality. In this fulfillment, the ultimate story is seen as a "Divine Comedy," a deeply satisfying happy ending.

MIDDLE AGES AND RENAISSANCE

This was the period of Lewis's professional teaching at Oxford University and later Cambridge. This teaching resulted in books like *English Literature in the Sixteenth Century, The Allegory of Love* and *The Discarded Image.* He was one of the most widely read of this period among his contemporaries. He drew eclectically upon the imaginative resources of this rich reading in creating the beings and settings of the Chronicles. His greatest inspiration from this vast period was Edmund Spenser's *The Faerie Queene,* feeding his hunger, as Doris Myers puts it, for fantasy, the "love for myth and marvel."

The Faerie Queene is an allegory, based upon features of chivalry, portraying stories that illustrate the perfect knight. Spenser intended to write twelve books, but only six exist, covering the qualities of holiness, temperance, chastity, friendship, justice and courtesy. The Faerie

Queene holds a feast over twelve days, and on each a complaint is presented. In Spenser's scheme, a different knight sets out to redress each injury, proving himself the hero of a particular virtue. Prince Arthur, a general hero, appears in every book. As in the Narnian Chronicles, the books are populated with characters from classical mythology, medieval romance and the writer's imagination. Like Narnia, it is a green world: a trackless wood features in most scenes, where adventures take place, such as killing dragons.

Literary scholar Doris Myers believes that Lewis "followed Spenser . . . in writing the Chronicles of Narnia. Having lived for so many years with Spenser's Fairyland, he created a parallel universe of his own, filled with images of life." She argues that the Chronicles "can be understood as a miniature *Faerie Queene.*" She points out that Lewis "uses different degrees of allegory, ranging from thoroughly externalised characters like Bacchus and Father Christmas to well-individualized persons like Eustace and Jill." Rather like Spenser, Lewis merges images from the Bible, classical and northern mythology, English and European literature, and Irish fairy tales. Both Lewis and Spenser, she believes, celebrate the virtues of Judeo-Christian and Western tradition, "faith, moderation, love and friendship, justice and mercy, courtesy, and especially courage."

UP TO THE MODERN PERIOD

Lewis acknowledged a huge debt to his reading in the period following Shakespeare, Spenser and their contempories. The poems of George Herbert; the allegories of John Bunyan, *The Pilgrim's Progress* and *The Holy War;* John Milton's English epic, *Paradise Lost;* the wit and wisdom of Samuel Johnson; and the Romantics Wordsworth and Shelley were just some of the writings that nourished him. He delighted also in the novels of Jane Austen, relishing for instance her depictions of what he called undeception (see chapter five).

MODERN PERIOD (POST-1830)

Though Lewis portrayed the watershed in Western history as around the first half of the nineteenth century, he acknowledged that the values of the "Old West," which he sought to embody in the Chronicles, did not dry up, though much of the stream was diverted to children's literature, which gained in strength in the latter half of the nineteenth century. The values were also retained in much popular literature. This period also saw a rich collecting of folk tales and popularizing of Celtic and northern mythology. Tales and myths gathered by the Grimm brothers, Jacob and Wilheim (published between 1812 and 1822), and Henry Longfellow's *Poets and Poems of Europe* (1863, including translations of Icelandic poetry and other verse based on northern mythology) became well known. One author whom Lewis regarded as his "master," George MacDonald, wrote for both children and adults. His adult fantasies, *Phantastes* and *Lilith,* are benchmarks of the genre. Lewis records how the former fantasy "baptised his imagination" as a teenaged atheist, presaging his eventual return to faith many years later. MacDonald's Curdie books for children find echoes in the Chronicles, particularly the intended assault upon Narnia from underground workings, where the enslaved Earthmen replace MacDonald's goblins. Lewis was also inspired by H. Rider Haggard, Robert Louis Stevenson and William Morris. Among his contemporaries, his greatest models were his fellow Inklings Owen Barfield, J. R. R. Tolkien and Charles Williams. He also owed much to G. K. Chesterton, particularly his popular theology, such as *The Everlasting Man.*

The matrix for the Chronicles was Lewis's reading of the books of the vast period of Judeo-Christianity and Western civilization up to his "Great Divide" between the "Old West" and the "post-Christian" West, what he simply called "old books." Let him explain why:

> Every age has its own outlook. It is specially good at seeing certain truths and specially liable to make certain mistakes. We all, there-

fore, need the books that will correct the characteristic mistakes of our period. And that means the old books. . . . We may be sure that the characteristic blindness of the twentieth century—the blindness about which posterity will ask, "But how *could* they have thought that?"—lies where we have never suspected it. . . . None of us can fully escape this blindness, but we shall certainly increase it, and weaken our guard against it, if we read only modern books. Where they are true they will give us truths which we half knew already. Where they are false they will aggravate the error with which we are already dangerously ill. The only palliative is to keep the clean sea breeze of the centuries blowing through our minds, and this can only be done by reading old books. . . . Two heads are better than one, not because either is infallible, but because they are unlikely to go wrong in the same direction. To be sure, the books of the future would be just as good a corrective as the books of the past, but unfortunately we cannot get at them.

Lewis writes the Chronicles with the virtues of the "old books," but in a manner attractive to contemporary people who may not realize the value of reading the old, thus allowing a different perception, a window—or should I say, a wardrobe door?—into other worlds.

Aslan, Narnia and Orthodoxy

C. S. Lewis was a literary critic who also had marked philosophical interests. Anything that he wrote on theology, such as *Miracles, The Problem of Pain, Reflections on the Psalms,* or *Mere Christianity,* he regarded as the offerings of a layperson. Some of his opinions he presented explicitly as speculation. He tried to set forward an orthodox theology, which he called "mere Christianity." This was a center ground of theology that he shared with his great friend J. R. R. Tolkien, who was a Roman Catholic. Lewis found this common ground in writers from the past he loved, such as the poets Edmund Spenser, George Herbert and John Milton; the storyteller and preacher John Bunyan; the Christian mystic Thomas Traherne and numerous others; and contemporary writers such as G. K. Chesterton, Charles Williams and Dorothy L. Sayers.

An important contribution that Lewis made to theology was on the nature of language, and how language pictures reality, including the deep reality of the world that we do not normally see. For him the Bible has the character of a revelation from God involving unique truth-claims, written in varied genres of the ancient world such as historical narrative, poetry, allegory, parable and apocalyptic. The Gospels spelled out for him the meaning of God's nature, sin, salvation and the atonement. The Gospels combined the qualities of a good story with being factual. His orthodoxy was a traditional Anglican kind, and, like Dorothy L. Sayers and G. K. Chesterton, he delighted in dogma.

At the center of the theology of Narnia is, of course, Aslan, who is the incarnation of the divine in bodily form (in the Narnian case, the body of a talking lion). Lewis saw the incarnation as the central doctrine of Christian faith, brilliantly portraying it in his book *Miracles*. "Every other miracle prepares for this, or exhibits this, or results from this," writes Lewis. "Just as every natural event is the manifestation at a particular place and moment of Nature's total character, so every particular Christian miracle manifests at a particular place and moment the character and significance of the Incarnation." Similarly, all events in Narnia turn out to point to Aslan, who is behind all the stories.

Lewis saw Christian faith as the fundamental presupposition of "Old Western" civilization after the arrival of Judeo-Christianity from the Near East. He spoke of the contemporary world in the West as being "post-Christian." The book of Christian faith, the Bible, is central to Lewis. (One of his books is specifically on the book of Psalms.) He draws on the literary content of the Bible frequently in the Chronicles, mainly in theme but sometimes in genre (when his stories contain apocalyptic, as in *LB*; creation narrative, as in *MN*; and prophecy, as in *LWW*, when it is foretold that two Sons of Adam and two Daughters of Eve will come into Narnia).

In the Chronicles there are explicit biblical parallels—allusions to creation, Eden, the Fall of humanity and the end of the world. In one place, in *VDT*, the lamb offering a breakfast of fish evokes John 21. There are also many implicit parallels, as when God appears hidden during the hundred years of winter in *LWW* or during the tyranny of the new Narnians under Miraz in *PC*. Aslan's return in *LWW* is like the spring of the year the Old Testament prophets refer to. There is a faithful remnant in *PC*, as there was in Israel's darkest hours. The four signs given to Jill echo the Ten Commandments, or the Law.

There are many more allusive references, as, in *VDT*, when Eustace casts off the dragon skin with Aslan's help or, in *SC*, when Jill drinks from the stream in Aslan's Country. Throughout the Chronicles small decisions eventually fix salvation or damnation, or at least destiny: as when Eustace slowly becomes a dragon even before arriving at Dragon Island, or Susan little by little moves toward rejecting Narnia's reality, or Edmund declines into eventual betrayal. Aslan's Table, with its crimson cloth and stone knife, recalls the Eucharist and the "daily bread" promised by God.

The Chronicles pick up on the biblical theme of evil as illusion and deception (and not an equal reality to good), which is connected with the biblical idea of idols and Satan's ability to appear as an angel of light. In the Narnian stories we find the deceptive beauty of witches like Jadis and the Green Witch (who captivates and enslaves Rilian in *SC*). In *LB* Puzzle apparently becomes Aslan, leading to the blasphemy of Tashlan, in which the evil Tash appears to be at one with Aslan. Related to this theme of deception and illusion is the necessity of undeception and a radical change in perception (see chapter five), which, in biblical terms, comes about through victory over sin and temptation. In *VDT* we find the alluring spell of Deathwater broken, just in time. In *SC* Puddleglum burns his foot in order to come to his senses (an allusion to Christ's injunction to cut out one's eye or even sacrifice one's life if necessary for the sake of truth). In *SC* the way of escape from the giants of Harfang is a tiny cave or crack in the earth, evoking the narrow gate to life that exists for those who can see it (with the help of God's instructions).

One of the sharpest indicators of the underlying theology of Narnia is given by Lewis himself to a child called Anne, in a letter of March 5, 1961.

Here Lewis explains to Anne that the whole Narnian series has foundational themes. In *MN* there is an account of creation and how evil enters Narnia at the very beginning. In *LWW* is a telling of Christ's crucifixion and resurrection. *PC* is concerned with "restoration of true religion after a corruption." The calling and conversion of a "heathen," is the subject of *HHB*. *VDT* portrays the spiritual life, especially in Reepicheep's quest for Aslan's Country. *SC* concerns the continuing spiritual battle against the dark powers. *LB* tells of the coming, in Shift the ape, of the antichrist, leading to the prophesied end of the world and Last Judgment.

As a literary critic, Lewis's insights are valuable in approaching the Bible as a literary text (though Lewis was skeptical of a simplistic "the Bible as literature" approach). His book *Reflections on the Psalms* provides a useful model in this. Lewis's observation about inspiration, that truth is scattered in many myths around the world and is not only in the Bible, deserves attention. It bears similarity with Calvin's view that truth is to be welcomed where it is to be found in non-Christian thinking. Lewis's *Miracles* provides fascinating insights into the wider implications of the doctrine of incarnation, God's supreme disclosure of himself. Language, story and myth, in God's grace, can be incarnations of truth, anticipating or echoing the incarnation of truth himself. In the Gospel records, true history and the greatest of all stories are one; myth becomes fact.

Lewis employs the Bible in his fiction, and particularly in the Chronicles, to refresh and renew, and even reorder, the reader's perception. He encourages, in a very basic, straightforward and ordinary way, what might be called a symbolic perception of reality—viewing reality *from* the frame of narrative, story, image and other symbolic elements. For him the wealth of images, stories, myth and other symbolic patterns from the past (see chapter two, "The Background to the Chronicles of Narnia") were intensified and fulfilled in the Bible. To give one instance, the hero of heroes of Scripture is the lamb that was slain from the creation of the world. In a profound sense, symbols such as the lamb are not merely poetic, but solidly real. The lamb that was slain, for instance, is linked in numerous ways to actual events in documented history, such as the crucifixion and resurrection of Christ in A.D. 33. Lewis employs the symbol of the lamb (who soon shifts shape to the lion, Aslan) at the end of *VDT*.

Lewis's imaginative work reinforces such a biblical emphasis upon a symbolic perception of reality. His symbolic world of Narnia, even though fictional, points to the solidly real. For this reason it takes us back to the ordinary world that is an inevitable part of our human living and experience, deepening both its wonders and its terrors. Our awareness of the meaning of God's creation and his intentions for us is enlarged. Lewis guides us, through the Narnia stories, in seeing our world with a thoroughly Christian understanding. His invented world of Narnia also illuminates what is revealed of God in the natural order. It speaks of God, Christ (in Aslan) and nature. Lewis also explores heaven and the character of religious experience. For Lewis, the literature of "romance" (including fairy tale, fantasy and some science fiction) had important theological implications (see chapter five, "Literary Features of the Chronicles").

1. GOD

Lewis observed how reluctant people are to move from the idea of an abstract and fuzzy deity to a living God who has a determinate character and makes demands upon us. He realized that fantasy and fairy story, like myth, have the remarkable power to make abstractions concrete and real. In the Chronicles the distinctiveness and particularity of God is demonstrated in the magical figure of Aslan, elusive but definite, wild, surprising and always shaping events providentially.

Throughout his life, Lewis loved particular things, distinctiveness in people and places, in books and conversations. In Lewis's book *Miracles,* which is key for understanding his view of God, many connections are made between the deep reality of particular things and the underlying factuality—the utter concreteness—of God. In many ways, the Chronicles are a fictive expression of that book, containing profound theology even though the stories are scaled for children.

Lewis felt that people often hide from the idea of a definite, personal God by calling the notion crude or primitive. For Lewis, however, God is fact, rather than the result of a rational argument. Rather than being an abstract concept or a human symbol, God is overwhelmingly concrete and real. The endlessly articulate nature of the universe, part of the wonder of scientific discovery, is a pale reflection of God's infinitely inner articulation. Often, Lewis felt, picture language and stories came closer to grasping the concreteness of reality, including God's overwhelming reality. This is why he poured his insights and experience of God into the format of children's fantasy.

The pre-Christian Lewis had felt the concreteness of God first of all through stories and myths—but his reason demanded that God's existence must be perceived in literal facts and events in the real world. This prepared him for finding God through the literal facts of Christ's incarnation, life, death and resurrection in first-century Palestine, without losing the magic of the sheer imaginative appeal of these facts. Like George MacDonald, Lewis saw God essentially as "the glad creator" and hence regarded the incarnation as the grand miracle, springing from God's involvement with his creation. He was able to explore this wonder of the incarnation in imaginative form in his creation of the Lion-God, Aslan, fully talking beast and fully divine. For many readers of Lewis, he is most memorable for the fresh images of God and Christ that he created, enabling people in our modern world to see again, or for the first time, the tangible meaning of God's reality. Lewis's delight in God's creation is at the heart of his fantasy writing and his theology of romance.

2. ASLAN, CREATOR-LION OF NARNIA

Narnia is a world of talking animals, even though humans enter it from our world from the beginning. Its creator is a talking lion, Aslan, who is also divine. Like Christ, he has two natures. In Aslan's case, these are his divine nature and his nature as a talking lion, endued with rationality. Aslan (Turkish for "lion") is intended to be a symbol of Christ, Christ not as he appeared and will appear in our world (as a real man), but as he appears in Narnia (as a "real" Narnian talking lion). He is sovereign, the High King of beasts, over the world in which Narnia is located.

Aslan's divine father is the Emperor-over-the-sea, dwelling beyond the Eastern Ocean, past Aslan's Country and the World's End. The symbol of the lion is a traditional image of authority. In his *The Problem of Pain,* Lewis writes: "I think the lion, when he has ceased to be dangerous, will still be awful." The emblem of the Lion is also found in Buddhist and Eastern art as a guardian figure of strength.

The biblical theologian Austin Farrer, a close friend of Lewis's, commented on the biblical roots of the lion Aslan at the request of Walter Hooper:

> The Seer of Revelation is shown Christ as a Lamb, not a Lion. But it is to be observed that as his first appearance the Lamb-Christ is introduced as a paradoxical substitute for a Lion-Christ. "One . . . saith unto me, Weep not: behold, the Lion from the Tribe of Judah, the Scion of David, has conquered; he can open the Book. . . . And I saw in the midst of the Throne . . . a Lamb standing as though slaughtered" (Revelation 5:5f). A Jewish seer of much the same date presents the straight picture of the royal Aslan: "And I beheld, and lo, as it were a lion roused out of the wood roaring; and I heard him send forth a human voice. . . . This is the Messiah whom the Most High has kept unto the end of the days, who shall spring up out of the seed of David" (2 Esdras 11:37; 12:32). The Lion-Messiah of

Jewish tradition derives from the Oracles of Jacob on his twelve sons. He praises Judah as the royal stem, a lion none does rouse, a hand from which the sceptre will never depart (Genesis 49:9).

There are many other biblical allusions surrounding Aslan in the Chronicles. In *PC,* when Aslan calls Lucy's name in the dead of night, it is an echo of the call of Samuel. When Aslan confers with the White Witch in *LWW* over the fate of Edmund, it is a distant allusion, perhaps, to the discussion between God and Satan at the heavenly court at the beginning of the book of Job. Aslan's loneliness and the trial of his feelings before he goes to his appointment with death unmistakeably recall Gethsemane. As Susan and Lucy look on the scene of Aslan's execution, the allusion is clear: the scene is like that of the faithful women at the cross. Aslan's tears over Digory's mother are reminiscent of Christ's sorrow over Lazarus.

There is a strong element of wildness in Aslan: he is not a tame lion. As Mr. Beaver says, he isn't safe. His wildness correlates with a numinous wildness in nature, represented by figures in Narnia from pre-Christian paganism such as Bacchus and Silenus from classical mythology and giants from northern and Celtic legend. Lewis balances Aslan's wildness and terrifying nature perfectly with his approachability, beauty and gentleness. In *LWW,* we are told, Lucy and Susan do something they would never have dared to do without Aslan's permission: they sink their cold hands into the sea of his beautiful mane to comfort him. After his resurrection, he romps with them, and Lucy afterwards can't make up her mind whether it was like playing with a thunderstorm or with a kitten. As for his awesomeness, Aslan's roar is magnificently portrayed in *PC.*

The sound, deep and throbbing at first like an organ beginning on a low note, rose and became louder, and then far louder again, till the earth and air were shaking with it. It rose up from that hill and floated across all Narnia.

Not only in his wildness does Aslan have a quality of the numinous. It is evident in other ways also. Even the mention of his name stirs the children deeply in *LWW,* even before they have met him. His numinous quality is associated with his scent, with music and with light. For Susan, his very name evokes a delicious smell or a delightful strain of distant music. When Shasta in *HHB* falls at the feet of the unknown lion, a strange and solemn perfume that hangs about the mane envelops him. As the voyagers in *VDT* approach Aslan's Country at the End of the World, the quality of light takes on a new dimension. It would be too bright to bear but for the strange, strengthening power of the sweet seawater they drink. In that light they can glimpse features of a blissful, heavenly country. According to Warren Lewis, the sweet scent and light associated with Aslan in his brother's stories were suggested by descriptions of the Holy Grail in Thomas Malory and in Tennyson's *Idylls of the King.*

Aslan is perceived in remarkably different ways by various characters in the stories. Indeed, how they perceive him becomes the ultimate indicator of whether they pass to his left or right on Narnia's Judgment Day in *LB.* That final choice, shaped by a myriad lesser choices, is prefigured many times in the stories. Nikabrik, for instance, perceives Aslan as a "performing lion" in *PC.* In *LWW,* the White Witch calls him the "Great Fool" before slaying him. Rabadash in *HHB* sees Aslan as a "demon" and a "horrible phantasm." Rather like some modern theologians, the Narnian talking horse Bree sees talk of Aslan as a lion as only figurative language (until he actually encounters him).

All seven of the Chronicles teem with Christian meanings found also in Lewis's other writings, such as the true character of God and the nature of humanity, nature, heaven, hell and joy (the longing he called *Sehnsucht*). The key to these meanings lies in the fact that Aslan is a figure of Christ, out of many possible figures of him. If a reader is unaware of this, he or she can still enjoy the stories in their own right; if he or she is aware, the meaning of Christian truths often comes strangely alive. Many readers are moved to tears for instance at the death of Aslan though they may be so familiar with the Gospel narratives as to be unmoved by the accounts of Christ's death.

3. NATURE

Central to Lewis's writings is the view that nature must take second place to its creator. Commenting about nature in a letter, Lewis said, with feeling: "All the beauty withers when we try to make it an absolute. Put first things first and we get second things thrown in: put second things first and we lose both first and second things. We never get, say, even the sensual pleasure of food at its best when we are being greedy." Edmund of course finds this out when he becomes addicted to Turkish Delight in *LWW*; his delight in the confection soon palls.

Nature in Lewis's eyes is a "second thing," the first being the person who created it. In fact, there could be very many worlds, with our universe being just one of them. In a sense, an artist reflects God in the making of many works. Shakespeare made *The Winter's Tale* as well as *Hamlet*. Hamlet-world has a consistent nature, as does the world of *The Winter's Tale*. These worlds could overlap; Shakespeare could have put in a character common to both stories. But they are independent as artworks.

In the *LWW*, Peter suddenly recognizes (see the discussion of recognition and undeception in chapter five, "Literary Features of the Chronicles") that there could be many natures after Lucy reports a world existing through the wardrobe:

> "But do you really mean, sir," said Peter, "that there could be other worlds—all over the place, just round the corner—like that?"
>
> "Nothing is more probable," said the Professor, taking off his spectacles and beginning to polish them, while he muttered to himself, "I wonder what they do teach them at these schools."

Because nature is a "second thing" does not lessen its reality. It is always particular, and everything in it is weighty with meaning. In one of his early scholarly works, *The Personal Heresy,* Lewis observed: "In space and time there is no such thing as an organism, there are only animals and vegetables. There are no mere vegetables, only trees, flowers, turnips, &c. There are no 'trees,' except beeches, elms, oaks, and the rest. There is even no such thing as 'an elm.' There is only *this* elm, in such a year of its age at such an hour of the day, thus lighted, thus moving, thus acted on by all the past and all the present, and affording such and such experiences to me and my dog and the insect on its trunk and the man a thousand miles away who is remembering it. A real elm, in fact, can be uttered only by a poem." Lewis discovered also that the reality or meaning of natural things can be articulated in stories, as well as poems. The Chronicles celebrate the sheer, exuberant existence of natural things like animals, trees and even the ingredients of meals.

One tragic result of the improper placing of nature as the primary thing is reductionism, or the attitude that sees through all things in nature and the human world until ultimately it sees nothing.

"In our world," said Eustace, "a star is a huge ball of flaming gas."

"Even in your world, my son," replied the old man, "that is not what a star is but only what it is made of."

The very history of the world, believed Lewis, is one of humanity's separation from God on the one hand and from nature on the other. Our separation from nature comes of a moral failure—from our wish to exalt ourselves and thus to belittle all else. We should reject materialism and recognize God's continued activity in the fecundity of natural things like trees, grass, flowers and shrubs.

Lewis believed that evil—whether from human beings or demonic forces—always results in the disruption or even the destruction of nature. In *LWW,* the White Witch kept Narnia in the blight of perpetual winter. In *LB,* places of natural beauty are despoiled for the sake of economic exploitation, expansion and so-called progress. In *MN* Digory's Uncle Andrew is indifferent to the fate of guinea pigs in his care. In 1947, Lewis complained, "The evil reality of lawless applied science . . . is actually reducing large tracts of Nature to disorder and sterility at this very moment." As a young atheist Lewis stoically accepted a bleak, colorless view of nature, and in his imaginative life, fueled by his wide reading, cared mainly about a contrasting world of gods and heroes and an ideal world of beauty. Many years later he eventually, and reluctantly, accepted a Christian universe. He soon realized the implications of commitment to this "real universe, the divine, magical, terrifying and ecstatic reality in which we all live."

What fixed the reality of the natural world forever was the incarnation of God himself as a fully human being in a fully real human body. Christ's resurrection meant that he retains this human body forever. The environment of his resurrected body, and that of his followers in the future, could be called a new nature, though believers, Lewis included, prefer to call this environment "heaven." C. S. Lewis was once interviewed by *Time* magazine (September 8, 1947). They wondered if his life at Oxford, a life of writing, walking, teaching and reading, was monotonous. Lewis's reply baffled them: "I like monotony."

It is, in fact, upon the humble and common things of nature that Lewis's wonderlands of the imagination—particularly the Chronicles—are based, "the quiet fullness of ordinary nature." He also saw the ordinary (he learned this from George MacDonald) as the basis of spirituality. In a letter, he wrote: "The familiar is in itself ground for affection. And it is good, because any natural help towards our spiritual duty of loving is good and God seems to build our higher loves round our merely natural impulses—sex, maternity, kinship, old acquaintances." Conversely, as he demonstrated vividly in the characters of Edmund, Eustace and Susan, small things are likely to play the main part in the downfall of a person (eventually leading, in Edmund's case, to a big action of betrayal). Because of the link between ordinary reality and imaginative creation, Lewis found himself on the defensive about fantasy. A common charge is that literary fantasy is escapism. In his book *Of This and Other Worlds,* Lewis says of *The Wind in the Willows* (the popular children's story by Kenneth Grahame): "The happiness which it presents to us is in fact full of the simplest and most attainable things—food, sleep, exercise, friendship, the face of nature, even (in a sense) religion." Such fantasy is the opposite of escapism. It deepens the reality of the real world for us—the terror as well as the beauty.

Closely linked to Lewis's zest for ordinary nature was his attention to the details of life and experience. This remarkable power of observation, and sensitivity to tone and mood, added detail after detail of exuberant creation to his imaginative writings. He was very aware of nature, seasons, weather, atmosphere and, of course, animals, and was able to allow his readers, through his verbal dexterity and power of storytelling, to experience sensations they had never previously had. He delighted in particular to put animal characters into his books. Narnia is a world of talking animals.

Lewis's letters are also full of references to animals. In a letter to an American lady, he recounted: "We were talking about cats and dogs the other day and decided that both have consciences but the dog, being an honest, humble person, always has a bad one, but the cat is a Pharisee and always has a good one. When he sits and stares you out of countenance he is thanking God that he is not as these dogs, or these humans, or even as these other cats!"

The natural world of God's creation, Lewis believed, imposes a boundary to the human imagination. We cannot, like God, create *ex ni-*

hilo, out of nothing. We can only rearrange elements that God has already made and that are overflowing with his meanings. Our proper mode of imaginative making is what Lewis's friend J. R. R. Tolkien dubbed subcreation. We create a kind of secondary nature.

Ultimately, there was, for Lewis, an inevitable connection between nature and joy since in nature heaven itself is foreshadowed:

> The settled happiness and security which we all desire, God withholds from us by the very nature of the world: but joy, pleasure, and merriment, He has scattered broadcast. We are never safe, but we have plenty of fun, and some ecstacy. It is not hard to see why. The security we crave would teach us to rest our hearts in this world and oppose an Obstacle to our return to God: a few moments of happy love, a landscape, a symphony, a merry meeting with our friends, a bathe or a football match, have no such tendency. Our father refreshes us on the journey with some pleasant inns, but will not encourage us to mistake them for home.

This sense of homelessness which for Lewis is invariably a pointer to heaven is vividly captured in the Chronicles, in Shasta's love of northern lands in *HHB* and in the mouse Reepicheep's desire to find Aslan's Country in *VDT.*

No one has better summarized Lewis's idea of nature than Kathryn Lindskoog, in her *The Lion of Judah in Never-Never Land:*

> Lewis's concept of nature is threefold. It consists of a romantic appreciation of untamed beauty, a rational acceptance of the supernatural, and a realistic awareness of the corruption and ultimate destruction of our present system. His concept of God is that of a creator, redeemer, and sustainer who is omnipotent, omniscient, and omnipresent. This personal God of love, simultaneously an awesome king, has the power to reveal Himself to his creation by

assuming an incarnate form. Lewis's concept of mankind is based upon mankind's relationship to God. Therefore it is reverential, yet critical. Man is prone to sin, and this keeps him from the full joy of fellowship with God. Man should resist the deceptions of evil and determine his behavior toward God, other men, and animals by love. The resurrected man will enjoy an eternal life of unbroken fellowship with God. These three concepts have been graphically presented in mythological form in the Narnian tales.

In the Chronicles we have the story of one invented nature—the world of Narnia—from its creation to its dissolution. We encounter the introduction of evil, the unfolding history of Narnia, the totalitarian grip of the witch's spell, its ending by Aslan's sacrifical death, and the long, slow processes of living out virtuous lives over the course of history. This simple picture of Narnia is in essence the story of our own complex, still unfolding world.

4. THE RELIGIOUS IMAGINATION

Awe. Lewis considered the emotion of awe to be close to fear, but implying no consideration of danger. It was caused by the presence of the numinous. Lewis expresses his belief, in *The Problem of Pain,* that awe is a direct experience of the supernatural. In the Chronicles, this was a natural response to the presence of Aslan.

Numinous. An all-pervasive sense of the other is focused in the numinous, a basic human experience charted by the German thinker Rudolf Otto in his book *The Idea of the Holy* (1923), which deeply influenced Lewis. The primary numinous experience involves a sense of dependence upon what stands wholly other to mankind. This otherness (or other-worldliness) is unapproachable and awesome. But it has a fascination. The experience of the numinous is captured better by suggestion and allusion than by a theoretical analysis. Joy *(Sehnsucht),* or inconsolable longing, is an important feature of the numinous experience.

Many realities captured in imaginative fiction could be described as having some quality of the numinous. C. S. Lewis realized this, incorporating the idea into his apologetic for the Christian view of suffering, *The Problem of Pain,* and he cited an event from Kenneth Grahame's fantasy for children, *The Wind in the Willows,* to illustrate it. The final part of *VDT* particularly embodies the numinous, as the travelers approach Aslan's Country across the Last Sea. The numinous is most realized in the Chronicles in encounters with Aslan, evoking awe, terror, worship, the desire to dance, joy or rejection.

Where the numinous is captured, its appeal is first to the imagination, which also senses it most accurately. It belongs to an area of meaning that we cannot easily conceptualize. Lewis found this when he read George MacDonald's *Phantastes,* describing in *Surprised by Joy* the effect of his reading as the baptism of his imagination. It was years later that he was able to reconcile this experience with his thinking.

Joy. The theme of joy is like a thread running through the Chronicles, and indeed through most of the writings of C. S. Lewis. It is the subject of his autobiographical *Surprised by Joy* and *The Pilgrim's Regress.* Lewis portrays it as a secret human longing that no experience can satisfy. Joy is a keen sense of homelessness that finds no home in the world. "The sense that in this universe," writes Lewis, "we are treated as strangers, the longing to be acknowledged, to meet with some response, to bridge some chasm that yawns between us and reality, is part of our inconsolable secret."

In the Chronicles this mysterious longing is most often associated with the presence, or even the hint of the presence, of Aslan, the Creator-Lion:

> Perhaps it has sometimes happened to you in a dream that someone says something which you don't understand but in the dream it feels as if it had some enormous meaning—either a terrifying one

which turns the whole dream into a nightmare or else a lovely meaning too lovely to put into words, which makes the dream so beautiful that you remember it all your life and are always wishing you could get into that dream again. It was like that now. At the name of Aslan each one of the children felt something jump in his inside. . . . Susan felt as if some delicious smell or some delightful strain of music had just floated by her. And Lucy got the feeling you have when you wake up in the morning and realise that it is the beginning of the holidays or the beginning of summer.

The sensation is most heightened in *VDT,* embodied in Reepicheep's quest for Aslan's Country, a desire that more and more grips the other voyagers. It reaches its intensity as they sail over the last sea, beyond Ramandu's country, where the water is sweet. When they drink the water, they feel "almost too well and strong to bear it." They need no food— the light itself sustains them. Then a sudden, short-lived breeze from the east, from Aslan's Country, carries a smell and music on it.

Edmund and Eustace would never talk about it afterwards. Lucy could only say, "It would break your heart." "Why," said I, "was it so sad?" "Sad!! No," said Lucy.

No one in the boat doubted that they were seeing beyond the End of the World into Aslan's Country.

Such joy, thought Lewis, inspired the writer to create fantasy. It is *Sehnsucht,* one of the manifestations of the numinous, explored in Rudolf Otto's *The Idea of the Holy. Sehnsucht* means "longing" or "yearning," evoking a sense of alienation that has spiritual and mystical implications. It is akin to nostalgia but is far more than emotion. It is a state of mind, which has important theological and philosophical implications. Characteristically, the experience of *Sehnsuct* carries with the "sweet desire" a sharp sensation of alienation or distance from the object of desire. What is desired is unobtainable, yet life appears empty without it.

In fact, *Sehnsucht,* seen as a yearning or longing that is a pointer to joy, was for Lewis a defining characteristic of fantasy. The creation of another world is an attempt to reconcile human beings and the world, to embody the fulfillment of our imaginative longing. Imaginative worlds, wonderlands, are "regions of the spirit." Lewis claimed in *Of This and Other Worlds* that "to construct plausible and moving 'other worlds' you must draw on the only real 'other world' we know, that of the spirit."

Lewis, in mapping joy in many writings, illuminates a state of mind that has been a recurrent theme in literature. This compulsive quest engenders both fleeting joy and a sensation like homelessness or exile—we realize that we are separated from what is desired. This separation lies at the heart of romanticism, which seeks the reconciliation of humanity and nature, and a knowledge that is personal as well as objective. Joy for C. S. Lewis is the master key both to the nature of human beings and to their creator. It is a pointer towards heaven.

In attempting to imagine heaven (one of the few contemporary writers to do so convincingly), Lewis discovered that joy is "the secret signature of each soul." He speculated that the desire for heaven is part of our essential (and unfulfilled) humanity:

> There are times when I think we do not desire heaven; but more often I find myself wondering whether, in our heart of hearts, we have ever desired anything else. . . . Are not all lifelong friendships born at the moment when at last you meet another human being who has some inkling (but faint and uncertain even in the best) of that something which you were born desiring, and which, beneath the flux of other desires and in all the momentary silences between the louder passions, night and day, year by year, from childhood to old age, you are looking for, watching for, listening for? You have never had it. All the things that have ever deeply possessed your

soul have been but hints of it—tantalizing glimpses, promises never quite fulfilled, echoes that died away just as they caught your ear. But if it should really become manifest—if there ever came an echo that did not die away but swelled into the sound itself—you would know it. Beyond all possibility of doubt you would say "Here at last is the thing I was made for." We cannot tell each other about it. It is the secret signature of each soul, the incommunicable and unappeasable want, the thing we desired before we met our wives or made our friends or chose our work, and which we shall still desire on our deathbeds, when the mind no longer knows wife or friend or work. While we are, this is. If we lose this, we lose all.

In portraying this theme of joy Lewis purposed, to use the words of one commentator, "to awaken a desire for love and goodness." It is particularly important of course that children are drawn toward love and goodness, and Lewis embodies the theme of joy throughout the Narnian tales. As well as a general longing for Aslan in the stories, and Reepicheep's quest in *VDT,* there are other manifestations of joy. In *MN,* during the creation of Narnia, Frank the cabby exclaims: "Glory be! . . . I'd ha' been a better man all my life if I'd known there were things like this." When Digory hears the sound of Aslan it was,

> beyond comparison, the most beautiful noise he had ever heard. It was so beautiful he could hardly bear it. The horse seemed to like it too; he gave the sort of whinny a horse would give if, after years of being a cab-horse, it found itself back in the old field where it played as a foal, and saw someone whom it remembered and loved coming across the field to bring it a lump of sugar.

In *LWW* the girls had longed ever since they met Aslan to bury their hands in his mane. In *HHB* the theme of longing is treated with beautiful subtlety. Bree, the exiled Narnian horse, and Shasta, the lost prince, long to travel to Narnia. Bree remembers it as a foal; Shasta's longing is based on a more mysterious longing (eventually explained by the fact that he is really from Archenland). The boy experiences the longing as a desire for northern lands. In *PC,* the longing often manifests itself as a desire for the Old Narnia, suppressed by the modernizing tyrant Miraz. We see this particularly in Caspian and in Doctor Cornelius, his tutor. In *LB,* Emeth, the virtuous Calormene, has since childhood desired to serve and know Tash, the false deity, and look on his face—a desire that is fulfilled when he meets Aslan. At the end of Narnia, Jewel the unicorn declares of Aslan's Country: "This is the land I have been looking for all my life, though I never knew it till now."

5. HEAVEN

In the Chronicles, heaven is associated with Aslan's Country. Lewis employs some of his most abiding images of heaven in describing the approach of the voyagers to the World's End. In the other sense of the end of the world, Lewis describes the creation of the New Narnia in *LB* in terms of a heavenly country.

Heaven, for Lewis, is a literal place, though, in our present, fallen situation, it will not be discovered by searching through the universe in space rockets. It is a new nature that God has planned, the ultimate context of a fully human life, bodies and all. The theme of heaven's reality runs through Lewis's writings, particularly his fiction, and is closely linked with his characteristic theme of joy or inconsolable longing.

In this present life, the situation is like being on the wrong side of a shut door, with heaven on the other side. Morning was one of Lewis's favorite images of heaven. We respond to the freshness and purity of dawn, but that doesn't make us fresh and pure. In *VDT,* Eustace, Edmund and Lucy are invited to breakfast by a Lamb. On the green grass near Aslan's Country a fire has been lit and fish is roasting on it. The setting evokes a breakfast long ago by the shore of Lake Galilee, to which the newly risen Christ invited the fishermen-disciples, one of the most numinous passages in the New Testament, yet fully real.

Lewis saw heaven as founded upon the paradox that the more we abandon ourselves to Christ, the more fully ourselves we become. Thus, while redemption by Christ improves people in this present life, the consummation of human maturity is unimaginable. In heaven, both the individuality and society of persons will be fulfilled, both diversity and harmony. Heaven is varied; hell monotonous. Heaven is brimful of meaning; hell is the absence of meaning. Heaven is reality itself, hell a ghost or shadow.

Heaven is probably unimaginable, Lewis believed, even though of course we have the biblical images to take us as far as they can. Parable, allegory and fiction are the closest that we can come to speaking of heaven. This is why he explored heaven so much through fantasy, as in *The Great Divorce, VDT, LB,* and *Perelandra.* In his prose, he particularly speaks of heaven in *The Problem of Pain* and *Letters to Malcolm* and in a sermon, "The Weight of Glory."

In *LB,* the children see the land of Narnia die forever and freeze over in blackness. They are filled with regret. Later, as they walk in a fresh morning light, they wonder why everything seems strangely familiar. At last they realize that this was again Narnia, but now different—larger and more vivid, more like the real thing. It is different in the way that a real thing differs from its shadow, or waking life from a dream.

Worldviews and Narnia

As well as being rich in theology, the Chronicles explore some basic worldviews, including the tenet of modern thinking—naturalism, or materialism. Every person has a worldview from which nature and other human beings are perceived. Lewis's own move from naturalism and atheism involved a growing recognition of the importance of pagan and mythological insights. This chapter will look first at naturalism, in relation to the Chronicles, and then Lewis's insights into paganism, which so shaped the creation of Narnia.

NATURALISM AND SUPERNATURALISM

Naturalism is Lewis's name, in his book *Miracles: A Preliminary Study,* for the view that nature is "the whole show," with nothing outside nature existing. Another name for such a worldview is materialism. This contrasts with supernaturalism, which admits other worlds or natures that overlap with the nature we know or are in some sense "above" it in a kind of hierarchy, or are "above" it in the sense that a third dimension is "above" a two-dimensional world. In Lewis's theistic, Christian view, nature is created by God, who is above it and has created at least one other world above it, the world of the spirit. God could have, and might well have, created other natures, or could have chosen not to create at all (in which case, I wouldn't be writing this book). For much of his life, Lewis was a naturalist, coming reluctantly at first to faith in theism and then in Christianity. He knew from the inside what a materialist faith felt and tasted like.

In the Chronicles, Lewis tends to portray the attitude of naturalism, once so familiar to him, as one that reduces something rich and multifaceted to a dreadfully poorer reality. Uncle Miraz in *PC* displays this attitude when he finds out that Caspian's nurse has been telling tales of Old Narnia:

> "That's all nonsense, for babies," said the King sternly. "Only fit for babies, do you hear? You're getting too old for that sort of stuff. At your age you ought to be thinking of battles and adventures, not fairy tales."

The Green Witch uses such reductionist arguments when she tries to persuade Eustace, Jill, Puddleglum and Prince Rilian that there is no world of Narnia above Underworld; there is no world where the sun shines:

> "What is this *sun* that you all speak of? Do you mean anything by the word?"
>
> "Yes, we jolly well do," said Scrubb.
>
> "Can you tell me what it's like?" asked the Witch. . . .
>
> "Please it your Grace," said the Prince, very coldly and politely. "You see that lamp. It is round and yellow and gives light to the whole room, and hangeth moreover from the roof. Now that thing which we call the sun is like the lamp, only far greater and brighter. It giveth light to the whole Overworld and hangeth in the sky."
>
> "Hangeth from what, my Lord?" asked the Witch; and then, while they were all still thinking how to answer her, she added,

with another of her soft, silver laughs: "You see? When you try to think out clearly what this *sun* must be, you cannot tell me. You can only tell me it is like the lamp. Your *sun* is a dream; and there is nothing in that dream that was not copied from the lamp. The lamp is the real thing; the *sun* is but a tale, a children's story. . . ."

Slowly and gravely the Witch repeated, "There is no *sun*."

Her argument echoes a central tenet of naturalism against faith in God, used by Feuerbach, Marx, Freud and others. This reverses the perspective of faith, seeing belief in God merely as a projection of human wishes onto the sky.

Another figure in the Chronicles who exhibits an attitude that smacks of naturalism (even though it is not full-blooded materialism) is Nikabrik the dwarf. He is a pragmatist; that is, he is concerned only with practical consequences and the interests of dwarfs. At one point he expresses the view that the power of the White Witch to create the hundred-year winter was very "practical" and praised her support for the dwarfs. He looked solely at measurable results:

"Do *you* believe in Aslan?" said Caspian to Nikabrik.

"I'll believe in anyone or anything," said Nikabrik, "that'll batter these cursed Telmarine barbarians to pieces or drive them out of Narnia. Anyone or anything, Aslan or the White Witch, do you understand?"

This leads him to an alliance with a Wer-wolf and a Hag (who, in a significant moral inversion, calls the White Witch the "White Lady").

PAGANISM AND MYTHOLOGY IN LEWIS

Plato, a famous Greek philosopher born about 427 B.C. in Athens, was admired by Lewis and is important to the imaginative structure of the Chronicles. He was a founding father of idealism in philosophy. His work provided much imaginative inspiration for Lewis, though Lewis was not a Platonist as such. Some forms of Platonism were deeply influential during the medieval period, which was Lewis's great love and the object of much of his scholarship. Belief in the immortality of the soul, as held by Lewis and the Christian tradition, is not in itself Platonism, nor is imaginative use of the Platonic idea of this world as a copy of a more real one. Lewis provides a remarkable reworking of Plato's Myth of the Cave (from his *Republic*) in *SC*, beautifully providing a Christian defense in answer to the claim of the naturalist that God is a projection of the human being. Professor Kirke bemoans the fact that the Pevensie children have learned nothing in their schools of the possibility of other worlds interlocking with ours. Knowing Plato would have taught them this.

Lewis regarded Plato as a pagan whose insights prefigured Christian beliefs in some respects. In the Chronicles, Lewis explored pre-Christian paganism, the idea of a natural affinity with a biblical worldview, what he called the *anima naturaliter Christiana*. Certainly, Lewis's success as a contemporary Christian writer reveals that such faith can strike a deep chord around the world today. Much of this success came from his assuming a natural affinity between our ordinary humanity and Christian belief. Lewis wrote during an age of modernism, and he was a lifelong antimodernist. This led him to an imaginative defense of Christian faith that stands in the tradition of a spirituality that is increasingly attractive to contemporary readers. Lewis's exploration of paganism depends upon a distinction between Christian and pagan spirituality. Christian spirituality has to struggle long and hard to be consistent with orthodox theology. This didactic element is usually integrated successfully into Lewis's storytelling: many children read the Chronicles without being aware of their strong Christian themes. Lewis discovered, by writing the first of his science-fiction stories in the 1930s, that for modern readers theological themes could be carried unobtrusively and could even be undetected by them.

Lewis's spirituality results in a vision that affects all his life, thought and experience. Christian spirituality has to reckon with the Word of God, the Logos, guaranteeing a dignity to the articulation of reality in language. God (and indeed the far reaches of nature) can be spoken of. This leads naturally to discourse and stories. In Christian mysticism, mystery is always relative. For Lewis (as he learned from his friend Tolkien particularly) all pagan insights are unfinished and incomplete, anticipating the greatest story, God's "spell," or the Gospel. As a Christian storyteller, he grappled with pagan insights, exploring how far the pagan imagination could go without the light of Scripture, God's special revelation. In grappling with and affirming pagan insights, his attitude belongs to the thought patterns of the Middle Ages, to an older world. It stands against modernism and happily connects with our current climate. Ultimately, for Lewis, grace successfully spiritualizes and transforms nature. Human storytelling is fulfilled and even verified in the supreme act of grace, documented in the Gospels. Lewis embodies this grace most successfully in his creation of Aslan, the numinous God in lion form who can sing worlds into being.

Before and after his conversion to Christian faith, Lewis wrestled with the anthropology of James G. Frazer (1854-1941), as represented in the widely influential *The Golden Bough: A Study in Magic and Religion* (abridged edition, 1922). Lewis came to see serious errors in Frazer's view of pagan mythology. Sir James Frazer explored magic and religions throughout the world in the hope of tracing an important part of the evolution of human thought. As a result, *The Golden Bough* (originally in thirteen volumes) is encyclopedic. In seeking a unified development, Frazer denied the value of asking whether religions were true or false. In his view, Christianity had no uniqueness. Lewis came to the conclusion that similarities between biblical teaching and ancient myths can argue for the truth of Christianity as well as against it, though at first they seemed devastating to Christian belief. He extensively made use of such similarities in the Chronicles, populating his stories generously with beings from classical, northern and Celtic mythology, beings such as Bacchus and Silenus, who romp wildly round Aslan in a Great Dance. Susan remarks to Lucy:

"I say, Lu—"

"What?"

"I wouldn't have felt safe with Bacchus and all his wild girls if we'd met them without Aslan."

"I should think not," said Lucy.

James Frazer had documented many myths of dying and rising gods throughout the world. As Lewis developed as a Christian thinker, he continued to reflect on such myths. He argued that "We must not be nervous about 'parallels' and 'pagan Christs': they ought to be there—it would be a stumbling block if they weren't."

A distinctive example of a dying god is Balder. In Scandinavian mythology, Balder was the god of light and joy. He was son of Odin and Frigg, king and queen of the gods. In a dream, Frigg was warned that Balder's life was threatened. Frigg made all the forces and beings in nature swear that they would not harm Balder. There was one exception that she overlooked however—the mistletoe. When the gods hurled darts and stones at Balder, Loki placed mistletoe in the hands of his twin brother, Hoder, the blind god of darkness. Balder was slain. Odin sent Hermod, another brother, to the underworld to plead for his return. It was granted that if everything in the world would weep for him, he could return from death. Everything did so but for one ancient giantess (said to be the mischievous Loki in disguise).

In *Surprised by Joy,* Lewis records the impact this story had upon him even in its barest form: "Instantly I was uplifted into huge regions of northern sky, I desired with almost sickening intensity something never to be described (except that it is cold, spacious, severe, pale, and remote)."

Lewis confessed that he loved Balder before he loved Christ. He came to see, however, that Christ's incarnation in history made abstract reality tangible to human beings much more successfully than mere myth, even though myth, like poetry, has the power to make concrete what would otherwise be abstractions and imponderables.

In one of his letters, Lewis speculates that some modern people may need to be brought to pre-Christian pagan insights in preparation for more adequately receiving the gospel. He writes:

> For my part I believe we ought to work not only at spreading the Gospel (that certainly) but also at a certain preparation for the Gospel. It is necessary to recall many to the law of nature *before* we talk about God. For Christ promises forgiveness of sins: but what is that to those who, since they do not know the law of nature, do not know that they have sinned? Who will take medicine unless he knows he is in the grip of disease? Moral relativity is the enemy we have to overcome before we tackle Atheism. I would almost dare to say "First let us make the younger generation good pagans and afterwards let us make them Christians."

The Chronicles were Lewis's main attempt at a "preparation for the Gospel," inculcating a kind of good paganism in its modern readers.

THE CENTRAL IMPORTANCE OF MYTH

Our word *myth* comes from a Greek word that means "story." J. R. R. Tolkien wrote a poem to C. S. Lewis about the making of myth ("mythopoeia") in which he argued that while speech is invention about objects and ideas, myth is invention about truth, transcending thought and transforming the objective into a quality rather than a quantity. Myth and language are part of one knowing process. Myth has the ability to make concrete what would otherwise remain abstract. In fact, without the shaping of our perception by myth, and other imaginative creations (such as metaphors and models), we would not know real things, only abstractions. There is therefore an intimate connection between myth and thought.

Lewis grew to accept his friend's view of the importance of myth. Tolkien and he placed the highest value on the making of myth in imaginative fiction and poetry. The appeal of the making of myth is that it implies the creation of an imaginative world in which the storyteller arouses a reader's imagination, leading to another dimension of understanding. In his *An Experiment in Criticism,* Lewis argued that some stories are outright myths—as is the story of Cupid and Psyche. Other stories have what Lewis called a "mythical quality." Examples he gave were the plots of *Dr. Jekyll and Mr. Hyde,* H. G. Wells's *The Door in the Wall,* Kafka's *The Castle,* the conceptions of Gormenghast in Mervyn Peake's *Titus Groan,* and the Ents and Lothlorien in Tolkien's *The Lord of the Rings.* Lewis tried to pin down the elusive features of myth in the same book: (1) It is independent of the form of words used to tell the story. (2) Narrative features such as suspense or surprise play little part in the distinctive pleasure of myth. (3) Our empathy with the characters of the story is at a minimum; we do not imaginatively transport ourselves into their lives. (4) Myth is alway fantasy, dealing with the impossible and preternatural. (5) Myth is never comic; though the experience may be joyful or sad, it is always grave. (6) The experience in fact is awe-inspiring, containing a numinous quality.

Lewis draws upon ancient mythology in elements of his Narnian stories, and in many of his characters, which are drawn from classical, Old Norse and Celtic mythology: Bacchus, Silenus, fauns, centaurs, giants, dwarfs and a Snow Queen, to name a few. His greatest imaginative achievement in the Chronicles is the creation of Aslan, who takes on the status of myth. A numinous quality surrounds him, one evidence of which is his smell and another his roar. Though he is not a "tame lion," the children delight in running their hands through Aslan's mane. Though his death is solemn and grave, he romps with the girls Lucy and Susan after his resurrection. His very name evokes a strange longing. He sings the world of Narnia into being.

At the heart of Christianity, Lewis believed, is a myth that is also a fact—making the claims of Christianity unique. In the Christian story myth is born and lives properly for the first time, rather than remaining merely figurative. The Gospels had all the qualities of great human storytelling. But they portrayed a true event—God the storyteller entered his own story, in the flesh, and brought a joyous conclusion from a tragic situation. Lewis became a Christian believer when he saw that the nourishment he had always received from great myths and fantasy stories was a taste of that greatest, truest story—of the life, death and resurrection of Christ.

By becoming fact, Lewis points out, the story of a dying God returning to life did not cease to be myth, or lose the quality of myth. Lewis praised John Milton for retaining the tangible quality of myth in most of *Paradise Lost,* his great epic, which is one of the most powerful of credal affirmations in Christian literature. Lewis strived to follow Milton's example in his own fiction, including the Chronicles.

In writing the Narnia stories, Lewis drew upon what he saw as pagan anticipations of the Gospel in myth. In *The Pilgrim's Regress,* written soon after Lewis's conversion, John the pilgrim is in the caverns near his journey's end. A voice speaks out, a voice (Kathryn Lindskoog points out) that is rather like Aslan's. John is troubled because Wisdom, an allegorical figure, has told John his experiences on his journey had been figurative and mythological, not actual happenings. The Voice explains, in answer to his puzzlement:

> Child, if you will, it *is* mythology. It is but truth, not fact: an image, not the very real. But then it is My mythology. The words of Wisdom are also myth and metaphor: but since they do not know themselves for what they are, in them the hidden myth is master, where it should be servant: and it is but of man's inventing. But this is My inventing, this is the veil under which I have chosen to appear even from the first until now. For this end I made your senses and for this end your imagination, that you might see my face and live. . . . Was there any age in any land when men did not know that corn and wine were the blood and body of a dying and yet living God?

Pagan insights into a dying god, drawn from cultures around the world, played an important part in Lewis's own recognition of the truth of Christianity, and this image of the dying god is one of many pagan myths that he built into Narnia's magical world.

Literary Features of
the Chronicles

Any amount of theology can be smuggled into people's minds under cover of romance without their knowing it." So Lewis dryly wrote to his friend Sister Penelope on July 9, 1939. He had been reading reviews of his *Out of the Silent Planet,* and only a tiny proportion (two of about sixty) seemed to realize the theological underpinnings of his idea of the fall of the Bent One.

By "romance" Lewis meant strongly imaginative stories that contained glimpses of other worlds, whether they be fantasy, fairy story or science fiction. Such stories are remote from everyday life, or at least unusual, in their strangeness, poignancy, heightened state or other qualities that appeal to the imagination. In keeping with this quality, H. G. Wells labeled his science fiction "scientific romances."

C. S. LEWIS'S THEOLOGY OF ROMANCE

In the light of his success in getting past people's barriers with his portrayal of Christian truth in his science-fiction stories, Lewis gradually worked out a theology of romanticism. He did this in practice, as a creative writer, but also suggested, more analytically in several places, how such a theology looked. His theological approach underpins his late literary work, *An Experiment in Criticism*. His theology of romance owed much to the nineteenth-century writer who was Lewis's mentor, George MacDonald. The designation "romantic theologian," Lewis tells us, was invented by his friend Charles Williams. What Lewis says about Williams applies also to himself.

> A romantic theologian does not mean one who is romantic about theology but one who is theological about romance, one who considers the theological implications of those experiences which are called romantic. The belief that the most serious and ecstatic experiences either of human love or of imaginative literature have such theological implications and that they can be healthy and fruitful only if the implications are diligently thought out and severely lived, is the root principle of all his [Williams's] work.

Lewis particularly worked out the theological implications of the experience of sweet desire he called "joy" (see chapter three). Like Charles Williams, he had a profoundly imaginative perception of life. "The imaginative man in me is older, more continuously operative, and in that sense more basic than either the religious writer or the critic," Lewis tellingly confessed in a letter written in 1954. His imagination had made him try to be a poet and after his conversion encouraged him "to embody my religious belief in symbolical or mythopoeic forms." These forms included the Chronicles. He chose to write for children, not to give them what they wanted, "but because the fairy-tale was the genre best fitted for what I wanted to say."

Lewis is a central twentieth-century example of a writer of Christian fantasy, along with his friends J. R. R. Tolkien and Charles Williams. These writers stand in a rich tradition, dating back to early stories of

King Arthur. Such writers give a high place to the imagination as a faculty of meaning.

In the light of a theological perspective on romance like Lewis's, the definition of *fantasy* in *The Encyclopedia of Fantasy* is helpful: "A fantasy text is a self-coherent narrative. When set in this world, it tells a story which is impossible in the world as we perceive it; when set in an otherworld, that otherworld will be impossible, though stories set there may be possible in its terms." This self-coherence requires belief in some kind of overarching story. Thus the fantasy text might well differ in its use of the fantastic from modernism and postmodernism, both of which, according to the *Encyclopedia,* question the very nature of story in their different ways.

The imagination for Lewis is concerned with apprehending realities (even if they belong to the unseen world), rather than with grasping concepts. Imaginative invention is justifiable in its own right. It does not have to be justified by being forced to carry a message.

This is why good works of imagination cannot be reduced to morals and lessons, although lessons can be derived from them, and the truer the works the greater and richer the applications that can be drawn from them by the reader. They instruct by pleasure, even though their wisdom and insight are a matter of suggesting (or even smuggling in) new perceptions and perspectives, rather than a matter of conceptual ideas. In a review of Tolkien's *The Lord of the Rings,* Lewis noted that "what shows that we are reading myth, not allegory, is that there are no pointers to a specifically theological, or political, or psychological application. A myth points, for each reader, to the realm he lives in most. It is a master key; use it on what door you like." Why then use fantasy to make a serious point? Because, Lewis answers, the writer wants

to say that the real life of men is of that mythical and heroic quality.
. . . And Man as a whole, Man pitted against the universe, have we

94

seen him at all till we see that he is like a hero in a fairy tale?

"The value of the myth is that it takes all the things we know and restores to them the rich significance which has been hidden by 'the veil of familiarity,'" he continued.

> The child enjoys his cold meat (otherwise dull to him) by pretending it is buffalo, just killed with his own bow and arrow. And the child is wise. The real meat comes back to him more savory for having been dipped in a story; you might say that only then is it the real meat. . . . By putting bread, gold, horse, apple, or the very roads into a myth, we do not retreat from reality: we rediscover it.

Similarly, although this sort of writing works with some readers but not with others, when it works, fantasy can "generalize while remaining concrete" and "at its best it can do more: it can give us experiences we have never had and thus, instead of 'commenting on life,' can add to it." This has a special importance for Christian communicators because fantasy can "steal past" the religious associations and demands that destroy one's ability to feel the truth of the Christian revelation as one should. "By casting all these things into an imaginary world, stripping them of their stained-glass and Sunday school associations, one could make them for the first time appear in their potency." The writer could, then, "steal past those watchful dragons."

Out of this belief about the nature and necessity of the imagination in storytelling, the features of Lewis's theology of romance emerge in the Chronicles: the symbolic depth he creates in the stories, his choice of the genre of fantasy, his concern to capture myth, his endeavors to shape imaginatively the reader's perception, and his conviction that imagination can enlarge our knowledge and even yield sensations never before experienced or else renewed and refreshed. These and other narrative features of the Chronicles are explored below.

ARE THE CHRONICLES ALLEGORY?

Lewis's friend J. R. R. Tolkien was critical of the Chronicles because he felt that they were too allegorical. Lewis denied a number of times that he was writing allegory; he was sensitive to this criticism. He argued rather that he was exploring what he called "supposals"—suppose, for instance, that there was a world of talking animals ruled over by the king of beasts, a talking lion who was also the maker of that world; suppose God had chosen to become bodily incarnate in that world appropriately as a lion.

Lewis did not intend Aslan to be an allegory of Christ. He explained why in a letter written a few days after Christmas, 1958:

> By an allegory I mean a composition (whether pictorial or literary) in which immaterial realities are represented as feigned physical objects; e.g., . . . in Bunyan, a giant represents Despair. If Aslan represented the immaterial Deity in the same way in which Giant Despair represents Despair, he would be an allegorical figure. In reality however he is an invention giving an imaginary answer to the question, "What might Christ become like, if there really were a world like Narnia and He chose to be incarnate and die and rise again in that world as he actually has done in ours?" This is not allegory at all.

In 1958 he replied to a letter from Lucy Barfield (to whom *LWW* is dedicated), one of many he received from children who had read one or more of the Chronicles. "You've got it exactly right. A strict allegory is like a puzzle with a solution; a great romance is like a flower whose smell reminds you of something you can't quite place. I think the something is the whole *quality* of life as we actually experience it." He referred to Tolkien's *The Lord of the Rings* as an example of a romance—a story that opens up the dimensions of other worlds. "I've never met Orcs or Ents or elves—but the feel of it, the sense of a huge past, of lowering danger, of heroic tasks achieved by the most apparently unheroic people, of distance, vastness, strangeness, homeliness (all blended together) is so exactly what living feels like to me."

Tolkien's criticism of the Chronicles was that too many allegorical elements (he felt) existed in the stories. As a genre, however, the Chronicles are not allegory but rather fairy tale, a branch of fantasy. As a genre, allegory is a figurative narrative or description sustained throughout a story, one that conveys a particular and well-signposted pattern of meaning, often moral and instructional. Notable examples in English literature are John Bunyan's *The Pilgrim's Progress* and Edmund Spenser's *The Faerie Queene* (both of which enormously influenced Lewis). Tolkien's short story "Leaf by Niggle" is in the genre of allegory, as is Lewis's *The Pilgrim's Regress*. It is possible for a symbolic story that is not in the genre to have allegorical elements. This is true for example of the biblical parables. There are a number of such elements in the Chronicles, as when the Wer-wolf initially introduces itself in a riddle. The creature explains himself in a "dull, grey voice":

> I'm hunger. I'm thirst. Where I bite, I hold till I die, and even after death they must cut out my mouthful from my enemy's body and bury it with me. I can fast a hundred years and not die. I can lie a hundred nights on the ice and not freeze. I can drink a river of blood and not burst. Show me your enemies.

Lewis pointed out that when Tolkien's *The Lord of the Rings* first appeared, some interpreted the one ring allegorically as meaning the atomic bomb. Tolkien corrected this view: "I think that many confuse 'applicability' with 'allegory'; but the one resides in the freedom of the reader, and the other in the purposed domination of the author." Contrasting myth and allegory, Lewis similarly wrote that a myth is a "story out of which ever varying meanings will grow" whereas allegory suggests one meaning. The Chronicles have a varied applicability, even though a Christian reader will be likely to recognize a Christian pattern of meaning. Lewis himself believed that the stories could inculcate a "good paganism" in a modern reader (see chapter four), a reader Lewis considered "post-Christian." This was part of his purpose in writing them.

FANTASY

Fantasy as a recognizable literary genre emerged in the nineteenth century and is associated with books for both adults and children, including *The King of the Golden River,* by John Ruskin (1851); *The Water Babies,* by Charles Kingsley (1863); *Phantastes,* by George MacDonald (1858); Lewis Carroll's "Alice" stories (1865, 1871); J. R. R. Tolkien's *The Hobbit* (1937) and *The Lord of the Rings* (1954-1955); Mervyn Peake's *Gormenghast* trilogy (1946-1949); and C. S. Lewis's Chronicles. Recent examples include J. K. Rowling's stories of Hogwart's School and Philip Pullman's *His Dark Materials* trilogy.

A dominant type of fantasy is Christian fantasy, the most well-known contemporary practitioners of which are Tolkien and Lewis, both friends and co-conspirators in a project to rehabilitate fairy stories for grownups. The project involved writing stories of the type grownups over a huge period of time have enjoyed, but which had only comparatively recently been relegated to children's reading. In fact, Tolkien remains in the vanguard of the entire modern adult-fantasy genre. Lewis also wrote fantasy for grownups with his science-fiction trilogy and his retelling of the myth of Cupid and Psyche, *Till We Have Faces.* He also demonstrated that even within the boundaries of children's literature, fantasy could burn with the intense fire of its origins, helping children to become more aware of the "beauties and terrors of the world," to use Tolkien's phrase.

Christian fantasy has a long and varied history. The literary origins are perhaps the Arthurian stories of the early Middle Ages. Its history includes Dante's fourteenth-century *The Divine Comedy,* the poignant Middle-English poem *Pearl,* Spenser's *The Faerie Queene,* Marlowe's *Dr. Faustus,* Bunyan's *The Pilgrim's Progress,* and George MacDonald's *Phantastes* and *Lilith.*

Lewis believed that when fantasy works well it approaches myth; that is, it can "generalize while remaining concrete" and "at its best it can do more: it can give us experiences we have never had and thus, instead of 'commenting on life,' can add to it." By this he meant that fantasy, like myth, can apply generally and universally even while retaining its distinctively concrete character. At its most successful it can achieve even more. It is able to offer us experiences and sensations that previously we have not had—fantasy can add to life rather than merely commenting on it. This idea appealed to him as he wrote the Chronicles. Fantasy, he believed, can "steal past" the religious associations and demands that destroy one's ability to feel the truth of the Christian revelation as one should.

One genre of fantasy is made up of "Arabian" tales—stories based on an Arabia that is more imaginary than real, populated by set pieces like oases and deserts, bazaars and slums, flat-topped dwellings, spreading Bedouin tents, olive-dark skins, and skylines dominated by minarets. The immediate imaginative source of such stories is the tales making up *The Arabian Nights,* but tales like this go back to the presence of conquering Islam in southern parts of Europe. Cities in such stories are often based on an imagined Cairo or Baghdad, bustling with beggars, eunuchs, caliphs, viziers and genies. Lewis drew on this genre in creating Calormen, to Narnia's south (reflecting the north-south location of Christendom and Islam in the Middle Ages). He also wrote his own Arabian fantasy in *HHB,* over half of which is set in Calormen, featuring its dry landscapes, its desert, and its crowded and noisy city of Tashbaan.

Aravis, a central protagonist, is a member of the Calormene nobility. Arabian tales are very much a Western fantasy, and this is reflected in Lewis's own use of the genre. He sometimes employs the worst stereotypes—in one place describing the breath of Calormenes as smelling of garlic and onions (a stereotype which used to be reserved by the English for the French). But he also, with great sensitivity, explores the imaginative insights of Calormene culture into the nature of God expressed in the spiritual quests of Aravis and Emeth, which lead them by different trails to Aslan, the creator and true ruler of the world in which Narnia and Calormen exist.

PERCEPTION SHAPED BY THE IMAGINATION

Commenting on how Uncle Andrew perceives the scene after Narnia has come into being, the narrator says, "What you see and hear depends a good deal on where you are standing: it also depends on the sort of person you are." Andrew is full of terror and, after some effort, cannot even hear the sounds of talking animals, including Aslan's, as speech or song. "He had never liked animals at the best of times, being usually rather afraid of them; and of course years of doing cruel experiments on animals had made him hate and fear them far more."

C. S. Lewis suggests that imaginative literature creates a symbolic perception of reality. He gave a very simple illustration of this kind of perception in his essay "On Stories" in explaining the logic of the fairy story, which "is as strict as that of a realistic novel, though different." Referring to *The Wind in the Willows*, he asked:

> Does anyone believe that Kenneth Grahame made an arbitrary choice when he gave his principal character the form of a toad, or that a stag, a pigeon, a lion, would have done as well? The choice is based on the fact that the real toad's face has a grotesque resemblance to a certain kind of human face—a rather apoplectic face

with a fatuous grin on it. . . . Looking at the creature we thus see, isolated and fixed, an aspect of human vanity in its funniest and most pardonable form.

The Encyclopedia of Fantasy points out the subversive nature of fantasy in encouraging a perceptual shift: "It could be argued that, if fantasy (and debatably the literature of the fantastic as a whole) has a purpose other than to entertain, it is to show readers *how to perceive;* an extension of the argument is that fantasy may try to alter readers' perception of reality." This point is explained more, as follows: "The best fantasy introduces its readers into a playground of rethought perception, where there are no restrictions other than those of the human imagination. . . . Most full-fantasy texts have at their core the urge to *change* the reader; that is, full fantasy is by definition a subversive literary form."

The Chronicles bring out strikingly different perceptions of the White Witch and Aslan. All the time, of course, the reader knows which is right, due to the skill of the narrator. In *LWW* there is a marked constrast between Edmund's and Lucy's perception of the White Witch. Over a millennium later Nikabrik the dwarf quite admires the White Witch, and the Hag calls her the "White Lady." All the beings of Narnia are ultimately judged by their perception of Aslan, passing to his right or left in *LB*.

The creatures came rushing on, their eyes brighter and brighter as they drew nearer. . . . But as they came right up to Aslan one or other of two things happened to each of them.They all looked straight in his face; I don't think they had any choice about that. And when some looked, the expression on their faces changed terribly—it was fear and hatred. . . . And all the creatures who looked at Aslan in that way swerved to their right, his left, and disappeared into his huge black shadow. . . . But the others looked in the face of Aslan and loved him, though some of them were very frightened at the same time.

Magic (associated with the White and Green Witches) often affects someone's perception rather than altering reality—they fall victim of illusion. Prince Rilian has only one hour per day when the spell of the Green Witch no longer holds him in illusion, and he has to be tied to a chair to prevent him from acting on the true knowledge he has then.

RECOGNITION AND UNDECEPTION

Connected to the imaginative shaping of perception is recognition. The premise behind recognition is that we live in a story-shaped world. In stories, the prime recognition is that someone is within a story of some kind. Aristotle saw recognition marking a fundamental shift in the movement of a story from a tangle of ignorance to knowledge. A protagonist recognizes that "the Story has been telling them"—a narrative structure precedes the event they are in, and will reach a conclusion subsequent to that event. Recognition is perhaps best illustrated by the moment in *LB* when the children and others realize that they are in a new Narnia, a Narnia that is also linked to England transfigured, the beginning of a new chapter in the great story. Throughout the Chronicles, this is the recognition that Aslan is behind all the stories of the individual characters; he shapes them. In *HHB,* when Shasta (now known as Prince Cor) tells Aravis the story of how he was found as a child, he recognizes that Aslan "seems to be at the back of all the stories."

For Lewis, and also for Tolkien, a key moment of recognition in the Gospels is Christ's resurrection—the sudden turn that denies final defeat. Lewis memorably captures this turn in the restoration of Aslan after his cruel death on the Stone Table.

Undeception is an important instance of the category of recognition. It is a quality that has theological implications.

Undeception was a favorite theme of Lewis, for whom a characteristic of the human condition is the state of being deceived by others, by sin, or by oneself. He refers to the concept of undeception in his essay "A Note on Jane Austen," in *Selected Literary Essays*. He finds the theme in her novels, which were favorite reading for him. Many of Lewis's fictional characters experience undeception, usually associated with salvation. In *SC,* Prince Rilian has an hour each day when the deception weaved about him by the Green Witch lifts. He has to be restrained in the enchanted Silver Chair to stop him from acting on this knowledge. Edmund, the betrayer of his brother and sisters, undergoes undeception in *LWW,* seeing the witch in her true nature. Eustace in *VDT* experiences undeception through the painful experience of turning into a dragon. In *HHB,* the talking horse Bree is undeceived when he perceives the true nature of Aslan upon encountering it at the Hermit's house.

Lewis regarded the purpose of his fiction as helping to undeceive modern people, who are separated from the past. He intended to provide knowledge of perenniel human values and an acquaintance with basic Christian teaching about the realities of sin, redemption, immortality, divine judgment and grace.

Amnesia and Lost and Distant Knowledge

Amnesia and partly apprehended knowledge is a plot device common in fantasy literature and employed by Lewis in the Chronicles, whether it is a spell representing bondage through forgetting, or the absence of important knowledge. In *SC,* Prince Rilian is kept in a state of amnesia about Narnia and his true status as a Narnian prince, only coming out of his forgetfulness once a day, when he is bound to a silver chair to stop him from acting on his knowledge. In *HHB,* Shasta is unaware that he is anything more than an ordinary Calormene boy, though he knows he is an orphan and that his skin color is different from the Calormenes he knows. He senses that he lacks some important knowledge about himself.

In the Wood Between the Worlds in *MN,* a borderland of many portals to various worlds, arriving travelers very quickly fall into a state of pleasant stupor and forgetfulness, although Jadis finds it a place of terror, particularly as her magic powers fail. In the wood, life becomes like something in a dream, where visitors are in danger of sleeping forever.

In *SC,* the Green Witch uses a weapon of amnesia or forgetfulness not only on Prince Rilian but, in a different way, upon the gnomes in Underland. This was originally a happy place. She brings Underlanders from the deep realm of Bism to a region nearer the world's surface, where they work for her in glum servitude, their memory of their past hidden from them by her enchantment.

In *VDT,* forgetfulness of sleep is a blessing for Lord Rhoop after his experiences on the Dark Island, where dreams come true.

Talking Animals

Talking animals have a long tradition in literature, mythology and folk tales. The ancient tales of Aesop are still read today. Narnia, of course, is a land of talking animals, and there are other examples in contemporary fantasy, such as the great figure of Iorek Byrnison, the armored bear in Philip Pullman's *Northern Lights.*

Talking animals are normally animals in this world that talk (as do the serpent and Balaam's ass in the Bible, and Mr. Toad and Badger in the Wild Wood). In another world setting they would simply be animals that had the feature of speech, as in the hrossa on Malacandra in C. S. Lewis's *Out of the Silent Planet.* In Narnia, talking beasts, even though they are in another world, are self-consciously talking animals, an awareness created by the presence of humans. At the very beginning of Narnia, beasts are dumb (with the exception of the Creator-Lion), and a selected group are subsequently given the gift of speech in the presence of humans. The gift can be taken away, as in the fearful judgment upon Ginger the cat in *LB*.

Lewis was constantly fascinated by the gap between humanity and the subhumanity of beasts. The title of his Narnian tale *The Horse and His Boy* tells it all, a title cleverly suggested by his publisher. The pronoun, "his," bridges the gap between animal and human; the boy, Shasta, belongs as much to the talking Narnian horse, Bree, as Bree belongs to Shasta. Lewis's fascination with this gap is evident in his magnificent concept of Narnia as a land of talking beasts created by the great talking lion, Aslan. Talking animals are normally found only in children's books, such as *The Wind in the Willows,* by Kenneth Grahame, a book much admired and quoted by Lewis, or in the tales of Beatrix Potter. In his science-fiction tale *Out of the Silent Planet*, however, Lewis smuggles in talking animals that are palatable to the adult reader. Most notably this is the case with the hrossa, who, though personal beings, also retain the qualities of animals.

Lewis regarded the invention of talking beasts as a feature of what his friend J. R. R. Tolkien called "sub-creation." Lewis once wrote: "We do not want merely to see beauty. . . . We want something else which can hardly be put into words—to be united with the beauty we see, to pass into it, to receive it into ourselves, to bathe in it, to become part of it. That is why we have peopled air and earth and water with gods and goddesses and nymphs and elves." And, we might add, the talking beasts of Narnia, including Aslan.

THE NARRATOR IN THE CHRONICLES

A story is always told from a point of view. A point of view in a story is the perspective adopted by the author in presenting characters, actions, setting and events that make up the narrative. In the Chronicles, Lewis chose to write in the third person, only very occasionally (and unobtrusively) reverting to a first-person perspective. This was more effective than an entire first-person narration located in a particular character in being able to have the broader facts to hand. If Lewis had decided upon a first-person narrator, he could have told the story from the viewpoint of a participant—presumably Susan could have been the choice of narrator, as she was the only protagonist not to be killed in the railway accident in 1949. (Lewis could have also chosen a first-person narrator more removed, such as Alberta Scrubb, who might have changed her ways after losing Eustace, or one of the more thoughtful Telmarines who returned to this world.)

Third-person narrators normally choose between a God-like perspective (knowing everything that is going on, including the thoughts in the minds of all the protagonists and other players) or a deliberately limited point of view (which might still give insight into the thoughts of a single character who is the focus of the story). Lewis generally adopts a somewhat limited point of view (having to ask characters about their adventures, and in one place reporting that he had not been able to find out why something had happened), but cleverly using a variety of alternative, limited perspectives, as when the story is told for a while through Eustace's diary or through Trumpkin the dwarf (four chapters of PC). In HHB, Aravis and Shasta take the platform to tell their stories. (Aravis, who has been trained in storytelling as part of her Calormene education, tells hers well; Shasta, poorly educated, badly.) In fact, the whole of HHB is, we are informed, a popular tale told in Narnia. Even in writing LB, where Lewis patently couldn't have discovered the events from a protagonist, as none return, he retains a limited point of view in the narration rather than being God-like. He occasionally uses the first person ("If one could run without getting tired, I don't think one would often want to do anything else") and at the very end candidly admits that he has come to the limits of what he knows: "As He spoke, [Aslan] no longer looked to them like a lion; but the things that began to happen after that were so great and beautiful that I cannot write them. And for us this is the end of all the stories."

The persona of the narrator of the Chronicles is attractive, rather like a kindly uncle who doesn't look down on his nephews and nieces but constantly takes them into his confidence and expresses forthright opinions (as when he explains Narnian time in relation to English time): "When the Pevensie children had returned to Narnia last time for their second visit, it was (for the Narnians) as if King Arthur came back to Britain, as some people say he will. And I say the sooner the better."

In his memoir of his childhood reading, *The Child That Books Built,* Francis Spufford captures the quality of the narrator of the Narnian tales perfectly:

> The author's voice in the Narnia books kindly explained things to the child reading. . . . It was a gorgeously certain voice, which in itself lent a wonderful solidity to Narnia's stars and sausages, so that they blazed in their spheres and swelled in their skins, but it never spoke with adult detachment. . . . The voice was as impassioned as you were. It breathed as hard as you did; it felt awe, surprise, fear, joy and worshipfulness as much as you did; it luxuriated as you did in the idea of lying on the air like a sofa while the clouds went by beneath like sheep grazing on a big blue field.

NARNIA AS A SUBCREATION

Subcreation is a concept developed by Lewis's friend J. R. R. Tolkien, and one that deeply influenced him. It is expressed in Tolkien's famous essay "On Fairy Stories."

Tolkien believes that the art of true fantasy or fairy-story writing is subcreation: creating another or secondary world with such skill that it has an "inner consistency of reality." A clue to the concept of subcreation lies in the fact that the word *fairy,* or more properly *faery,* derives from "the realm or state where faeries have their being." A faery story is not thus a story that simply concerns faery beings. The beings are in some sense otherworldly, having a geography and history surrounding them. Tolkien's key idea is that Faery, the realm or state where faeries have their being, contains a whole cosmos, a microcosm. It contains the moon, the sun, the sky, trees and mountains, rivers, water and stones, as well as dragons, trolls, elves, dwarfs, goblins, elves, talking animals and even a mortal person when he or she is enchanted.

Tolkien's view, and the expression of it in *The Lord of the Rings,* was Lewis's inspiration for the creation of Narnia. Tolkien called the result of subcreation a secondary world. It is an imagined other world that is thoroughly consistent and plausible on its own inner terms. Tolkien's idea had an enormous influence on Lewis. Narnia, like Middle-earth, is a secondary world. Tolkien focused the storyteller's desire to have a well-imagined world as a context for the story, in which its symbolic geography heightened the events. Pre-Tolkienian fantasies or symbolic stories often have a rudimentary but discernible secondary world, as in John Bunyan's *The Pilgrim's Progress* (1678) or George MacDonald's *Phantastes* (1858). C. S. Lewis's Narnia is an outstanding example of a successful secondary world, created with Tolkien's views in mind.

In imaginative literature an island is a common device for locating a secondary world of some kind (as in Caliban's island in Shakespeare's *The Tempest*) or a secondary world within an imagined world, as in the islands visited in *VDT* in the Chronicles. Islands provide a boundary for a heightened situation within a story or as a setting for a story. In the Chronicles each island encountered by the voyagers in *VDT* has a distinct character, representing distinctive dangers or opportunities. In the context of a journey, the islands represent stages of growth and discovery, for individuals and for a company. Eustace is tested and transformed on Dragon Island, and Lucy's transformation occurs on the Island of the Voices, where, with Aslan's help, she is able to make the islanders visible again. Caspian's trial happens when he glimpses the beauty of the World's End. The test is whether he will return, as promised, to Ramandu's Island, and to Ramandu's daughter, with whom he has fallen in love.

For Lewis, the inspiration for a voyage between islands, motivated by a distant quest, was twofold: the Celtic *Immram* (particularly the Voyage of Saint Brendan, which formed the basis of a long poem by his friend J. R. R. Tolkien) and Homer's *The Odyssey,* in which Odysseus slowly journeys back from Troy, encountering adventures on islands and in strange lands.

A secondary world presupposes a relationship of some kind with the primary world—the world we inhabit, and touch, taste, smell, hear, see, investigate and think about. A portal into a secondary world is a common feature of fantasy literature and is more specific than a threshold or borderland between worlds (like the Wood Between the Worlds, or Aslan's Country). A portal could be a mirror, a door, a gate, a tunnel, a picture, a labyrinth, a film or television screen, or (in science fiction) a wormhole in space-time. Portals in the Chronicles include the wardrobe (in *LWW*), a picture (in *VDT*), a South Sea island cave (in *PC*), a stable door (in *LB*), a railway station (in *PC* and *LB,* perhaps because it marks the junction of branch lines), or a door in the air (in *PC*). A portal is sometimes transportable, as with an amulet, a ring or a book. In the Chronicles, such a portal is evidenced in Uncle Andrew's magic rings. The idea of the portal is central to the conception of Narnia, and an important part of the imaginative attraction of the Chronicles. When someone goes through a portal, furthermore, he or she must face wonders and strangeness. These are abundant in the themes, concepts and images embodied in the land of Narnia.

Themes, Concepts
and Images in Narnia

Themes, concepts and images in the Chronicles range from the moral and spiritual to the literary. C. S. Lewis is not averse to addressing ideas of the past or the modern world in his themes. This chapter is supplementary to the preceding three chapters, exploring further images and themes arising out of Lewis's theological, philosophical and literary interests. The remarkable thing of course is that, far from remaining in the specialist, academic and relatively inaccessible realm of the scholar, these features are made concrete and tangible in the stories of Narnia.

MASTER ELEMENTS

Certain images, ideas and themes in a narrative have an integrating purpose, pulling together what would otherwise be disparate elements. They work together with the story line, or plot, to capture the richness that constitutes a good story. An important such master element in the Chronicles is that of the quest.

The quest often takes the form of a journey in symbolic literature. In fiction such as Lewis's, life and experience have the character of a journey, and this character can be intensified by art. The Christian possibilities of the quest have been explored by Thomas Malory (in *Morte d'Arthur*), by John Bunyan (in *The Pilgrim's Progress*), as well as by J. R. R. Tolkien—to name a few writers.

The quest motif is a hallmark of Lewis's writings, both fiction and nonfiction. *MN* records Digory's double quest for the magic apple and to save his dying mother; *VDT* also concerns a double quest, to find the lost lords and to discover Aslan's Country; *HHB* chronicles Shasta's journey to the north, to Narnia; *SC* tells of the quest of Eustace and Jill to find the long-lost Prince Rilian; and Lewis's autobiography, *Surprised by Joy*, tells of his personal quest for an elusive joy.

In *VDT* the quest is communal. The company on the *Dawn Treader* owes something to the Fellowship in *The Lord of the Rings*. Without losing the overall theme of quest, Lewis cleverly shifts in focus to different characters as they are tested and go through trial—first Eustace, then Lucy, and finally Caspian and Reepicheep.

Metamorphosis is a radical shift in shape that is willed by the being undergoing the change. Thus the Green Witch in *SC* intentionally appears as an alluring and beautiful young woman, to entice and capture Rilian, and at another time she becomes a green serpent to murder the queen, Rilian's mother. At one stage in *VDT* Aslan shifts shape from a lamb. The masterwork of such change is Ovid's *Metamorphosis* (c. A.D. 1-8).

Transformation is not the same thing as metamorphosis: it happens to a being through an external agent and, like metamorphosis, can be good or bad. The White Witch transforms many talking beasts and other creatures like fauns into statues. Aslan transforms the cabby's horse, Strawberry, into a flying horse (renaming him Fledge and giving him the gift of speech). At the creation of Narnia many beasts are transformed into talking animals and acquire a larger stature than that of their dumb counterparts. Most interestingly, Eustace Scrubb is transformed into a dragon and requires the intervention of Aslan to become a real boy again. This marks a deeper transformation from the boorish, self-centered Eustace to a boy with Old Narnian and Old Western values of courtesy, gentleness and honor, that is, Christian (or, should we say, Aslanian?) values.

Children who stumble into Narnia through portals from this world, or are called there to help, represent the humble and meek. Of such, in Lewis's view, is the kingdom of heaven. They are not perfect, having obvious faults, flare-ups and bickerings. Those who do serious wrongs (like Digory awakening evil in Charn and Edmund betraying his siblings) and those morally flawed (like Eustace, spoiled by a modern education and modern parents) go through a process of redemption or recompense. Lewis displays great skill in shaping events around a group of children, or a pair in company with Narnians, rather than telling the story of an individual. The interaction within a company or fellowship adds complexity and depth to the narrative. Lewis adds to the richness by introducing children from the world of Narnia into the story in *HHB*. The focus is upon Shasta and Aravis, with only tangential interaction with the human children Lucy, Edmund and Susan.

More than any other of his writings, the Chronicles reflect Lewis's love of *animals.* Throughout his adult life he was an inveterate keeper of dogs. At The Kilns the household ruled by Mrs. Moore kept chickens. (There are chicken coops on board the *Dawn Treader.*) A bear dubbed Mr. Bultitude by Lewis and his brother Warren featured at Whipsnade Zoo, and the brothers liked to visit to see him, the wallabies nearby and many other animals. Lewis was opposed to vivisection (see his essay on the subject in *Essay Collection*). Misuse of animals is deplored in the Chronicles, and not just physical abuse—Shift's employment of the simple Puzzle as a false Aslan evokes censure. The character of Jadis is disclosed in *MN* through her treatment of Strawberry, the cabby's horse:

"She was flogging the horse without mercy. Its nostrils were wide and red and its sides were spotted with foam." Poignantly, when Lucy and Susan go to the corpse of Aslan, murdered on the stone table, there is foam around the lion's mouth, marking his terrible suffering. Lewis's concern about animals is in the very fabric of the stories, in a detail like Digory and Polly's concern over the guinea pigs used by Uncle Andrew. Lewis celebrates animals most, of course, in the talking animals of Narnia (see chapter five), where animals and even trees can be beings endued with rationality.

In the world in which Narnia lies there is an important contrast of *east and west*. Aslan, it is well known, appears from the east. In fact, his country lies to the uttermost east, the goal of Reepicheep's quest in *VDT*. This orientation reflects medieval geography, in which Eden and paradise lie far to the east. In *PC* we are told of the land of Telmar, to the west, from which danger came to Narnia. It is likely that the portal through which the mariners from this world entered Narnia was close by the boundary between worlds.

In the larger scheme, the boundary to other worlds lies all around Narnia's earth, characterized by immense mountain ranges. This might explain why, in *MN,* Digory travels westward to find the magic apple in the Land of Youth, and in *LB* the way further up and deeper in to the new Narnia is also westward. It seems that the eastern and western borderlands to other worlds are closer to Narnia. Traveling north or south leads only to perils.

SPIRITUALITY

Many of the important themes in Narnia concern the spiritual or transcendent elements of human life. In an important way, they add dimensions to Lewis's theological and philosophical preoccupations. Like his friend J. R. R. Tolkien, Lewis believed that storytelling is the most natural way to convey spirituality and truth about the nature of reality. This can be seen for example in the use of *prophecy* in the Chronicles. In fantasy, prophecy and prediction are always of deep significance, central elements in the plot. Foretelling points normally to the processes of fate, but in Narnia (as in Tolkien's Middle-earth) prophecy signposts the workings of divine providence. The issue of individual freedom and agency is played out in relation to a personal and intelligent hand in the processes of events (even if mysterious), rather than against a blind fate. This creates a quality of hope rather than stoic endurance, a quality that can be as courageous as stoicism. In the Chronicles, providential events are always associated with Aslan.

A fundamental feature of fantasy and fairy stories is *restoration* or *recovery*. What is being recovered may be a land that has been blighted (as when spring reaches Narnia after a hundred years of deep winter) or a society in spiritual decline (as when the Old Narnians remove the rule of the Telmarines under the tyrant Miraz). For C. S. Lewis (as for his friend J. R. R. Tolkien) the template for all good stories is the biblical motif of restoration from a primeval fall into sin and wickedness, a restoration involving sacrifice. Very often in fantasy the force behind blight in land and society is a dark figure like Sauron in *The Lord of the Rings*. In the Chronicles it is the White Witch in *LWW,* the Green Witch in *SC,* and Shift the ape (unleashing the demonic terror of Tash) in *LB*. In *LB* Lewis portrays the horrific process of Narnia's subjection to Calormene overlords, as living trees are destroyed and noble talking beasts are taken into slavery.

Restoration or recovery brings about a healing of the wounds fundamentally caused, Lewis believed, when we act through the blindness of sin. Lewis rejected what he saw as the restless quest of the modern world to be original. Indeed, meaning was to be discovered in God's created world, not somehow to be created by human beings, and in this discovery imagination working through fantasy was an effective aid. G. K. Chesterton, in his book *Orthodoxy,* speaks of the way that children normally are not tired of familiar experience. In this sense they share in God's energy and vitality; he never tires of telling the sun to rise each morning. The child's attitude, in fact, is a true view of things, and dipping into the world of story can restore such a sense of freshness. Lewis explains that the child "does not despise real woods because he has read of enchanted woods: the reading makes all real woods a little enchanted." Similarly, for Lewis's friend J. R. R. Tolkien, fairy stories help us to make such a recovery—they bring healing—and "in that sense only a taste for them may make us, or keep us, childish."

Lewis was convinced that, through story, the real world becomes a more magical place, full of meaning. We see its pattern and color in a fresh way. The recovery of a true view of things applies both to individual things like hills and stones and to the cosmic—the depths of space and time itself. For in subcreation, as Tolkien taught him to believe, there is a "survey" of space and time. Reality is captured in miniature. Through subcreative stories—the type to which the Chronicles and his science fiction belong—a renewed view of reality in all its dimensions is given—the homely, the spiritual, the physical, the moral.

Healing is a common feature of fantasy tales, closely related to recovery and restoration, and often embodied in the central movement of the story. It occurs after the very worst has happened: the wasteland may become green again; spring may end a bitter, extended winter; a hero or leading character may emerge from a state of illusion or amnesia, or may escape from chains or bondage. Tolkien saw the ultimate expression of healing in fantasy and fairy story as *eucatastrophe* (literally, "good catastrophe"), the sudden turn in the story from the worst to the best. In the Narnian stories the ultimate turn or healing is that of the resurrection of Aslan on the stone table.

In the Chronicles, Lucy is a healer. Her gift from Father Christmas is a beautiful small diamond flask, containing healing cordial. The cordial has a pleasant smell, and Lucy employs it many times in her ministry, healing minor ailments like Eustace's seasickness and major injuries like life-threatening battle wounds.

THEMES OF THE MODERN WORLD

A number of Lewis's themes in the Chronicles illuminate the nature of modern society (see also chapter four, "Worldviews and Narnia"). Lewis indeed intended that the created world of Narnia, with its incipient stories, should provide a perspective from the "outside" on our modern world. Narnia embodies values and virtues of an older West and even further back in history, before the West (see "Images and Themes and Ideas from a Lost World" in this chapter, below).

Lewis believed that one of the strongest myths of our day is that of progress. Change is considered to have a value in itself. We are increasingly cut off from our past (and hence a proper perspective on the strengths and weaknesses of our own age). These attitudes lead to *chronological snobbery*. Lewis expressed this concern with the myth of progress in his inaugural lecture at Cambridge University, *"De Descriptione Temporum."* In the Chronicles this characteristically modern attitude is particularly exemplified by Eustace Scrubb and his parents, and by the Telmarine regime of Miraz, Caspian's uncle. His friend Owen Barfield made Lewis aware that he was corrupted with this attitude. Lewis explains:

> Barfield . . . made short work of what I have called my "chronological snobbery," the uncritical acceptance of the intellectual climate common to our age and the assumption that whatever has gone out of date is on that account discredited. You must find out why it went out of date; was it ever refuted (and if so by whom, where and how conclusively) or did it merely die away as fashions do? If

the latter, this tells us nothing about its truth or falsehood. From seeing this one passes to the realization that our age is also "a period," and certainly has, like all periods, its own characteristic illusions. They are likeliest to lurk in those wide-spread assumptions which are so ingrained in the age that no one dares to attack or feels it necessary to defend them.

Lewis makes a number of references to modern *education* in his fiction. Experiment House, for instance, in the story of *VDT,* embodies his dislike of modern educational methods. A similar distaste is evident in his portrayal in *PC* of the girl's school in Beruna, administered by the Telmarine regime. (Tight, uncomfortable clothes, in this case, school uniforms, are always an indicator of the unnatural in Lewis's writing.) Gwendolen is obviously a true Narnian, constricted by new Narnian education, which is drearily preoccupied with dry facts and lists rather than true learning. Judged only by his satire, Lewis might seem bilious. This is misleading. His powerful essay, *The Abolition of Man,* reveals antihuman values being unwittingly embodied in some typical school textbooks of his day.

Lewis nowhere more clearly put forward his vision of education than in his early essay "Our English Syllabus," in *Rehabilitations and Other Essays.* He confesses:

Human life means to me the life of beings for whom the leisured activities of thought, art, literature, conversation are the end, and the preservation and propagation of life merely the means. That is why education seems to me so important: it actualizes that potentiality for leisure, if you like for amateurishness, which is man's prerogative. You have noticed, I hope, that man is the only amateur animal; all the others are professionals. . . . The lion cannot stop hunting, nor the beaver making dams, nor the bee making honey.

When God made the beasts dumb He saved the world from infinite boredom, for if they could speak they would all of them, all day, talk nothing but shop.

IMAGES AND THEMES AND IDEAS FROM A LOST WORLD

In the Chronicles, Lewis attempted to capture the imaginative splendor of the Middle Ages and other features from the more ancient past of the Judeo-Christian and classical worlds, providing a contrast with the values of the modern world, as we also explored in chapter two, "The Background to the Chronicles of Narnia." A number of images and themes help to give solidity to this portrayal of a lost world.

One such theme is *astrology*. The night sky in Narnia is modeled upon a medieval one, with living stars and a world that is commonly perceived as flat (even though, in the Middle Ages, scholars were aware that the earth was a globe). The planets were ruled by intelligences, great lords and ladies (rather like the planets in Lewis's science-fiction trilogy). There is not a modern separation, therefore, between astronomy and astrology. Heaven and the starry skies were one. Signs in the skies are taken with utmost seriousness in Narnia. Centaurs have a remarkable facility in reading the portents.

Michael Ward has argued that the Chronicles playfully embody medieval astronomy. While his case might seem rather stretched, Ward does draw out Lewis's interest in medieval imagery. Each of the stories, Ward argues, represents one of the seven planets of astrology. In this scheme the seven astrological planets (the Moon, Mars, Mercury, Jupiter, Venus, Saturn and the Sun—the Roman days of the week) influenced people, events and the metals in the earth, each in a distinctive way. Ward argues that Lewis uses the astrological planets as spiritual symbols. In *VDT,* for instance, the voyagers head toward the sunrise, gold (the metal of the sun) tempts Eustace and provides the curse on Deathwater Island, and light takes on a numinous quality as the adventurers approach the End of the World and Aslan's Country.

Lewis saw the *centaur* as an appealing illustration of how nature might one day be harmonized with Spirit (*Miracles,* chap. 14). The mingling of human and natural delighted Lewis's imagination, which was oriented toward the premodern period—particularly the medieval and ancient world. For Lewis the characteristic feature of the modern world is the machine: it is perhaps significant that the modern imagination mingles the machine and humanity, rather than nature and humanity—a process Lewis prophetically explored through the growth of a sinister technocracy in *That Hideous Strength.*

In the Chronicles the centaurs of classical mythology are considerably softened. They are particularly associated in Lewis with prophecy (see, for example, "Roonwit" in part three: "The A-Z of Narnia").

The resounding images and vignettes of the *apocalypse,* depicting the end of the world, or great tribulation (where huge populations are affected), have had a powerful influence upon fantasy stories. The book of Revelation (written c. A.D. 95) is itself an example of a genre of apocalyptic, produced in a particularly turbulent period of Jewish history around 200 B.C. to A.D. 200. It is not surprising that Lewis, a daily reader of the Bible, draws upon the book of Revelation and other apocalyptic sections of the Bible in *LB.* This tells of the end of Narnia, and many images are easily recognizable from Revelation, as when the stars fall from the sky. There is, too, an antichrist, first in Shift the ape, then in the spiritual deceit of Tashlan.

The image of *apples and apple trees* is likely to be one of many signposts that Lewis deliberately placed in the Chronicles, pointing to the Christian pattern of meanings underlying the stories. It also may recall his childhood love of Irish fairy tales and folklore, in which the Isle of Apples, the Land of Eternal Youth, is a hint of the country of heaven.

The overgrown apple orchards of Cair Paravel, now in ruins, feature in *PC*. They help the children remember their previous visit to Narnia in *LWW,* when they were kings and queens. Also, the apples provide sustenance in their hunger. At the beginning of Narnia, Digory, in the far west, is sent to pluck an apple from a tree bearing silver apples. His temptation to use the healing apple to save his mother alludes to the ancient temptation of Eve, recorded in the Bible. Apples in Narnia signify what is beneficial and also indicate salvation. In an old poem, the apple tree signifies Christ, reversing the ancient curse upon humanity and reflecting biblical imagery in the Song of Songs:

> The tree of life my soul hath seen,
> Laden with fruit, and always green:
> The trees of nature fruitless be
> Compared with Christ the apple tree.
>
> This fruit doth make my soul to thrive,
> It keeps my dying faith alive;
> Which makes my soul in haste to be
> With Jesus Christ the apple tree.

PART TWO

ALL ABOUT
THE CHRONICLES
OF NARNIA

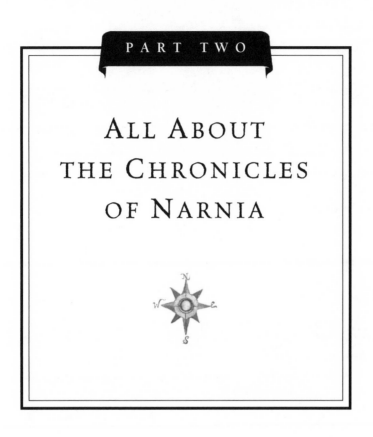

An Overview of
the Chronicles of Narnia

The seven tales for children by C. S. Lewis cover almost half of the twentieth century and over two and a half millennia of Narnian years from its creation to its final days. In order of Narnian time, the titles are *The Magician's Nephew; The Lion, the Witch, and the Wardrobe; The Horse and His Boy; Prince Caspian; The Voyage of the "Dawn Treader"; The Silver Chair;* and *The Last Battle.* Opinions vary about what order one should follow in reading the books. The first to be written was *LWW,* which is perhaps the best reason to read it first. The books are introduced below in order of publication. Note that *MN* was the second of the Chronicles to be attempted by Lewis, but because of some structural problems in the writing, he delayed finishing it, and so it was not published until 1955.

THE LION, THE WITCH, AND THE WARDROBE (1950)

This first tale of Narnia that Lewis wrote, *LWW,* began with a picture that he saw in his head of "a faun carrying an umbrella and parcels in a snowy wood." Four children, Peter, Edmund, Susan and Lucy Pevensie, are evacuated from wartime London to stay with Professor Digory Kirke. In one room of his vast house is a bulky wardrobe. Through this wardrobe the children enter a snowy wood in Narnia's Lantern Waste.

Lucy is the first to enter (in the stories she is the most spiritually perceptive of all the children) and soon comes across Mr. Tumnus near a lamp post (the origin of which is explained in *MN*). When she returns, discovering that no time in our world has passed at all, the others do not believe her story of a magical world through the wardrobe. Later, Edmund enters Narnia too, but is too mean-spirited to admit afterward to the others that he has, leaving Lucy more miserable than ever. Finally, however, all four pass through the portal into the land of fauns, wolves, beavers and other talking animals. Three of them join forces with those animals who are loyal to Aslan, the great talking lion, creator of Narnia. Edmund, however, turns traitor and goes over to the White Witch, who has Narnia in her spell, so that it is always winter and never Christmas.

Aslan pays the terrible cost of Edmund's treachery by sacrificing his own life to break the witch's magic. Narnia is freed as Aslan returns to life: the witch is destroyed after a battle in which Peter is tested in combat. The creatures that she had turned to stone are unpetrified by the lion. The Pevensie children spend many years in Narnia, growing up into young adults and reigning as kings and queens during Narnia's Golden Age. They have many adventures, including a visit to Calormen to the south (a visit that plays a part in the story of *HHB*). Eventually the four return to our world and find, as Lucy had before, that no time had passed here.

Professor Kirke reassures them with a proverb that reveals he knows a lot about Narnia: "Once a King in Narnia, always a King in Narnia." He says that sooner or later they will discover another entrance into that magical land. Why Kirke knows so much is revealed in *MN*, for it turns out that he had entered Narnia as a boy, forty years before.

PRINCE CASPIAN (1951)

A year after their first adventure in Narnia, the four Pevensie children are called back to help Caspian, the true heir to the throne, whose life is in danger from the tyrant Miraz, who holds control over Narnia. He has suppressed the Old Narnians who remained loyal to the ancient memory of Aslan and Narnia's past Golden Age, when the children had been kings and queens at Cair Paravel. Over a thousand years have passed in Narnian time since that era. This story reveals much about the history of Narnia over more than a millennium and how humans had come to dominate over the talking animals, as a result of Telmarines stumbling into Narnia from our world long before.

The depth of Narnia's historical past is vividly evoked for the children by the ancient ruins of Cair Paravel, the home of the four when they were kings and queens. There they are joined by a dwarf, Trumpkin, who has been sent by Prince Caspian to see if help has come from another world. Caspian has called for help by blowing the horn of Queen Susan, left behind from the Golden Age. Caspian is under siege from his uncle, Miraz, a Telmarine brutally suppressing any trace of Old Narnia. The children join Caspian and, with the return of Aslan in the nick of time, defeat the enemy with the help of walking trees.

THE VOYAGE OF THE "DAWN TREADER" (1952)

The sequel to *PC*, this is the story of a double quest, for seven lords of Narnia who disappeared during the reign of the wicked King Miraz and for Aslan's Country at the end of the world over the Eastern Ocean. Reepicheep the mouse is particularly seeking Aslan's Country, and his quest embodies Lewis's characteristic theme of joy. During the sea journey of the *Dawn Treader*, various islands are encountered, each with its own kind of adventure. The story has the character of an Old Irish *Immram*, a voyage among islands (such as the Voyage of Saint Brendan, which Lewis admired). It also owes something to Homer's ancient *The Odyssey*. Of the original Pevensie children, only Edmund and Lucy return to Narnia in this story. Their spoilt cousin, a "modern boy" named Eustace Clarence Scrubb (who almost deserves his name), is also drawn into Narnia. At one stage he turns into a dragon, and he becomes sorry for his behavior. Only Aslan, the great lion, is able to peel off his dragon skin and restore him.

The children join the ship on its journey between Narnia and the Lone Islands. Here they fall into the hands of slave traders. Beyond the Lone Islands they encounter a great storm, and the bedraggled *Dawn Treader* limps into the haven of Dragon Island (where Eustace becomes a better boy). Pursuing their quest eastward, and beyond Burnt Island, they are endangered by a great sea serpent. Nearby, at Deathwater Island, they find a missing lord turned to gold and narrowly miss the same fate. Yet farther east they come across the mysterious Island of Voices, where Lucy reads a great magician's book, in one of the most delightful episodes in the Chronicles. Further on, after the nightmare adventure at Dark Island, they find refreshment at World's End Island. Here they meet Ramandu, a star, and his beautiful daughter, who later becomes Caspian's queen. After sailing across the final Silver Sea, they approach Aslan's Country, the end of Reepicheep's quest.

VDT, like J. R. R. Tolkien's *The Fellowship of the Ring*, is a communal quest, even though there are elements of the individual journey of the kind we find in *The Pilgrim's Regress*. As the voyage progresses, there are skillful shifts in focus to different characters as they are tested and go through trial, in particular Eustace, Lucy and Caspian. This balance of fellowship and individual testing is part of the structural balance of *VDT*. *VDT* most expresses the beautifully crafted unity-in-diversity that is a hallmark of the Chronicles (see chapter five, "Literary Features of the Chronicles"). The rich mix of adventures never distracts from the forward movement of the narrative, concerned with the quest.

THE SILVER CHAIR (1953)

This sequel to *VDT* concerns Eustace Scrubb and another unfortunate pupil of Experiment House (a "modern school," Lewis tells us). Jill Pole is called into Narnia with Eustace to take part in a quest for the long-lost Prince Rilian, son of Caspian X, the Caspian of the previous adventure, now in his old age (for many years have passed in Narnia during the few months since the last adventure). The children's search takes them into the wild lands north of Narnia and eventually into a realm below the earth called Underland. The two children are accompanied by one of Lewis's most memorable creations, Puddleglum the Marsh-wiggle. They encounter and destroy the Green Witch, murderer of Rilian's mother. Before that, they narrowly escape being eaten by the giants of the city of Harfang, for whom man is a delicacy; even the tough Marsh-wiggle is in their cookery book.

The theme of *SC* very much concerns recognition (see the subsection "Recognition and Undeception" in chapter five) and perception, in the face of the misleading and the illusionary. Another central theme is obedience to the clear instructions of Aslan concerning the quest, even in the face of confusion.

THE HORSE AND HIS BOY (1954)

Set in the period of Narnia's Golden Age, most of the story unfolds in the cruel southern land of Calormen. A lost son of King Lune of the friendly country of Archenland, north of Calormen, has been brought up by a poor fisherman. He has the name Shasta and knows nothing of his true origin and real name (Prince Cor), but has a strange longing to travel to the northern lands.

The story also concerns a high-born Calormene girl, Aravis, who runs away from home to flee an unpleasant marriage. Both children independently encounter Narnian talking horses, in captivity in Calormen, who tell them about the freedom of Narnia's pleasant land and who escape with the children. The two pairs of horses and their children meet up, seemly by accident, but by Aslan's design, on the road, all on a quest to reach Narnia.

When passing through Calormen's capital, Tashbaan, Aravis uncovers a treacherous plot to conquer Archenland and Narnia, led by the spiteful Prince Rabadash, foiled in his suit of Queen Susan of Narnia. With great courage, and some failures, the children are able to warn the two northern countries of their danger. The Calormene plot fails; Shasta is restored to his father; the two horses, Bree and Hwin, return to their talking companions in Narnia; and Cor and Aravis marry, to become king and queen of Archenland after Lune's death. Bree particularly has hard lessons to learn about himself and about the true nature of Aslan. He is the most well-defined talking animal created in the Chronicles, with the exception of Aslan himself. He interacts convincingly with Hwin, Shasta and Aravis on their long journey. Aravis learns to recognize (see "Recognition and Undeception" in chapter five) the qualities of the seemingly lowborn Shasta.

Several of the characters familiar to readers of *LWW* appear in this book, including most of the Pevensie children and the faun, Mr. Tumnus. Both the skeptical horse Bree and the disdainful Aravis have to encounter Aslan.

This tale reveals some of the extent to which the geography of the world of Narnia is drawn from the late medieval picture of reality that Lewis loved so deeply, as portrayed in his brilliant study, *The Discarded Image*.

THE MAGICIAN'S NEPHEW (1955)

This tale tells of the creation of Narnia by Aslan. It also tells us about the Victorian childhood of Digory Kirke, and about how the London gas lamp post comes to be in Narnia at all. Also it speaks of the origin of the White Witch and explains the arrival of evil in Narnia—showing the evil as older than that world.

Digory and his dying mother are staying with his Uncle Andrew and Aunt Letty in London, his father being in India. He has made friends with Polly Plummer, his neighbor, and the two are tricked into an experiment with magic rings by the uncle, an eccentric magician.

At first they find themselves in the dying world of Charn, blighted by Jadis, the White Witch, whom Digory awakes from a spell, despite warnings from Polly. They are unable to leave her behind as they return to London with the aid of the rings. There Jadis wreaks havoc until the children are able to whisk her back to the Wood Between the Worlds, but not before she has wrenched off a handle from a lamp post, intending to use it to punish those who oppose her. The trio, along with Frank, a London cabby; his horse, Strawberry; and Uncle Andrew, end up in an empty world of Nothing, in time to hear Aslan's creation song. At the words and music of the lion's song, mountains, trees, animals and other creatures come into being to make Narnia and the world of which it is part. The sequence is reminiscent of passages from J. R. R. Tolkien's *The Silmarillion,* parts of which Lewis was familiar with in unfinished form.

Aslan gives Digory the opportunity of undoing the evil he had brought into Narnia. His task is to find a magic apple, the seed of which would produce a tree to protect the young world from Jadis for many a year. Polly joins him on the adventure, which requires journeying into the mountains of the Western Wild to find a delightful valley. In a garden there, on a hilltop, grows an apple tree bearing the magic apples. To help them, the cabby's horse, Strawberry, renamed Fledge by Aslan, is transformed into a flying and talking horse to carry them.

Upon the children's return, Aslan allows Digory to bring back an apple from the tree (which had immediately sprung up from the apple's seed) to restore his dying mother. Lewis's own mother, Flora Hamilton Lewis, died when he was a boy in Victorian Belfast (see chapter one, "The Life of C. S. Lewis").

In the fecundity of new growth associated with Narnia's creation, the metal pole brought by the Witch grows into a lamp post in Lantern Waste, and a great apple tree grows in England from the core of the magic apple eaten by Mrs. Kirke. Many years later, after the great tree falls, Digory has it made into a large wardrobe, the very same wardrobe that features in *LWW* as a portal into Narnia.

THE LAST BATTLE (1956)

LB tells of the passing of Narnia and the beginning of the New Narnia. Based upon biblical prophecies of the end of the world, this story tells the end of one world, the world of which Narnia is a part, how all worlds are linked, and how the great talking lion Aslan is the key to this link. Thus the Chronicles draw to their conclusion, and the consistency of their otherworldliness is established.

LB recounts the attempt of Shift the talking ape to delude the creatures of Narnia that Aslan has returned. Shift drapes Puzzle, a simple donkey, in a lion skin found floating in the river. He then persuades the talking animals that Puzzle is Aslan returned, and that he, Shift, is his spokesperson. Worse, he forms an alliance with Narnia's traditional enemy, Calormen. Young King Tirian, the last of the Narnian rulers, and seventh in descent from Rilian, hears of evil things happening—talking trees cut down, Narnian animals enslaved—and cannot believe that Aslan has returned and that this is his will. With his loyal unicorn, Jewel, he resists the Calormenes and is captured. Like several before him in previous ages, he calls for help from our world.

Tirian knows that in Narnian history children from another world are brought into Narnia to help or to rule. In this case, Eustace Scrubb and

Jill Pole come from our world. They are sent by Aslan in answer to Tirian's prayer. Aslan later also returns. Back in our world, Professor Digory Kirke and Polly Plummer, the very first visitors to Narnia (as recounted in *MN*), have called together those who had been in Narnia, "The Friends of Narnia." There is a train crash, which kills all those who answer the call, both those in an arriving train and those awaiting it at the station. All go in to be present after the end of Narnia, though only Eustace and Jill return to be active participants in the final battle against evil, helping Tirian, Jewel and the loyal Narnians. The visitors see Aslan's judgment of all the inhabitants of Narnia and its other countries and then are called "further up and further in" to a New Narnia. They discover that it is now permanently linked to their own, familiar world of England. They would never again have to part from Aslan, though now they see him in a new form.

LB shows the influence of George Orwell's *Animal Farm* (1945), admired by Lewis, in picturing modern tyranny over people and the land through the events that unfold in Narnia through the coalition between Shift and the Calormenes. The *Animal Farm* aspect of *LB* moves seamlessly on to the apocalyptic ending of Narnia, brilliantly giving variety in a wider unity.

One of the strangest features of the story, a twist reminiscent of Charles Williams, is that all the principal characters from our world are already dead as a result of a train accident. There are some similarities with Lewis's *The Great Divorce,* in that events after death are imagined and a vision of heaven is presented.

LB won the high-ranking Carnegie Medal for the best children's book of its year.

The History of Narnia

This chapter describes the history of Narnia, then provides chronologies of events in twentieth-century England and in Narnia.

A BRIEF SUMMARY

Because the time of earth is different from that of Narnia, the children who are drawn into that magical land of talking animals on a number of occasions find themselves at various parts of its history. Thus, although the Chronicles cover only about fifty years of our history (from the beginning to the mid-twentieth century, 1900-1949), we get a picture of the entire history of Narnia from its creation to its unmaking (1-2555 N.T.) and the new creation of all worlds, including Narnia and England.

Narnia's creation in year 1 N.T. is recounted in *MN*. Twelve-year-old Digory Kirke and eleven-year-old Polly Plummer enter the old and dying world of Charn through a pool in the Wood Between the Worlds after finding their way by accident into a Land of Nothing. Here, gradually, Narnia is created before their eyes by the song of Aslan, culminating in Aslan giving the gift of speech to many of the newly created animals. Unfortunately, Digory brings evil into that perfect world in the form of Jadis, destroyer of Charn, whom he previously awakened in that world. Jadis goes off to the northern fringes of Narnia but reappears in later ages as the White Witch who puts a spell over Narnia of winter that never comes to Christmas. The arrival of the four Pevensie children through the wardrobe in the year 1000 N.T. (told in *LWW*) coincides with the return of Aslan and the beginning of the end of her curse. Aslan's death on behalf of Edmund Pevensie, and his return to life by a deeper law than the one by which she operates her magic, leads to her defeat and death. Narnia's Golden Age follows as the children take their thrones as kings and queens, as Aslan had ordained.

We are told in *LWW* that the Pevensies legislated wisely, instituting sound laws and preserving peaceful relations with other countries. They conserved the environment ("stopped good trees from being unnecessarily cut down") and fostered neighborliness. As they carried on their Narnian lives joyfully their recollections of this world faded, becoming like the memory of a dream.

But the day comes when the children do return to their world, and long after their departure Narnia slowly falls into disorder. The Telmarines, led by Caspian I, occupy the land and silence the talking beasts and trees around 1998 N.T. "Old Narnia" only survives under cover as Aslan's remnant keep faith alive that he will return. Prince Caspian (his story is told in *PC*) is brought up by his wicked Uncle Miraz and Aunt Prunaprismia, who have deposed his father Caspian IX. The young prince learns of the "myth" of Old Narnia and longs for it to be true. In 2303 N.T. he escapes a plot by Miraz to kill him and joins forces with the Old Narnians. In the nick of time, help comes from the four Pevensie children drawn back into Narnia by his call for help on the Horn of Narnia. He becomes Caspian X after the civil war into which the children are caught up and during which Aslan returns to ensure victory for Old Narnia.

After defeating the Northern Giants in 2304 N.T., Caspian decides to set out in search of the seven lost lords. His adventures at sea are recounted in *VDT,* in which he is joined by Edmund, Lucy and their cousin Eustace Scrubb. On that voyage Caspian meets his wife and true love, Ramandu's daughter, whom he takes back to Narnia. She is murdered in 2345 N.T. by a serpent, a shape taken by the Green Witch, who wishes to conquer Narnia. This witch is of the line of Jadis. Caspian's son, Prince Rilian, is kidnapped and held under enchantment in an underworld for ten years by the witch. She plots to take over Narnia by using him as a puppet king. *SC* tells of his rescue by Eustace and his school friend, Jill Pole, who are brought into Narnia for this task.

After two hundred years, the last king of Narnia, Tirian, and indeed Narnia itself, are threatened in 2555 N.T. by a devilish plot that uses a counterfeit Aslan and links up with the Calormene forces (who are a constant threat to Narnia's security). This is Narnia's darkest hour. As told in *LB,* Tirian prays for help from the Sons and Daughters of Adam, and Aslan brings Eustace and Jill to his aid. Aslan himself finally intervenes and dissolves the whole world. This turns out to be a beginning rather than an end as the new, more splendid Narnia is revealed, this one linked with the real, or spiritual England, bringing together humans and talking animals forever.

CHRONOLOGY OF EVENTS

Events in England are in italic type. Note: These dates are based on C. S. Lewis's own timeline.

A.D. 1888	*Digory Kirke born.*
A.D. 1889	*Polly Plummer born.*
1 N.T.	Creation of Narnia. Some animals given gift of speech. Digory plants the Tree of Protection. The White Witch Jadis enters Narnia but flees into the far north. Frank I becomes king of Narnia. *Polly Plummer and Digory Kirke carried into other worlds by magic rings and witness Narnia's birth, A.D. 1900.*
180 N.T.	Prince Col, younger son of King Frank V of Narnia, leads some followers into Archenland (not then inhabited) and becomes first king of that country.
204 N.T.	Outlaws from Archenland cross the southern desert and set up the new kingdom of Calormen. *Peter and Susan Pevensie born, A.D. 1927 and 1928.*
300 N.T.	The empire of Calormen spreads dramatically. Calormenes colonize the land of Telmar to the west of Narnia. *Edmund Pevensie born, A.D. 1930.*
302 N.T.	The Calormenes in Telmar behave wickedly, and Aslan turns them into dumb beasts. King Gale of Narnia delivers the Lone Islands from a dragon and, as a result, is made emperor. *Eustace Scrubb and Jill Pole born, A.D. 1933. Lucy Pevensie born year previously.*
407 N.T.	Olvin of Archenland kills the Giant, Pire.
460 N.T.	Pirates stumbling into Narnia's world from ours take possession of Telmar.
898 N.T.	The White Witch Jadis enters Narnia again out of the frozen north.
900 N.T.	The Long Winter begins.
1000 N.T.	The Pevensies arrive in Narnia. Edmund turns traitor, and Aslan sacrifices himself. The White Witch is defeated, ending the Long Winter. Peter becomes high king of Narnia. *The Pevensies, staying with Digory (now Professor) Kirke, reach Narnia through the magic wardrobe, A.D. 1940.*
1014 N.T.	King Peter successfully raids the troublesome Northern Giants.

Queen Susan and King Edmund visit the Calormene court. King Lune of Archenland is reunited with his long-lost son, Prince Cor, and rebuffs a treacherous attack by Prince Rabadash of Calormen.

1015 N.T.	The Pevensies hunt the White Stag and disappear from Narnia.
1050 N.T.	Ram the Great follows Cor as king of Archenland.
1502 N.T.	Queen Swanwhite of Narnia lived around this time.
1998 N.T.	Invading Telmarines overwhelm Narnia. Caspian I becomes king of Narnia.
2290 N.T.	Prince Caspian, son of Caspian IX, born. Caspian IX murdered by his brother Miraz, who takes the throne.
2303 N.T.	Prince Caspian flees from his Uncle Miraz. Civil war falls upon Narnia. Caspian summons the Pevensie children with Queen Susan's magic horn. By their aid and that of Aslan, Miraz's forces are defeated and he is killed by his own side. Caspian becomes King Caspian X of Narnia. *The Pevensies are again drawn into Narnia by the call of the magic horn, while returning to school for the summer term A.D. 1941.*
2304 N.T.	Caspian X defeats the Northern Giants.
2306-7 N.T.	Caspian X's great voyage to the end of the World. *Edmund, Lucy and Eustace reach Narnia again and take part in Caspian's voyage, A.D. 1942.*
2310 N.T..	Caspian X marries Ramandu's daughter.
2325 N.T.	Prince Rilian born.
2345 N.T.	The queen killed by a serpent (the Green Witch). Rilian disappears.
2356 N.T.	The quest to find Prince Rilian. Death of Caspian X. *Eustace and Jill, from Experiment House school, are caught into Narnia, A.D. 1942.*
2534 N.T.	Outlaws become common in Lantern Waste. Towers are built to guard that region.
2555 N.T.	Rebellion of Shift the ape. Eustace and Jill come to King Tirian's aid. Narnia falls into the hands of the Calormenes by confusion. The last battle and end of Narnia. End of the World. *Serious rail accident involving the Bristol train, in which the Friends of Narnia die, A.D. 1949.*

The Geography of Narnia

Narnia is a valley country, extending from the Lantern Waste in the west to Cair Paravel on the shores of the Great Eastern Ocean. It is a pastoral, green world full of trackless woods inhabited by talking animals. In *LWW,* an inspiring sight met the eyes of Peter and Aslan from the eastern edge of the open hillside on which stood the Stone Table. Aslan was showing Peter a far-off glimpse of the castle where he would soon reign. The hill also gave a good view of Narnia.

Because the sun was setting behind them the landscape below caught the evening light. Peter could see forested hills and valleys. A great silver river snaked away eastwards towards the sea, many miles away. Beyond the distant sea the cloud-filled sky was just then beginning to turn a delicate rose as it reflected the setting sun. Peter's attention was caught by something that shined on a little hill, where Narnia's land met the ocean. What shined, he realized suddenly, were the many windows of a castle that looked out in Peter's direction, catching the low sunlight. To Peter the castle looked like a huge star resting upon the ocean shore. It was his first sight of Cair Paravel, the seat of the kings and queens of Narnia.

Narnia's small valley land has Archenland and then Calormen lying to its south. (Calormen is a country dominated by caste and a slavery economy, in stark contrast to the freedom enjoyed in Narnia.) Narnia is a land inhabited by both talking and dumb beasts and trees, the chief of all its creatures being also its creator, Aslan, a talking lion. To the far west once lay the land of Telmar. Nearer is the Western Wild—a mountainous region covered with dark forests or with snow and ice. From this region rushes a river that becomes a waterfall, under which is Caldron Pool. From this flows the river of Narnia, which runs all the way to the Eastern Ocean.

Narnia's capital is Cair Paravel, the seat of kings and queens, always human, at Aslan's decree. It is located at the mouth of the river of Narnia. The Marsh-wiggles (found only in Narnia) live to the north of Cair Paravel. More northerly lies the river Shribble, and then the forelorn moorland of Ettinsmoor. Further north still is a mountainous region and Harfang, a stronghold of giants. Near Harfang is the ruins of a once-great city, under which lie a number of subterranean lands, including the kingdom of the Green Witch, dissolved in the time of Prince Rilian, son of Caspian, the tenth Telmarine king. To Narnia's east lies the vast Eastern Ocean, in which are many islands, and finally the Silver Sea and the World's End, where is Aslan's Country.

In the geography of Narnia, Lewis has captured something of the Ulster that he loved from childhood, particularly County Down. The Reverend Cosslet Quinn, a former Rector of Saint Mark's, Dundela, recalls vividly Lewis's love of the lore of Ulster: "I still remember from one occasion when I met C. S. Lewis, seeing the flash in his eyes as he spoke of the two-thousand-year-old Epic of Cuchulain, and what it ought to mean for an Ulsterman."

To the uttermost east and west of Narnia are boundary territories to other worlds. The entire world is ringed by tall mountains. Narnians perceive their earth as a flat world—in fact, Caspian's imagination is captured by the idea of a globe-shaped world that the kings and queens of Narnia came from. To the north and south are territories associated with danger—the White Witch dwells in the north for hundreds of years, and terrifying giants live there, while far south Calormen represents a constant threat to Narnian security. Narnia is a middle-world in which the qualities of ordinary life and freedom are nourished. For Aravis, in despair over her prospects in Calormen, Narnia represents hope. Narnia's middle-world between dangers to north and south echoes the *Mappa Mundi* that Lewis had created many years earlier in his story, *The Pilgrim's Regress*. Narnia is also the name of a small Italian town mentioned by Livy.

Other Writings of C. S. Lewis in a Narnian Context

W hen C. S. Lewis wrote the seven Chronicles of Narnia the whole person was engaged—the scholar as well as the storyteller. Thus one of the best ways to understand the intellectual and imaginative context of his children's stories is to read his other books. This chapter briefly looks at a wide range of his writings—literary scholarship, fiction for grown-ups, popular theology, essays and shorter pieces, autobiography, poetry, even his childhood writings—that mirror back his Narnian tales in varied and sometimes surprising ways.

THE ABOLITION OF MAN (1943)

Based upon a series of three Riddell Memorial Lectures for 1943, given at the request of University of Durham, Lewis expresses disquiet over values being presented in textbooks for students of English Literature in British sixth-forms (the upper years of high school). If values are objective, argues Lewis, one person may be right and another wrong. Judging goodness or badness is not simply a matter of opinion. He argues indeed that there is a universal acknowledgment of good and bad over matters like theft, murder, rape and adultery, a sense of what Lewis called the Tao. Though Lewis took the term from the East, he intends the "Way" to stand for a universal acknowledgment of natural law. It not only refers to the beliefs of the Old West (as Lewis calls it in his *De Descriptione Temporum*). With the abandonment of this perennial human wisdom, identity values like freedom and dignity become meaningless; the human being is merely part of nature. The book concludes with an appendix featuring various illustrations of the Tao from representative cultures around the world, gleaned from the thirteen-volume *Encyclopaedia of Religion and Ethics,* edited by James Hastings (1908-1926). Lewis seeks to embody the Tao in the values and virtues celebrated in the Chronicles (see chapter two, "The Background to the Chronicles of Narnia").

In his book *The Pilgrim's Regress* (see below), Lewis maps the distortions of the Tao in human life in terms of northern and southern biases, a geography that is evoked in the Chronicles, where the mid land of Narnia represents the balance of a healthy society.

BOXEN

Boxen is an imaginary kingdom created by Lewis as a young child, in collusion with his brother, Warren Lewis. The stories have been collected and edited by Walter Hooper into a book of the same name (1985). In his autobiography, *Surprised by Joy,* Lewis describes the origin of Boxen. The first stories were written, and illustrated, "to combine my two chief literary pleasures—'dressed animals' and 'knights-in-armour.' As a result, I wrote about chivalrous mice and rabbits who rode out in complete mail to kill not giants but cats." In creating an environment for the tales, a medieval Animal-Land was born. In order to include Warnie in its creation and shaping, features of the modern world like trains and steamships had to be included. Thus a history had to be created, and so on. The Boxen stories are less like the Chronicles than might be supposed—the young Lewis deliberately excluded any qualities such as wonder associated with "romance" in literature to make the tales "grown-up."

"DE DESCRIPTIONE TEMPORUM" (1954)

This was C. S. Lewis's inaugural lecture as professor in the newly formed Chair of Medieval and Renaissance English Literature at the University of Cambridge. It was broadcast later on BBC radio and published in several collections of his essays, including *Selected Literary Essays*. The lecture reveals his sympathies with an earlier age, the "Old West," even though he was ever concerned to communicate as a writer to a modern reader. Lewis argued that he was a relic of Old Western Man, a museum piece, if you like; that even if one disagreed with his ideas, one must take account of them as being from a rare (and therefore valuable) specimen of an older world. There is a Great Divide between that world and our modern one, where the machine has been absorbed into our inner lives as an archetype. Just as new and better machines replace older ones, so too (believes the modern) do superior ideas, beliefs and values (see "chronological snobbery" in chapter six, under the subhead "Themes of the Modern World"). The modern world is postpagan and post-Christian, Lewis believed, and carries an agenda that might well abolish humanity in the future.

The Chronicles seek to rehabilitate values of the older world in a manner attractive to a modern reader (see chapter two, "The Background to the Chronicles of Narnia").

THE DISCARDED IMAGE: AN INTRODUCTION TO MEDIEVAL AND RENAISSANCE LITERATURE (1964)

The Discarded Image arose out of a series of university lectures C. S. Lewis gave many years earlier on the medieval world image, which provided a background to literature up to the seventeenth century. Lewis employed the medieval world model in his science-fiction trilogy and in the Chronicles. Lewis helps his readers to feel the imaginative power of this model. It has an integrated picture of the heavens, the earth and humankind itself, with the human being as a miniature world, a microcosmos.

C. S. Lewis concludes *The Discarded Image* by hoping that no one thinks that he is recommending a return to the medieval model. He has only sought a proper regard of world models, respecting each and making an idol of none. Each age inevitably has its own "taste in universes." Thinking of chronological snobbery, Lewis added: "We can no longer dismiss the change in Models as a simple progress from error to truth. No Model is a catalogue of ultimate realities, and none is a mere fantasy. Each is a serious attempt to get in all the phenomena known at a given period, and each succeeds in getting in a great many. But also, no less surely, each reflects the prevalent psychology of an age almost as much as it reflects the state of that age's knowledge." Our world model will eventually change, like others before it.

English Literature in the Sixteenth Century (Excluding Drama) (1954)

C. S. Lewis contributed volume three of *The Oxford History of English Literature*. As well as providing a thorough history of the sixteenth century, the book is notable for its introduction, "New Learning and New Ignorance," which adds to the themes laid out in *The Discarded Image* and in his inaugural lecture to the Chair of Medieval and Renaissance Literature at Cambridge, *"De Descriptione Temporum."* He points out, for example, a transformation in the concept of magic that happened with the influence of a new empiricism. This new empiricism is what eventually led to the rise of modern science.

Writing this volume allowed him to expound one of his favorite authors, Edmund Spenser, though space severely restricted him. Lewis concludes that the period "illustrates well enough the usual complex, unpatterned historical process; in which, while men often throw away irreplaceable wealth, they not infrequently escape what seemed inevitable dangers, not knowing that they have done either nor how they did it." Sixteenth-century literature and its values particularly form part of the background to the Chronicles, in terms of its inspiration and literary models. Though the sixteenth is a transitional century, in which the Renaissance impacted English literature, the essential values and imaginative cast of the Middle Ages were retained and transformed in a new vitality. This resulted in exploration and the beginning of the rise of the new science. This "Golden Age" was represented particularly for Lewis by Edmund Spenser and his *The Faerie Queene,* which served as an inspiration and partial model for the Chronicles (see chapter two, "The Background to the Chronicles of Narnia").

AN EXPERIMENT IN CRITICISM (1961)

C. S. Lewis argues that literature exists for the enjoyment of readers and that books, therefore, should be judged by the kind of reading that they evoke. Good reading has something in common with love, moral action and the growth of knowledge. Like all these, it involves surrender, in this case by the reader to the work being read. Looking at reading in this way does better justice to the wide variety of reading taste (which encompasses fantasy as well as stories "about life") than is found in the literary establishment of his day.

Lewis tries to present the evidence of his own lifetime's reading, and adds: "I regret that the brutes cannot write books. . . . In reading great literature I become a thousand men and yet remain myself. Like the night sky in the Greek poem, I see with a myriad eyes, but it is still I who see. Here, as in worship, in love, in moral action, and in knowing, I transcend myself; and am never more myself than when I do."

The book presents Lewis's foundational ideas about myth, fairy story and fantasy, which underlie the creation of the Chronicles. Though he couldn't find books written by animals, he gave vivid life to talking animals in Narnia, including memorable characters like Bree and Puddleglum the Marsh-wiggle.

"IT ALL BEGAN WITH A PICTURE . . ."

In this article, written for the *Radio Times* and reprinted in *Of This and Other Worlds,* C. S. Lewis explains how he came to write *LWW.* He reveals that all seven Chronicles "began with seeing pictures in my head." The first image had come to him around the age of sixteen—that of a faun in a snowy wood carrying parcels and an umbrella.

"THE LEFAY FRAGMENT"

This fragment, named after the appearance of Mrs. LeFay in it, was written with the intention of explaining various elements in *LWW,* such as the lamp post and how Narnia came to be. This was a difficult artistic problem. In it Digory is rather like Curdie in George MacDonald's *The Princess and Curdie* when he shoots a white pigeon and feels sorry afterwards. In Digory's case he cuts a limb of his friend, the oak tree. As a result he loses his gift of understanding the speech of living things, animals and trees. Lewis abandoned it after a few thousand words as, artistically, it didn't work as a Narnia story—perhaps because the magic is in this rather than another world. The fragment reveals much about Lewis's creative processes—he wrote intuitively, inspired by vivid mental pictures. In many cases he was able to sustain the story from such a beginning, but sometimes not, as in this case and that of another fragment, "The Dark Tower," which was intended as another story about Elwin Ransom in the science-fiction sequence.

MERE CHRISTIANITY (1952)

One of the most well known of C. S. Lewis's books, *Mere Christianity* is a revised and enlarged edition of three previous books of talks given on BBC radio, *Broadcast Talks* (1942; called *The Case for Christianity* in the United States), *Christian Behaviour* (1943) and *Beyond Personality* (1944). It is straightforward and lucid, and sets out the essence of what Lewis believed as a Christian. He tried to remain within the core beliefs of Christians of all orthodox denominations. In Lewis's words, the broadcasts were "an attempt to convince people that there is a moral law, that we disobey it, and that the existence of a Lawgiver is at least very probable and also (unless you add the Christian doctrine of the Atonement) that this imparts despair rather than comfort." Lewis attempted to restrict the theology underlying the Chronicles to this same common ground, as he saw it.

NARRATIVE POEMS (1969)

C. S. Lewis wrote both lyrical and narrative verse, and originally hoped to make his name as a poet. This volume contains four stories, including "Dymer," "Launcelot," "The Nameless Isle" and "The Queen of Drum"— about the escape of a queen from a dictator into fairyland. None perhaps is really successful, and even "Dymer" is only minor verse. Lewis comes to his own in prose storytelling, in which his poetic sensibility is allowed freer rein. This is true from his earliest fiction, *The Pilgrim's Regress*. "The Nameless Isle" concerns a shipwrecked sailor and his adventures on a magic island, an island adventure theme he took up in *VDT*. "The Queen of Drum" is a fairy story. (See also *"Poems."*)

OF THIS AND OTHER WORLDS (1982)

This title is a posthumous collection of Lewis's short fiction and essays and brief pieces on narrative fiction edited by Walter Hooper. It includes a number of essays that cast light upon the Chronicles, including "It All

Began with a Picture . . ." and "Sometimes Fairy Stories May Say Best What's to Be Said."

"On Juvenile Tastes" (1958)

This article, collected in *Of This and Other Worlds,* is of interest in revealing Lewis's views of children's tastes. There is no one literary taste, he argues, common to all children (some for example might like fantasy, and others not), but storytelling does appeal to children. Many writers will write for children because they want to tell a story, and storytelling—the narrative art—is out of fashion, he says, with the literary establishment.

"On Science Fiction"

This essay was originally a paper presented in 1955. It is collected in *Of This and Other Worlds* and includes insights into the appeal of science fiction to Lewis (a science-fiction writer himself). Those he likes best cater to an age-old human love for fantasy and fairy story. They are able to offer a "keen, lasting, and solemn pleasure." Rather than merely commenting on life, like a good novel, "good stories of this sort (which are very much rarer) are actual additions to life; they give, like certain rare dreams, sensations we never had before, and enlarge our conception of the range of possible experience." It was this kind of marvelous story of another world that Lewis attempted in each of the Chronicles.

"On Stories" (1947)

This essay, collected in *Of This and Other Worlds,* is a forerunner of Lewis's late work, *An Experiment in Criticism.* He is concerned to highlight the existence of qualities that stories are able to capture that are more, say, than simply excitement. A world embodied in the story is part of the nature of its interest to the attentive reader. That world is built upon a consistent logic and is as important as, if not more so than, the construction of plot. The plot is merely a net to capture an elusive quality. In the tale of "Jack the Giant Killer," for example, what is presented is not mere danger, but danger from *giants*.

In constructing and writing the Chronicles, Lewis was concerned to embody elusive qualities like northernness, the presence of heaven, joy, recognition or worship.

"ON THREE WAYS OF WRITING FOR CHILDREN" (1952)

This essay, collected in *Of This and Other Worlds,* reveals much of the thinking underlying his decision to write the Chronicles, and his approach to the writing. Rather than writing for a market, a children's author is better (1) to have a story that grows out of a tale told orally to particular children, or (2) to write from a recognition that a children's story is the best artistic form for what one has to say. Lewis himself composed the Chronicles from such a recognition. The essay is of great interest in revealing Lewis's great debt to his friend J. R. R. Tolkien for ideas like subcreation and for the belief that fairy story as a genre has been unfairly relegated to the nursery. He also draws on Tolkien's forthright rebuttal that fantasy and fairy story are escapism.

OUT OF THE SILENT PLANET (1938)

This is the first volume of C. S. Lewis's science-fiction trilogy. Dr. Elwin Ransom, a philologist don from Cambridge University, is kidnapped while on a walking holiday in the midlands and taken to Malacandra (Mars) by Dick Devine and Edward Weston, the latter a famous physicist and materialist. They are under a misapprehension that the unseen ruler of Malacandra wants a human sacrifice—a fantasy created by their dark minds.

After escaping his captors, Ransom is at first terrified and disoriented by the red planet and its diversity of terrain and inhabitants—various forms of rational life related in a harmonious hierarchy. The inhabitants—sorns (or, more properly, seroni), hrossa and pfifltriggi—turn out to be civilized and amiable. Ransom, as a linguist (partly modeled on J. R. R. Tolkien, and perhaps at times resembling Lewis himself), is soon able to pick up the rudiments of their language. They are talking animals presented appropriately for a science-fiction genre.

In *Out of the Silent Planet,* as in the Chronicles, Lewis imaginatively reconstructs the medieval picture of the cosmos for modern readers. He later set out this world picture in his book *The Discarded Image.*

PERELANDRA (VOYAGE TO VENUS) (1943)

This, the second volume of C. S. Lewis's science-fiction trilogy, is set on the planet Perelandra (Venus), a paradisiacal, oceanic world of floating islands as well as fixed lands. Dr. Elwin Ransom is transported there to rebuff the attacks of the forces of evil incarnate in the human form of his old enemy, Edward Weston. Perelandra, Ransom discovers, has its own, green-fleshed equivalent of Adam and Eve. Ransom plays a key part, much to his surprise, in frustrating the devilish plans of the bent Oyarsa of earth to corrupt the unspoiled world. Eventually Ransom realizes, to his dismay, that he must engage Weston in a physical fight to the death. Lewis's study of John Milton's great epic poem, *A Preface to Paradise Lost,* had dealt with the fall of humanity and key themes such as hierarchy. *Perelandra* portrays the imaginative splendor of Milton's themes in a way designed to bewitch the modern reader, bypassing our prejudice against the past—what Lewis dubbed our "chronological snobbery." Similarly, the Chronicles try to rehabilitate the imaginative world image of the Middle Ages, which has a deep affinity with Milton's themes.

The story beautifully climaxes in a vision of the "Great Dance" of the universe, in which all patterns of human and other life interweave. The idea of the music of creation is found in *MN*, in the song of Aslan that brings Narnia into being.

THE PILGRIM'S REGRESS: AN ALLEGORICAL APOLOGY FOR CHRISTIANITY, REASON AND ROMANTICISM (1933; NEW EDITION, 1943)

C. S. Lewis was researching the method of allegorical poetry and story-telling for his study *The Allegory of Love* when he wrote this book. In fictional and more general form, it covers the ground of his later account of his life up to his conversion, *Surprised by Joy.*

The Pilgrim's Regress is an intellectual, early twentieth-century version of John Bunyan's great allegory. Instead of Christian, the central figure is John, loosely based on Lewis himself. Like *The Pilgrim's Progress,* the quest can be mapped. Indeed, Lewis provides his reader with a *Mappa Mundi,* in which the human soul is divided into north and south, the north representing arid intellectualism and the south emotional excess. A straight road passes between them. Needless to say, John's route strays far off the straight and narrow. Like the young Lewis, he tends toward intellectual rather than sensual follies. The story gives a vivid picture of Lewis's intellectual climate of the 1920s and early 1930s.

This book was Lewis's first work of fiction and popular Christian communication. In writing it, he began honing skills that were further refined in composing his science-fiction trilogy. This development of his skills allowed him eventually to achieve the creation of the Chronicles. The quest theme, as John travels in search of the island he glimpsed, anticipates elements of the Chronicles, such as Caspian's longing for the Old Narnia in *PC* and Reepicheep's quest for Aslan's Country in *VDT.* The text of *The Pilgrim's Regress* is interspersed with poetry. One poem, "The Dragon Speaks," was quoted by J. R. R. Tolkien with pleasure in early drafts of his famous essay on *Beowulf.* The subject of the poem has certain similarities with the creature on Dragon Island in *VDT* that lives in a cave near a rocky pool.

The events of the story take place in an imagined geography, which

150

Lewis mapped as a *Mappa Mundi.* This map is found inside the endpapers, and it echoes the geography of Narnia. Theologian J. I. Packer describes the world the *Mappa Mundi* depicts as "the personal world of wandering and return that the story explores." In his preface to the third edition of *The Pilgrim's Regress,* Lewis explains the map as a scheme of "the Holy War as I see it." It depicts "the double attack from Hell on the two sides of our nature" (the mind and the physical sensations). Packer presciently points out that the idea of the Holy War, drawn from Bunyan and others, as well as Lewis's war experience, not only informs *The Pilgrim's Regress,* but "gives shape and perspective to Lewis's output as a whole." The attacks on the soul from north and south represent, in Lewis's words, "equal and opposite evils, each continually strengthened and made plausible by its critique of the other." The northern people are cold, with "rigid systems whether sceptical or dogmatic, Aristocrats, Stoics, Pharisees, Rigorists, signed and sealed members of highly organized 'Parties.'" The emotional southerners are the opposite, "boneless souls whose doors stand open day and night to almost every visitant, but always with the readiest welcome for those . . . who offer some sort of intoxication. . . . Every feeling is justified by the mere fact that it is felt: for a Northerner, every feeling on the same ground is suspect."

Both tendencies actually dehumanize us, a thesis he explored in *The Abolition of Man.* To remain human we have no choice but the straight and narrow, the "Main Road": "With both the 'North' and the 'South' a man has, I take it, only one concern—to avoid them and hold the Main Road. . . . We were made to be neither cerebral men nor visceral men, but Men."

In the world in which Narnia is located, dangers come from the north and the south, as on the *Mappa Mundi.* The threats from the north are witches (first the White Witch, and later the Green Witch) and giants, or ettins. To the south the threat comes from the troublesome Calormenes.

POEMS (1964)

This volume contains most of C. S. Lewis's lyrical verse, with the exception of the early cycle of poems entitled *Spirits in Bondage*. They reveal a great variety of themes, including "Narnian Suite," which is in two parts—"March for Strings, Kettledrums, and Sixty-three Dwarfs" and "March for Drum, Trumpet, and Twenty-one Giants."

THE PROBLEM OF PAIN (1940)

This book is important in setting out theological ideas that underpin the Chronicles, such as the doctrine of the fall of humanity, explaining the reality of evil. C. S. Lewis's purpose in writing it was to "solve the intellectual problem raised by suffering." He had never felt himself qualified "for the far-higher task of teaching fortitude and patience."

For a such a small book, Lewis ranged far and wide, discussing God's control over all human events, including suffering, the goodness of God, human wickedness, human pain, hell and heaven. His concern for animals is evident in his section on animal pain. Austin Farrer comments that Lewis presents "a world haunted by the supernatural, a conscience haunted by the moral absolute, a history haunted by the divine claim of Christ." It contains fine passages on heaven, joy and the sense of the numinous that is present in so much of Lewis's fiction, including the Chronicles. It argues from the starting point of God's relationship to the universe that he has made and is uncompromising in its supernaturalism (see chapter four, "Worldviews and Narnia").

"SOMETIMES FAIRY STORIES MAY BEST SAY WHAT'S TO BE SAID" (1956)

This little article, collected in *Of This and Other Worlds,* throws valuable light on the processes behind Lewis's writing of the Chronicles. A person as author begins with an idea or an image, and he or she as total person (of which being an author is only part) questions the value of undertaking the project before proceeding. With the Chronicles, the pictures always came first, and then a sense of the best form for the story. Fairy story struck Lewis as the best form for the tales of Narnia. (He points out that fairy story is not specifically for children: it is an adult genre that has been relegated to the nursery. He wrote the Chronicles for all who might enjoy them, but deliberately limited and scaled it to what children would like and understand.) Only then did he think about the aspect of Christian communication. After the form had been decided, it occurred to him as total person (rather than simply as author) that "casting all these things into an imaginary world, stripping them of their stained-glass and Sunday school associations, [suppose] one could make them for the first time appear in their real potency? Could one not thus steal past those watchful dragons? I thought one could."

SPENSER'S IMAGES OF LIFE (1967)

This book is based on C. S. Lewis's Cambridge lectures on Edmund Spenser's great poem, *The Faerie Queene.* He intended to turn his material into a book but did not live to do so. Lewis's holograph notes were expanded and edited into this book by his friend Alastair Fowler of Brasenose College, Oxford.

The Faerie Queene is one of the greatest poems in the English language and the literary work that perhaps most influenced the nature of the Chronicles (see chapter two, "The Background to the Chronicles of Narnia"). Lewis, in this academic study, approaches *The Faerie Queene* as a splendid and majestic pageant of the universe and nature, which celebrates God, to use Lewis's own phrase, as "the glad creator." Lewis considers *The Faerie Queene* to be perhaps the most difficult poem in English, above the demand of great literature for both a simple and a sophisticated response.

SURPRISED BY JOY: THE SHAPE OF MY EARLY LIFE (1955)

This records C. S. Lewis's autobiography up to his conversion to Christianity at the age of thirty-one. *Joy* is a technical term used by Lewis to help define an inconsolable longing that contradicted the atheism and materialism that his intellect embraced. In first theism and then Christianity both his intellect and his imagination were fulfilled. A key moment in his journey to faith was the discovery of George MacDonald's *Phantastes*.

Prior to that reconciliation Lewis portrays the "two hemispheres" of his mind in turbulent conflict. "On the one side a many-islanded sea of poetry and myth; on the other a glib and shallow 'rationalism.' Nearly all that I loved I believed to be imaginary; nearly all that I believed to be real I thought grim and meaningless."

In his account Lewis records much of his childhood reading as well as people and experiences that shaped his early life. The person who emerges is very much recognizable as the person who created Narnia.

THAT HIDEOUS STRENGTH (1945; ABRIDGED PAPERBACK VERSION 1955)

This is the final volume of the science-fiction trilogy, begun in *Out of the Silent Planet* and *Perelandra (Voyage to Venus)*. It continues C. S. Lewis's presentation of the problem of good and evil and is subtitled a "modern fairy tale for grown-ups."

This book, as a sequel to the previous stories, set on other planets, brings matters "down to earth," under the influence of Lewis's friend, Charles Williams. It is set on Thulcandra, the silent planet Earth, so called because it is cut off by evil from the beatific language and worlds of Deep Heaven. In another sense, matters are brought "down to earth" because Lewis takes pains in characterizing the marriage and personalities of Mark and Jane Studdock, the focus of the novel.

As Lewis makes clear in his preface, his story illustrates the point that he made in one of his most forceful studies of ethics, *The Abolition of Man* (1943). This is that a world that rejects objective principles of right and wrong, beauty and ugliness, also rejects what constitutes humanity's very nature and creates an unhumanity. Lewis embodies this rejection of values in The National Institute of Coordinated Experiments (NICE). The same principles are at work in *LB,* in the alliance between Shift and the Calormenes. In the latter case, the consequences are slavery and the despoiling of nature, particularly the destruction of the living trees. In both *That Hideous Strength* and *LB,* animals are treated with cruelty.

TILL WE HAVE FACES (1956)

In *Till We Have Faces,* C. S. Lewis retells the ancient story of Cupid and Psyche from Apuleius's *The Golden Ass.* In Apuleius's story, Psyche is so beautiful that Venus becomes jealous of her. Cupid, sent by Venus to make Psyche fall in love with an ugly creature, himself falls in love with her. After bringing her to a palace, he visits her only in the dark and forbids her to see his face. Out of jealousy, Psyche's sisters tell her that her lover is a monster who will devour her. She takes a lamp one night and looks at Cupid's face, but a drop of oil awakes him. In anger, the god leaves her. Psyche seeks her lover throughout the world. Venus sets her various impossible tasks, all of which she accomplishes except the last, when curiosity makes her open a deadly casket from the underworld. At last, however, she is allowed to marry Cupid.

In *Till We Have Faces,* Lewis essentially follows the classical myth but retells it through the eyes of Orual, Psyche's half sister, who seeks at first to defend her actions to the gods as being the result of deep love for Psyche, not jealousy.

The novel explores the depths of insight possible within the limitations of the pagan imagination, which foreshadows the marriage of myth and fact in the Gospels. Lewis takes up this same theme in his portrayals of the Calormenes Aravis in *HHB* and Emeth in *LB,* both of whom are able to acknowledge Aslan when they encounter him.

A Who's Who of the
Making of Narnia

This chapter supplements chapter one, "The Life of C. S. Lewis," and chapter two, "The Background to the Chronicles of Narnia," and is not intended to be comprehensive because of the complexities of the influences on Lewis's making of Narnia.

BARFIELD, OWEN (1898-1997)

A close friend of Lewis's and fellow Inkling, Owen Barfield shaped Lewis's thinking about the imagination through a "Great War" in the 1920s, helping to prepare the ground for his eventual acceptance of Christian faith. (Lewis at that time was an atheist.) Barfield had become an anthroposophist, an advocate of the mystical school of thought developed by Rudolf Steiner, who founded the famous Steiner schools. As with Tolkien, his main intellectual stimulus came from language. While an undergraduate, Owen Barfield experienced what has aptly been described as an "intellectual epiphany" while studying the romantic poets. Owen Barfield recalled this revelation in 1966: "What impressed me particularly was the power with which not so much whole poems as particular combinations of words worked on my mind. It seemed like there was some magic in it; and a magic which not only gave me pleasure but also reacted on and expanded the meanings of the individual words concerned." Language, he believed, had the power to transform human consciousness and to embody historic changes in this consciousness. His book *Poetic Diction* (1928) deeply influenced Lewis and Tolkien, and its power can still be felt in the vision underlying the Chronicles. Lewis attempted to popularize the rather arcane ideas of *Poetic Diction* in chapter ten of *Miracles,* entitled "Horrid Red Things."

Owen Barfield and his wife, Maud, adopted two children and fostered a third. The daughter, Lucy (to whom *LWW* is dedicated), had multiple sclerosis.

Lewis's debt to Owen Barfield was enormous. He paid tribute to him in *Surprised by Joy* and earlier in *An Allegory of Love* ("the wisest and best of my unofficial teachers"). More recently Owen Barfield has been appreciated as a leading twentieth-century thinker by figures as diverse as Saul Bellow, Theodore Roszak, G. B. Tennyson and Norman O. Brown.

BAYNES, PAULINE DIANA (B. 1922)

Lewis chose Pauline Baynes to illustrate his Narnia books after seeing her illustrations for a story by his friend Tolkien, *Farmer Giles of Ham.* Commenting on her work for *SC,* Lewis observed: "There is, as always, exquisite delicacy." As George MacDonald had done with the artist Arthur Hughes, Lewis found an illustrator whose imagination complemented his own.

Pauline Baynes played an important part in visualizing the world of Narnia. Working from a basic sketch map by Lewis, she drew a Narnia map for the end papers of the original hardback books, a popular poster map (1968) and a map of the voyage of the *Dawn Treader.*

CHESTERTON, GILBERT KEITH (1874-1936)

Chesterton was a celebrated convert to Christianity who influenced C. S. Lewis's thinking. "I liked him for his goodness," Lewis observed in *Surprised by Joy.* Chesterton wrote, like Lewis, in defense of Christian faith and fantasy. (Chesterton's chapter "The Ethics of Elfland" from *Orthodoxy* particularly contains insights explored and put into practice in the stories of Lewis and his friend J. R.R. Tolkien.) An essayist, critic, novelist and poet, his best-known writings include *The Everlasting Man, Orthodoxy,* the Father Brown stories, *The Man Who Was Thursday, The Napoleon of Notting Hill* and biographies of Robert Browning and others. Typical of his astuteness as a critic is his comment on George MacDonald in his *The Victorian Age in Literature:* "a Scot of genius as genuine as Carlyle's; he could write fairy-tales that made all experience a fairy-tale. He could give the real sense that every one had the end of an elfin thread that must at last lead them into Paradise. It was a sort of optimist Calvinism."

Chesterton's *The Everlasting Man* was once listed by Lewis as one of the ten most influential books that shaped his thinking and vocational attitude.

ENDICOTT, LIZZIE

Lizzie Endicott was C. S. Lewis's nurse, who told the infant stories from her roots in County Down, stories of Irish lore about leprechauns and their crocks of buried gold; the faerie folk; and Cuchulain, the hound of Ulster. One day, when drying the young child and his older brother, Warren, she threatened to spank their "pigieboties" or "piggiebottoms" because of their idling. This greatly amused the boys, who decided that Warren was the "Archpiggiebotham" and Lewis the "Smallpiggie-botham." "APB" and "SPB" they remained to each other for the rest of their lives.

EVACUEES

The children at the center of events in *LWW* are evacuees from a wartime city who are billeted with Professor Digory Kirke. During the war, Lewis, his brother, Mrs. Moore and Maureen Moore lodged evacuees at different times in their Oxford home, The Kilns. The first two—Patricia Boshell (later Heidelberger) and Marie Bosc—arrived in September 1940. Later in the war June Flewett (later Freud) was billeted there and eventually stayed nearly two years. She was just sixteen when she arrived, with no opinion, as she put it, of her intellectual ability. "Lewis," she recalls, "was the first person who made me believe that I was an intelligent human being and the whole time I was there he built up my confidence in myself and in my ability to think and understand." Lewis began a draft of what later became *LWW* after the arrival of the evacuees, though he didn't pick up the story again until after the war.

GREEN, ROGER LANCELYN (1918-1987)

Roger Green was biographer (with Walter Hooper) of Lewis, friend and sometimes visitor to the Inklings. Lewis and his wife, Joy Davidman Lewis, visited Greece with Green and his wife shortly before Joy's death. Green was a pupil of Lewis's who became a friend, and the two had a common taste in reading. He wrote an authoritative study of children's literature, *Tellers of Tales* (1946, updated 1953) and wrote many books for children himself. After hearing Lewis read early chapters of *LWW*, Green encouraged Lewis to complete it. Many of Green's books introduce children to myth and legend. *The Land Beyond the North* (1958) follows the Argonauts to the realm of Britain. His other fiction includes *From the World's End* (1948), his most mystical piece.

GREEVES, JOSEPH ARTHUR (1895-1966)

A friend of Lewis's from teenage years, Greeves shared the secret of joy;

the inconsolable longing; and a similar taste in reading and all things "northern," such as Old Norse mythology. Greeves's skill was in visual art rather than words (he was a talented fine artist), though he was an appreciative reader of a life-long correspondence from Lewis (collected in *They Stand Together*). Greeves lived at a house called Bernagh, almost opposite Lewis on the outskirts of Belfast. Lewis continued to meet up with Greeves until his death. Between 1921 and 1923 Arthur Greeves studied at the prestigious Slade School of Fine Art in London. Later he exhibited with the Royal Hibernian Academy in Dublin. Lewis did not share his faith (according to Lewis, Arthur came from a Plymouth Brethren background) until 1931, and later Arthur explored varieties of faith, concluding his life as a Quaker.

KIRKPATRICK, WILLIAM T. (1848-1921)

C. S. Lewis's tutor from 1914 to 1917, Kirkpatrick was dubbed "the Great Knock" by Lewis because of the impact of his stringent logical mind on the teenager. Kirkpatrick was then retired as headmaster of Lurgan College, in the north of Ireland, where Albert Lewis, Lewis's father had attended. He lived in Great Bookham, Surrey, England, where Lewis lodged happily during the tutorage. Lewis held a great affection for Kirkpatrick, describing him as the person who came closer to being a "purely logical entity" than anyone else he had ever met. Kirkpatrick's method was to combine language study with firsthand experience of major works; he guided Lewis in German, French, Italian, Latin and Classical Greek. His rationalism and atheism reinforced Lewis's own beliefs at that time, though Lewis's imagination continued to have an independent, contradictory life (for instance, he discovered George MacDonald's *Phantastes* during this period).

Kirkpatrick made his mark on Lewis's fiction, to be seen, for instance, in some characteristics of the learned Professor Digory Kirke.

LEWIS, WARREN HAMILTON "WARNIE" (1895-1973)

Warren was Lewis's only brother and a lifelong friend. He was also a gifted writer, producing a number of books on French history. His diaries provide a unique and essential insight into Lewis's life and meetings of the Inklings. As a child he collaborated with his younger brother on the Boxen stories.

Warnie Lewis began his military career when he entered the Royal Military academy shortly before the outbreak of World War One. After the war he served in Sierra Leone and Shanghai before retiring from the army in 1932 with a pension. He joined the unusual household run by his brother and Mrs. Janie Moore at The Kilns, in Oxford. After Lewis's death, he prepared a fascinating memoir of his brother, now housed in the Wade Center, Wheaton, Illinois (with a copy in the Bodleian Library, Oxford). An abridged version of the *Memoirs* is published in *Letters of C. S. Lewis*.

MACDONALD, GEORGE (1824-1905)

The Scottish writer (poet, novelist and fantastist) George MacDonald was born in Huntly in rural Aberdeenshire, the son of a weaver. C. S. Lewis regarded his own debt to MacDonald as inestimable. Like Lewis and Tolkien, he was a scholar as well as a storyteller. George MacDonald made a memorable appearance in Lewis's *The Great Divorce,* for Lewis regarded him as his "master." MacDonald's sense that all imaginative meaning originates with the Christian Creator became the foundation of Lewis's thinking and imagining, indirectly influencing the creation of Narnia. Lewis as a teenager had stumbled across a copy of MacDonald's *Phantastes* (1858), resulting in what he described as a baptism of his imagination. This is one of ten books Lewis once listed as particularly influencing his thinking and vocational attitude. One of MacDonald's last books, *Lilith* (1895), is among his greatest, a fantasy with the same power as *Phantastes* to move and to change a person's imaginative life.

The poet and critic W. H. Auden observed: "To me, George Mac-Donald's most extraordinary, and precious, gift is his ability, in all his stories, to create an atmosphere of goodness about which there is nothing phony or moralistic. Nothing is rarer in literature." It was this quality of goodness that attracted Lewis from the beginning, and he tried to emulate it in writing the Chronicles.

MOORE, MRS. JANIE KING ASKINS (1872-1951)

C. S. Lewis adopted Mrs. Moore as a mother in fulfillment of a promise made to her son, a billetmate of Lewis's during the Great War. Mrs. Moore, along with her surviving child, Maureen, governed Lewis's household from soon after World War One in a kind of benign, but often intense, matriarchy that rankled on Lewis's brother, Warren. Her companionship with Lewis forms the basis of the diaries he kept for several years in the 1920s, published in *All My Road Before Me*. With her practical turn of mind, there was something of Mrs. Beaver in her character.

NESBIT, E[DITH] (1858-1924)

Author of novels and stories for children, Edith Nesbit created the Bastable family in *The Story of the Treasure Seekers* and a sequence of fantasy tales, *Five Children and It, The Phoenix and the Carpet* and *The Story of the Amulet*. The tone of her stories influenced Lewis in writing the Chronicles, and *MN,* set in the period of many of her stories, is a conscious tribute to her. At the beginning of *MN,* Lewis writes: "In those days Mr. Sherlock Holmes was still living in Baker street and the Bastables were looking for treasure in the Lewisham Road."

PAXFORD, FRED (1898-1979)

Handyman and gardener at The Kilns, Fred Paxford was employed by

162

Lewis and Mrs. Moore in 1930 and remained there until Lewis's death. In his diary, Warren Lewis records his irritation with Paxford, but Lewis found his gloomy manner amusing, vividly modeling Puddleglum the Marsh-wiggle upon him.

POTTER, BEATRIX (1866-1943)

Beatrix Potter was born in London and introduced to the Lake District (where she eventually lived) on holiday in her teens. Late in life she observed: "It sometimes happens that the town child is more alive to the fresh beauty of the country than a child who is country born. My brother and I were born in London. . . . But our descent, our interest and joy were in the north country." She drew and painted from an early age, and her journals display her literary skill. In childhood she would smuggle animals (such as rabbits, mice and a hedgehog) into her house. She started sketching her pet animals dressed in clothes and taking part in human activities, whence came the idea of her stories, which began in letters to children. After self-publishing a little book about Peter Rabbit, a London publisher, Frederick Warne & Co., picked it up and produced their own edition in 1902. It quickly became a success, followed by the publications of *The Tailor of Gloucester* and *The Tale of Squirrel Nutkin* in 1903. Copies soon reached the Lewis household on the outskirts of Belfast. In *Surprised by Joy,* Lewis records that an early glimpse of joy—the inconsolable longing that so features in his writings—"came through *Squirrel Nutkin*; through it only, though I loved all the Beatrix Potter books. . . . It administered the Shock. . . . It troubled me with what I can only describe as the idea of Autumn." Like an earlier experience, it made him aware of nature as "something cool, dewy, fresh, exuberant." The Beatrix Potter stories also helped Lewis see the potency of talking animals, so central to the Chronicles.

TOLKIEN, J. R. R. (1892-1973)

John Ronald Reuel Tolkien was one of C. S. Lewis's closest friends, who, like Lewis, valued friendship highly. Their friendship lasted nearly forty years, from soon after their first meeting in 1926 to Lewis's death in 1963, though in the latter years there was some cooling of the relationship, for complex reasons. Before the publication of *The Hobbit* in 1937, Professor Tolkien was known mainly to a few learned scholars. Now, in the post-*Hobbit* era, he has been read by many millions of people throughout the world, a readership swelled by the appearance of the accomplished film version of *The Lord of the Rings* by Peter Jackson (2001-2003). It is likely that but for the influence of Tolkien on his friend the Chronicles would not have been written. Ironically, Tolkien disliked the stories because he considered them too allegorical, too consciously concerned to communicate the truth-claims of Christianity.

It was largely through Tolkien's influence that Lewis was persuaded of the truth of Christianity. For many years he had been an atheist. Before the friendship, Lewis was a minor poet and an academic. After knowing Tolkien, Lewis turned to fiction and the popular communication of Christian faith for which he is so well known. The Chronicles were inspired by hearing his friend read to him the chapters of *The Lord of the Rings* as they were written, and by Tolkien's remarkable concept of sub-creation (see chapter five). Lewis's science-fiction stories were written as the result of the challenge Tolkien and he set each other—Tolkien to write of time travel and Lewis of space.

PART THREE

THE A-Z
OF NARNIA

Beings, Places,
Things and Events

An asterisk (*) refers the reader to another entry in this section.

Adam and Eve In the Bible, Adam and Eve are the first humans, with all people in every part of the world descending from them. Narnia is a land of talking beasts, but humans are there from the beginning, having come from another world, this world. The original humans who witness the creation of Narnia in *MN* are Digory Kirke*; Polly Plummer*; Digory's uncle, Andrew Ketterley*; and a London Cabbie, Frank.* Jadis,* late of Charn,* is also with them; it is through her that evil is introduced into Narnia at its very beginning. Frank is chosen to be the first king of Narnia by Aslan. Aslan decrees that all kings or queens of Narnia have to be human ("Sons of Adam or Daughters of Eve"), reflecting a hierarchy by which Narnia is ordered. Frank's wife, Helen, is the first human to be drawn into Narnia by Aslan's call. From Frank and Helen many humans, including future kings and queens, are descended, but other humans, the Telmarines, stumble into Narnia through a portal, in this case a cave in a South Sea island.

Ahoshta Tarkaan In *HHB,* an elderly lord (tarkaan) of Calormen, and the Tisroc's Grand Vizier, or chief counselor. He is due to marry Aravis* in an arranged marriage. Base born, he works his way up the social hierarchy by intrigue and flattery. His appearance has little to attract the reluctant Aravis: he is short and wizened with age, and has a humped back.

Alambil One of the two planets visible at night in Narnia, the name of which means "Lady of Peace." When in conjunction with the star Tarva, it spells good fortune for Narnia.

albatross This large seabird leads the *Dawn Treader* out of the terrifying blackness surrounding the Dark Island after Lucy calls in desperation to Aslan for help. It is one of many signs of Aslan's providence in Narnia. There is a long maritime tradition of the albatross as guide and harbinger of good fortune (featured in Samuel Taylor Coleridge's *The Rhyme of the Ancient Mariner*).

Alimash A captain of the chariots in Calormen and the cousin of Aravis.* The horse Bree* remembers him as a worthy nobleman who, after an important battle, the capture of Teebeth, filled his nosebag with sugar.

Andrew, Uncle *See* Ketterley, Andrew.*

animals Animals are central to the magical world of Narnia, as it is a country of talking beasts, ruled over by the divine lion, Aslan.*

See also chapter six, "Themes, Concepts and Images in Narnia."

animals, talking   *See* chapter five, "Literary Features of the Chronicles."

Anradin   A Tarkaan of Calormen in *HHB* and crimson-bearded master of Bree,* the stolen talking horse of Narnia.* He treats Bree badly and tries to buy Shasta.* Later he supports Rabadash* in the battle of Anvard.*

Anvard   The capital of Archenland,* the seat of King Lune* featured in *HHB.* Anvard is a small, many-towered castle at the foot of the Northern Mountains. The ancient stronghold is protected from the north wind by a wooded ridge. The visitor should note its warm, reddish brown stone. Pleasant green lawns extend to the front of the entrance gate, but it has no moat.

Aravir   In *PC,* the morning star of Narnia,* which gleamed like a little moon. *See* astronomy of Narnia.*

Aravis   Only daughter of Kidrash Tarkaan, lord of the Calormene* province of Calavar, and descended, she is taught, from the god Tash.* She is important in *HHB,* along with Shasta* and the Narnian talking horses, Bree* and Hwin.* Aravis runs away from home when her mother arranges a marriage to Ahoshta*—sixty years old, with a face like an ape. She meets up with and eventually marries Shasta (Cor) and becomes queen of Archenland.* Aravis, despite her faults, displays the qualities of the virtuous pagan, also found later (in *LB*) in Emeth.* She is as true as steel and would never abandon a companion. She is also attracted to Aslan, even though the first hint of his existence comes through Bree's frequent expression, "By the Lion's Mane." Aravis discovers that Aslan has guided her, and also wounded her with the same welts her unfortunate maidservant received after Aravis ran away, awakening her from her indifference. When she meets Queen Lucy* they become instant friends.

Archenland   To Narnia's* south, and connected by a high mountain pass, Archenland is ruled over by King Lune* from Anvard* during the time of the co-regency of Peter, Edmund, Susan and Lucy Pevensie,* in *LWW* and *HHB.* Leading to the high mountains are pine-covered slopes and narrow valleys. The highest peaks are Stormness Head and Mount Pire. In Archenlandian mythology the twin-peaked Mount Pire was once a two-headed giant turned to stone. Archenland's southern boundary is marked by Winding Arrow River. Beyond this lies a vast desert that separates Archenland and the troublesome Calormen.* Travelers en route to Archenland from Calormen can use the conspicuous double peak of Mount Pire as a landmark. Archenland's wine is highly regarded and is so potent that water has to be mixed with it before drinking.

Ardeeb Tisroc Paternal ancestor of Aravis.*

Argoz In *VDT* he is one of the seven lords* of Narnia sought by Caspian* X. One of the three sleepers, he is eventually discovered slumbering a deep sleep of years at Ramandu's Island.*

Arlian In *PC,* one of the Telmarine* lords of Caspian* IX, executed for treason by the usurper Miraz.*

Arsheesh In *HHB,* an unpleasant Calormen* fisherman who raises the apparently orphaned Shasta.* Near his cottage is a narrow estuary with mud banks. Beside the cottage is a single tree and a donkey's stable.

Aslan Lewis's invented world of Narnia* contains many talking lions, the kings of beasts, but Aslan (Turkish for "lion") is not only this but also the creator and ultimate sovereign of the land. His father is the Emperor-over-the-sea, dwelling beyond the Eastern Ocean, past Aslan's Country* and the World's End. Aslan is a central presence in the Chronicles, his character and significance becoming clearer as the stories unfold.

Lucy Pevensie's* response to Aslan, such as hugging him, is one of the secrets of the lion's success as an imaginative creation. C. S. Lewis fashions a figure of authority, the creator and true sovereign of Narnia, who is eminently approachable by the innocent and good. Those also, like Edmund and later Eustace, who approach him in fear and repentance, find a friend like no other.

See chapter three, "Aslan, Narnia and Orthodoxy."

Aslan's Country This lies high up and beyond Narnia's* Eastern Ocean. It features in *VDT.* Also, Jill Pole* and Eustace Scrubb* arrive there when they are drawn out of our world in *SC.* Seen from the World's End,* Aslan's Country appears to be made up of mountains of enormous height, yet forever free of snow, clothed in grass and forests as far as the eye can glimpse. The highest peak is known as the Mountain of Aslan. Clouds above the Eastern Ocean viewed from its summit look like small sheep because of the mountain's height. The distinctive water of Aslan's Country quenches hunger and thirst. Approaching visitors find a deepening and splendid brightness that confers increasing youthfulness to those long exposed to it. Its brightness is like that experienced by Elwin Ransom* in Deep Heaven in Lewis's science-fiction trilogy. The quality of light in Deep Heaven and near Aslan's Country reminds us that Lewis was very much inspired by the medieval imagination, with its marked response to brightness, rather than the modern imagination, with its awe at the vastness of deep space or large quantities.

In *VDT* Aslan* in his country appears to the children, Edmund and Lucy Pevensie* and Eustace, first as a lamb and then as the familiar great lion. Because his country is a borderland of worlds, including the children's England, he partly reveals his this-worldly identity by appearing as a lamb.

Aslan's How A huge mound, in *PC,* which during the course of ages has been built over the Stone Table* where Aslan,* the great talking lion, was sacrificed. It is located in the Great Woods of Narnia,* but in open space, and has hollowed galleries and caves. From its top the traveler can see the forests of Narnia and, to the east, the great ocean. A "how" is the old name for a mound or cairn, and indeed the how has the character of a Celtic shrine. It is one of many reminders of the sweep of Narnia's history. Caspian bases himself here with his loyal fighters during the threat from the forces of his Uncle Miraz.

Aslan's Table The voyagers in *VDT* come across this table on Ramandu's Island,* laden with uneaten food. Sprawled over it are three sleepers, missing lords of the seven sought by King Caspian.* It runs the length of a clearing, with open sky above. A crimson cloth covering the table highlights the stone knife* lying on it, once used to slay Aslan. The food on it is replenished magically each sunset.

astronomy of Narnia The astronomy of Narnia reflects a medieval model, particularly of the sixteenth century that Lewis loved. Narnia itself is located on a flat world (or, at least, its inhabitants perceive it as flat). The planets and stars are living beings. One of them, Ramandu, a retired star, is encountered on his island in *VDT.* That there is some scientific study of the night sky is suggested by the instruments found in the house* of the magician in *VDT.* Doctor Cornelius* is well-versed in astronomy in *PC,* tutoring Caspian* in the subject. As in the late medieval and Renaissance period, astronomy and astrology coexist in Narnia, with astrological portents being given significance. Centaurs* are skilled in rendering the meaning of such omens. Lucy is well versed in Narnian astronomy: in *PC* she notices several summer constellations, the Ship, the Hammer, and the Leopard (a favorite with her).

Atlantis Even in the dawn of time, according to Uncle Andrew, Atlantis was a splendid city with palaces, temples and scholars. In Lewis's *That Hideous Strength,* Atlantis was the origin of Logres, the spiritual and true Britain, established during the time of King Arthur and Merlin. Merlin's magical art was a last survival of the older and different realm of Atlantis, or Numinor, as it is sometimes called, which existed in the preglacial period before primitive Druidism. It was brought to western Europe after the fall of Atlantis and differed greatly from the Renaissance magic with which we are familiar. The Chronicles retain the idea of a spiritual or essential England in *LB,* and a corresponding real Narnia, which is made visible at the end of the world.

In *MN* the magical rings that allow Polly Plummer* and Digory Kirke* to travel to other worlds, including Charn* and the space that becomes Narnia,* are made from Atlantean dust, passed onto Uncle Andrew by his godmother. They are linked to the Deep Magic that has existed in Narnia from its dawn.

Lewis employs the image of Atlantis being overwhelmed by flood to describe the impact of his mother's death, in his autobiography *Surprised by Joy.**

Avra A sparsely inhabited island in *VDT,* the third of a group known as the Lone Islands and the location of the estates of Lord Bern.* Avra has a medieval-like economy and social structure, where pleasant slopes reach down to the shoreline. Lord Bern's people are all free, working happily in the fields, resulting in a prosperous and contented fief.

Axartha Tarkaan In *HHB* he was Grand Vizier of Calormen* before Ahoshta.*

Azaroth A minor Calormene* deity.

Azim Balda To the south of the capital of Calormen,* a town at the junction of many roads. It is an important center of communications and the core of the country's postal system. Mounted messengers of the House of Imperial Posts carry letters throughout the vast country.

Azrooh A Calormene warrior supporting Rabadash* in the battle of Anvard,* slain by King Lune.*

Bacchus The classical god of wine (Roman, *Bacchus;* Greek, *Dionysus*), who makes an emphatic but fleeting appearance in Narnia (*LWW, PC*), representing the wild and pagan side to nature, which Aslan rules firmly but doesn't suppress. He is accompanied usually by Silenus* and the Maenads,* with whom he dances in joyful and exuberant celebration of the plenitude of nature, a dance and feast revolving around Aslan.

Bar In *HHB,* the chancellor of jolly King Lune.* He turns traitor and kidnaps the infant Prince Cor (named Shasta* by those who found him in Calormen*) when he hears that Cor will save Archenland.* Later Lord Bar is slain in battle.

Battle of Anvard In *HHB,* the unsuccessful attack by Rabadash the Calormene using two hundred horsemen, attempting to secure Anvard,* as part of a plan to go on and conquer Narnia.

Battles of Beruna Two battles are recorded in the Chronicles. The first is that in which the White Witch is defeated, in *LWW,* at the Fords of Beruna.* These fords are later bridged, and a second battle near Beruna is chronicled in *PC.* This takes place during the War of Deliverance. The Telmarines* surrender after finding that the bridge has disappeared.

bears *See* Bulgy Bears.*

Beaver, Mr. and Mrs. Loyal Narnian talking beavers who lead Peter, Lucy and Susan to the meeting point with Aslan in *LWW,* after feeding them and the traitor Edmund in their home at Beaversdam.* Mr. Beaver is a hard-working, warm-hearted and direct creature who tells the children some of the history of Narnia. Mrs. Beaver is the archetypal homemaker, busy with her sewing machine, domestic and hospitable. She delays their escape from Maugrim and his police as she packs carefully for the journey, much to the others' frustration.

Beaversdam Built by Mr. Beaver in *LWW,* the original dam spanned the still, wide upper reaches of The Great River* in a steep, narrow valley. It becomes the site of a historic settlement bordered to its north by fertile grasslands. The town has an important marketplace. Two Telmarine* lords, called the Brothers of Beaversdam, rule there during the reign of Caspian* IX.

beaver's house In *LWW* this is an odd little house perched on the top of the dam built by Mr. Beaver* (*see* Beaversdam*). It resembles an enormous beehive, and smoke from its fire emerges from a hole in its roof. The snug house has one room, in the corner of which Mrs. Beaver* habitually works her beloved sewing machine. There is a meal table, covered with a clean, rough cloth, and nearby an oven built into a range that accommodates the kettle and cooking pots. Instead of beds, the room has bunks built into the wall. Hams and strings of onions hang from the curved roof. Against the walls are clustered Mr. Beaver's paraphernalia: gumboots, oilskins, hatchets, shears, spades, fishing rods, nets and the like.

Belisar In the reign of Caspian* IX, a great Telmarine lord who is murdered at Miraz's instigation during a hunting party. The event, recorded in *PC,* is made to seem like an accident with arrows.

bell and the hammer *MN* tells how Digory* and Polly* come across in Charn* a little golden arch on a stone pillar from which there hangs a small bell made of gold. A hammer lies beside the arch. An enchanted verse is cut into the stone, the words of which tempt Digory to strike the bell, awaking Queen Jadis* and all her evil.*

Bern In *VDT,* one of the seven lords* of Caspian* IX. The voyagers find him living on Felimath, one of the Lone Islands.* His estate is called Bernstead.* After the removal of Gumpas,* Caspian* X makes him a duke.

Bernstead The estate on Felimath* Island, governed by Lord Bern. His people are free in a climate of slavery on the Lone Islands, and enjoy prosperity and happiness.

Beruna A small and snug red-roofed town half a day's march from Aslan's How.* Established by Telmarines,* it is walled and gated, with an important marketplace. It is near the meeting of the Great River and its tributary, the Rush River. The few Old Narnians* living there are delighted when Aslan delivers the town as Caspian's* forces grapple with Miraz's army.

Beruna Bridge A bridge build over the original ford by Beruna (*see* Beruna, Fords of*) in Miraz's modernizing regime. It is destroyed in *PC* by Aslan, freeing the River-god.* A more appropriate bridge is allowed later in Narnia.

Beruna, Fords of Fords over the river of Narnia, later bridged, near the Stone Table.* During the night of Aslan's* terrible death, his loyal forces encamp here. At the time of the events recorded in *PC* and *SC,* there is a town of Beruna located here.

birds Birds play an important role in Narnia. As with other animals, some are talking beasts. Some are messengers; eagles rescue or survey battles. Owls like Glimfeather* feature strongly in *SC,* including their Parliament of Owls.* In *MN,* Digory* sees a phoenix* in the garden.

birds of morning These large white birds appear each morning on Ramandu's Island* in *VDT.* They bring fire-berries that renew Ramandu, then they pick clean what food is left on Aslan's Table.* This is an implicit allusion to Isaiah 6, where one of the seraphs attending God's heavenly throne brings a live coal to purify Isaiah's mouth.

Bism An underground world deep below Narnia,* not be be confused with the Green Witch's* perverted Underland,* which lies above Bism. The word in Greek means "bottom," hence *abyss,* "bottomless." The children in *SC* catch a glimpse of Bism through a chasm in the earth. Here the bright gems of all colors are alive. It is the home of gnomes. Through Bism runs a river of fire inhabited by salamanders. In medieval lore, salamanders were the one creature able to live in fire, as birds in air and fish in water.

black dwarfs One of three types of dwarf in Narnia, with hard, thick horselike hair. They include Nikabrik,* Griffle,* Diggle* and the driver of the White Witch's* sleigh. They tend to be obstinate and cynical.

Black Woods In *PC,* woods near the ruins of Cair Paravel* and the sea. It is rumored by the Telmarines* that the woods are full of ghosts. Telmarines fear the sea, and they let the woods grow to protect them from it.

boggles These are summoned in *LWW* by the Witch Witch* to the execution of Aslan* on the Stone Table.* They are evil spirits, and the term covers a variety of demonic frighteners that people would boggle at in horror, such as specters, bogeymen and hobgoblins.

Bramandin In *MN,* a city of the ancient dead world of Charn.*

Bree Bree is a talking Narnian horse, one of the most sustained talking-animal characters in the Chronicles. A dappled horse, he disguises his true nature after being stolen and becoming the horse of Anradin* Tarkaan in Calormen.* He runs away with Shasta,* and the two come across Aravis* and Hwin* (another Narnian talking horse). Bree is haughty and skeptical about Aslan's reality, though he constantly swears "by the Lion's Mane." He is also concerned about his dignity when his tail has to be cropped (paralleling Reepicheep's* humiliation in losing his tail). His redeeming feature, however, is his love of rolling in the grass. Bree believes that all the talk of Aslan being a talking beast and a lion is merely metaphorical language—it only means he is as fierce or as strong as a lion. He is undeceived (*see* the subhead "Recognition and Undeception" in chapter five) when Aslan appears in all his reality.

Brenn The second of the Seven Isles,* with its main town being Redhaven.*

Bricklethumb Red dwarf* in *HHB* who, with his brother Duffle,* feeds Shasta* when he first comes into Narnia.*

Bromios Another name for Bacchus.*

Buffin A much-respected clan of giants* of Narnia.* This ancient family makes up for its lack of brains with its rich traditions.

Bulgy Bears In *PC,* three sleepy bears who are among the loyal Old Narnians. They offer Caspian* honey.

Burnt Island In *VDT,* a low, green island within sight of Dragon Island.* Here the only living creatures the travelers discover are rabbits and goats. Ruins of stone huts, several bones and broken weapons between the fire-blackened areas suggest that it has been inhabited fairly recently. A small coracle found there is given to Reepicheep,* befitting his diminutive size.

cabby Name given to a London horse-and-cab driver in the Edwardian period in which *MN* is set.

    See Frank, King.*

Cair Paravel Capital of Narnia,* the beautiful castle stands on the estuary of the Great River. In *LWW,* it is the seat of High King Peter* and the other ruling kings and queens. Originally it was situated between two streams, but erosion and a Telmarine channel turned its location into a small island. When the children return to Narnia ages later (as told in *PC*), the castle is in ruins. Caspian* X rebuilds it to its former splendor. In their subsequent visit, recounted in *SC,* Eustace Scrubb* and Jill Pole* hear told the ancient tale of *The Horse and His Boy.*

    Visitors should note its splendid Great Hall, restored by Caspian, with its ivory roof, floor paved in many colors and walls covered in tapestry. The West Door of this banqueting hall is hung with peacock feathers and the East Door opens to the direction of Aslan's Country* over the ocean. Cair Paravel is like the Court of Arthur, with a round table and embodying the ideal of equal rule. Lewis may have been inspired by the description of the Arthurian court at the beginning of the medieval poem *Sir Gawain and the Green Knight. Caer,* from which *Cair* derives, is Welsh for castle. In *LWW* Peter saw at it at sunset from a distant vantage point resting like a great star on the seashore.

Calavar In *HHB,* a province of Calormen* ruled by Kidrash Tarkaan, Aravis's father.

Caldron Pool In *LB,* a large pool under the cliffs at the western end of Narnia.* It owes its name to the bubbling and dancing movement of its churning water.

Calormen A huge, hot land to the far south of Narnia (the Latin word *calor* means "hot"). Calormen is ruled by a dark-skinned and sometimes cruel people, with a rich civilization. Its capital is Tashbaan,* and it has many provinces, each ruled by a tarkaan, or lord. Calormen is the setting of *HB.* To its north lies Archenland,* from which it is isolated by a large desert.

    Unlike the free lands of Narnia and Archenland to its north, Calormen has a rigidly hierarchical, caste society. The darker-skinned peasant majority have little or no rights, and slavery is common. It is basically an agricultural society, though fishing, crafts and trade have an important place. A troublesome country, Calormen historically has coveted the northern lands of its peaceable neighbors and particularly becomes a threat in the period described in *LB*. Calormen originated in the Narnian year 204, when outlaws fled south from Archenland.

Calormene Inhabitant of Calormen.* Calormenes have dark faces, and the men have long beards and wear flowing robes and orange-colored turbans. As a people, they express mixed qualities of wisdom, prosperity, courtesy and cruelty. Their speech is full of elaborate expressions, such as "May fountains of prosperity water the gardens of virtue and prudence." The narrator tries hard to overcome some prejudices he feels towards Calormenes but just occasionally succumbs, as when he speaks of their breath smelling of garlic and onions. The noblest of Calormenes are represented in the Chronicles in the persons of Aravis* and Emeth.*

Camillo A talking hare who in *PC* attends the Great Council.* He senses a man nearby, who turns out to be the half-dwarf Doctor Cornelius,* Caspian's* loyal tutor.

Carter In *SC,* a bullying pupil at Experiment House* who particularly seems to enjoy torturing animals.

Caspian The name of the first ten of the Telmarine* kings in *PC*. The last Caspian (born 2290 N.T., ruled 2303-2356 N.T. and died 2356 N.T.) becomes Caspian X after defeating the usurper Miraz.* He appears also as a central figure in *VDT* and, in old age, in *SC*. Caspian X marries the daughter of Ramandu,* later murdered by the Green Witch* of the line of Jadis.* He is succeeded by his son, Rilian,* who is for many years the prisoner of the Witch.*

The first of the kings of Telmar, Caspian I conquers Narnia* and silences the talking animals,* its proper inhabitants. Caspian IX, Caspian's father, is murdered by his brother Miraz.

See also chapter eight, "The History of Narnia."

Castle of the White Witch Edmund* finds the castle on a tributary of the Great River.* It is a stone building with high walls, with a courtyard and many towers. The courtyard is cluttered with unfortunate Narnians turned to stone by the witch. The castle is a police stronghold, controlled by Maugrim* (Fenris Ulf), complete with dungeons and smelling of fear. The castle is entered by high iron gates. Aslan however leaps over the walls to unpetrify the statues.

cats Two contrasting cats feature in the Chronicles. The first is Aslan in another form: the cat at the Tombs of the Ancient Kings* in *HHB*. The second is associated with Aslan's enemy, the Calormene god Tash*: this is Ginger* the cat, who is eventually turned into a dumb beast for his role in supporting Shift* in misleading the Narnians.

centaur The half human-half horse creature of classical mythology. Centaurs in the Chronicles have a prophetic role, as with the star-gazer Glenstorm.* Other named centaurs are Cloudbirth* and Roonwit.* They are knowledgable about the properties of roots and herbs, and about Narnian astronomy* and astrology. In the Chronicles the centaurs of classical mythology have been softened and made more gentle.

Charn In *MN,* a dead world and its city, which is the domain of Jadis,* later known as the White Witch. Charn was once the city of the king of kings, and wonder of all worlds. It has become a gloomy world, dominated by a giant red dying sun. As far as the eye can see, ruins extend. A great river had once flowed through Charn, but now only a wide ditch of gray dust remains. In Charn, Digory Kirke* awakes Jadis and all her evil by striking a forbidden bell.* Through him, she is drawn first into our world and then into Narnia.*

The blight of Charn represents evil before Eden, as in John Milton's epic poem *Paradise Lost* and medieval poetry like *Genesis*. In the Wood Between the Worlds,* the drying up of the pool that leads to Charn signifies its complete annihilation, a terrible lesson of the contingency of worlds. The term *Charn* alludes to the Charnel-House, where corpses or bones were piled.

Chervy the stag In *HHB* he informs King Edmund,* Queen Susan* and Prince Corin* of the Calormen* attack on Anvard.*

Chief Voice In *VDT,* the leader of the Dufflepuds,* who tells brave Lucy Pevensie* their history. All the other Dufflepuds repeat what he says, which is usually inane, with approval.

Chippingford In *LB,* a market town down the river from Caldron Pool,* where Shift* the ape sends Puzzle* the ass to buy food.

Chlamash In *HHB,* a Tarkaan or lord of Rabadash's,* who supports him in the battle of Anvard* and is forced to surrender to King Edmund.*

Cholmondeley Major In *SC,* a member of the bullying gang of pupils at Experiment House* who cause misery for Eustace Scrubb* and Jill Pole.*

choriambuses In *VDT,* instruments of the magician Coriakin* for measuring a choriambus—a metrical foot made up of two short syllables between two long. This and the other instruments of the magician are a joke on Lewis's part at the idea of a mechanical instrument for such tasks!

Christmas, Father In *LWW* this familiar figure appears in Narnia* as the White Witch's* curse of perpetual winter begins to break with Aslan's reappearance. Her boast had been that it would be ever winter but never Christmas. Father Christmas is a portent of change. Also, he gives magical presents to three of the four Pevensie* children who will become kings and queens of Narnia.

See Gifts of Father Christmas.*

chronology The time frame of Narnia runs independently of our world. Thus, when humans enter Narnia, no time at all passes in this world while they are there, even if many years pass in Narnia (as happens in *LWW*, when the children stay so long they grow to adulthood, but revert to their original ages when they return).

See chapter eight, "The History of Narnia."

chronoscopes In *VDT*, instruments of the magician Coriakin* for observing and measuring time.

City Ruinous In *SC*, a great ruined city of giants close by Harfang* in the northern wastelands. According to the Green Witch,* a king who once dwelt there had the following words inscribed on the ruins: "Though under Earth and throneless now I be, / Yet, while I lived, all Earth is under me." The Green Witch's Underland* lay beneath it. Only the words "UNDER ME" remain. The letters are so large that Jill and Eustace walked through one of the letter E's, thinking it a trench. Only from the high vantage point of Harfang are the letters recognizable.

classes of Narnian creatures In *PC* Doctor Cornelius,* Caspian's tutor, sets out nine classes of beings (reminiscent of the hierarchies of medieval classification): walking trees, visible naiads, fauns, satyrs, dwarfs, giants, gods, centaurs and talking beasts. Because Digory* brings evil into the newly created world in the form of Jadis,* it is decreed that humans should try to set things right. Accordingly, kings and queens of Narnia are to be human, so they are highest in terms of sovereignty. As rational beings, however, humans and talking beasts are equal. One volume title cleverly suggested by Lewis's publisher points to this fact—*The Horse and His Boy*. Shasta is as much Bree's boy as Bree is Shasta's horse.

Clipsie In *VDT*, the little daughter of the Chief Voice,* the leader of the Duf-flepuds.* She spoke the spell that made the Dufflepuds invisible.

Clodsley Shovel In *PC*, a loyal Old Narnian* mole. He leads the loyal moles to the Great Council.*

Cloudbirth In *SC*, a centaur* and renowned healer who tends the burnt foot of Puddleglum.*

Coalblack In *SC*, the horse of Prince Rilian.*

Col According to Lewis's sketch of Narnian history, a Prince Col in 180 N.T. leads a company of Narnians to settle in the fertile, uninhabited region later called Archenland.* The younger son of King Frank V of Narnia, Col becomes Archenland's first king. In *MN*, Lewis inconsistently states that Archenland's first king is the second son of King Frank I.

   See chapter eight, "The History of Narnia."

Cole In *HHB* he fights along with his brother Colin against the Calormenes.*

Colin In *HHB* he fights, together with his brother Cole, for King Lune* against the troublesome Calormenes.*

Colney Hatch In *MN*, a reference to a well-known lunatic asylum near London at that time (early in the twentieth century), as Jadis* is dubbed by someone in the crowd the "Hempress of Colney 'Atch."

Cor *See* Shasta.*

Coriakin In *VDT*, a magician who, like Ramandu,* was once a star of the sky. As a punishment for an unnamed wrong, Aslan* gave him the difficult task of governing the Dufflepuds.* He is elderly, with a waist-length beard; garbed in a red robe; and crowned with oak leaves. His many instruments reflect his scientific interests.

Corin In *HHB*, the younger twin brother of Shasta* (i.e., Prince Cor, who was lost for years in Calormen*). He would have been heir to the Archenland* throne had Cor not been restored, but is quite content not to become king. He is nicknamed Thunder-Fist because he is a great boxer.

Cornelius, Doctor In *PC*, a half-dwarf who is the tutor of Caspian,* later King Caspian X. He is loyal to the "Old Narnia"* and teaches the young prince the true history of the kingdom. As a true scholar, he is never without pen and ink.

Corradin In *HHB*, a member of Rabadash's assalt against Anvard,* who is slain by King Edmund.*

creation of Narnia In *MN* there is an account of the beginning, in which Narnia* is sung into being by Aslan.*

cruels In *LWW,* hair-raising supernatural beings called to Aslan's* execution by the White Witch.*

Dancing Lawn In *PC,* the setting of the Great Council* of Caspian* and his Narnian friends, west of the River Rush.* The neat circle of grass is ringed by elms. It is the favored site of feasts and councils in Narnia.

Dar Brother of Darrin in *HHB,* he fights in defense of Anvard* against the Calormenes* led by Rabadash.*

Dark Island In *VDT,* an island that appears to the voyagers first as a dark spot in the ocean. Here, in the darkness permanently engulfing the island, dreams come true (dreams we have while sleeping, including nightmares, not idle daydreams). Lord Rhoop* is rescued from this place of despair, and Lucy calls upon Aslan to lead them out of the darkness.

Darrin Brother of Dar in *HHB,* he fights in defense of Anvard* against the Calormenes* led by Rabadash.*

Daughter of Eve In the Chronicles, the name by which female humans are formally addressed. The Narnian throne may only properly be occupied by Sons of Adam* and Daughters of Eve.

daughter of Ramandu *See* Ramandu's daughter.*

Dawn Treader In *VDT,* the galleon in which the children Edmund* and Lucy* Pevensie and Eustace Scrubb* sail almost to Aslan's Country,* lying beyond the World's End. Shaped like a dragon, it has green sides and a purple sail. Pauline Baynes provided a useful cut-away illustration of the ship for the book. There are two long, large hatches fore and aft of the tall mast. In fair weather they are left open to allow air and light to penetrate the ship's belly. Below deck there are benches for rowing (for when the wind failed and for maneuvering in and out of harbor). Cabins are in the ship's stern. Caspian's is the finest, which he gallantly hands over to Lucy for her use. Instead, he takes the lowest galley, sharing it with Edmund and Eustace. The name of the ship is highly significant for the story, which is about the journey eastward toward Aslan's Country.* The ship treads toward dawn, the utter east.

Deathwater Island In *VDT,* an island to the east of Burnt Island,* and not more than twenty acres in size. The voyagers discover that it is rocky and rugged with a tall central peak. Its only flora are perfumed heather and coarse grass. Only seagulls appear to live there.

Two streams are found, one of which flows from a small mountain lake guarded by cliffs. To the horror of the visitors, anything dipped into the lake turns to solid gold. This explains the naked gold statue lying in its waters. It is the transformed body of one of the missing seven lords,* Restimar.* As a result of this grisly discovery, Reepicheep* gives the island its name.

Deep Magic In the Chronicles, the moral order by which the world of Narnia is made and sustained. One of its inner laws is that unless the Witch is given blood for every treachery committed all Narnia will fall apart, perishing in fire and water. The Deep Magic has affinities with Old Testament law.

Deep Realm Part of the lands lying under Narnia, deeper than the Marches, but with Bism* below it.

See Underworld.*

Deeper Magic In the Chronicles, a deeper principle than the natural moral order that sustains the world. This is a principle resembling the New Testament notion of grace, which fulfills and perfects the older law. Thus this Deeper Magic allows a willing victim to die in place of a traitor. This is why Aslan is able to die in Edmund's place. The White Witch sees the aspect of the Deeper Magic that fulfills the demands of the Deep Magic but fails to see the dramatic impact of the Deeper Magic, which is to overturn her grip of winter over Narnia and allow Aslan to return to life and continue his rule.

Deplorable Word In *MN,* a secret word that is known only to the great kings. When spoken, it destroys all living things except the speaker of the word. Jadis* utters the word in Charn* during a battle with her sister, creating a frozen enchantment that includes herself. She is awakened when Digory strikes the bell he discovers.

Destrier In *PC,* Caspian's* horse, a dumb beast. After bolting during a thunderstorm, it returns to its stables in Miraz's castle, revealing Caspian's escape.

Diggle In *LB,* the spokesman of a company of dwarfs who survive the Last Battle* only to be thrown into the Stable.* These dwarfs believe in nothing but themselves.

Digory Kirke *See* Kirke, Digory.*

D.L.F. In *PC,* an abbreviation of "Dear Little Friend," a nickname given to Trumpkin* the dwarf by Edmund.

dog-fox In *LWW,* a talking dog-fox (male fox) present at a party in the woods in which all partiers are turned into stone by the White Witch.

door in the air In *PC*, a portal between Narnia and this world created by Aslan* to allow the exodus of those Telmarines who wished to return to the South Sea island from which they came. The children Peter, Edmund, Susan and Lucy use the same portal to return to the railway station from which they were called into Narnia.

Doorn In *VDT*, the chief among the Lone Islands,* a group of islands some four hundred leagues to the east of Narnia. These islands had been under Narnian rule since the tenth king of Narnia, Gale,* freed the islanders from a dragon.* The town of Narrowhaven is Doorn's major settlement. Caspian* and the other voyagers are displeased to discover Narrowhaven a center of a slave trade to Calormen.* After skillfully deposing the governor, despite inferior forces, Caspian gives Lord Bern* the post.

dragon In *VDT*, an old and dying dragon is discovered by Eustace Scrubb* on Dragon Island.* (It later appears that one of the lost Narnian lords—Octesian*—for whom the party of voyagers is searching, transformed into this hideous shape.) Upon the dragon's death, the unpleasant Eustace himself becomes a dragon, and only Aslan* is able to restore him to his boy nature.

Dragon Island Discovered and named by Caspian* of Narnia* in *VDT*, it lies to the east of the Lone Islands.* It is named after the resident sad dragon,* which is the transformed shape of the missing Narnian Lord Octesian.* The mountainous island has deep bays rather like Norwegian fjords, ending in steep valleys that often have waterfalls. Cedars and others trees cover what little level land exists. Beside the ill-fated dragon, a few wild goats live there.

Drinian In *VDT*, Caspian's* loyal captain of the *Dawn Treader* and a lord of Narnia. In *SC*, he is featured in the court of his king. He is a trusted friend of Prince Rilian,* and advises him not to pursue his quest to find the serpent who killed his mother.

dryads In classical mythology, wood nymphs who live in trees and preside over woods. They live and die with the trees they animate. In the Chronicles they are sometimes referred to generically as wood people. In *LWW* the winter spell of the White Witch* makes them disappear, and in *PC* they are also subdued by the modernizing New Narnians of Miraz.* They are awakened by Aslan along with hamadryads* and Silvans.* In *LB* many die as their trees are cut down by order of the false Aslan instigated by Shift* the ape. The term *dryad* in Greek derives from the word for tree, *drus.*

duffers *See* Dufflepuds.*

Duffle In *HHB,* a practical and kind red dwarf who feeds and looks after Shasta* when he first enters Narnia. He is the brother of Rogin* and Bricklethumb.*

dufflepuds Encountered on the Island of Voices* in *VDT,* these monopods (one-footed creatures) had been made invisible by a spell. Lucy Pevensie* is persuaded to find the spell in the magician's book to make them visible again. They have a humorous way of talking about the obvious. The name is a contraction of their original title, Duffers,* and the new name of Monopods, given them by the voyagers.

dumb beasts Originally, at the very beginning of the creation, all animals were dumb, but Aslan chose some of them to receive the gift of speech. Smaller talking animals are noticeably larger in stature than their dumb relations. When Ginger* the cat is made dumb by Aslan,* this is the worst that can happen to a talking beast. Dumb beasts may be eaten for food, but never talking beasts.

Dumnus In *PC,* a faun.* With other fauns he dances around Prince Caspian.*

dust from Atlantis In *MN,* a box from Atlantis* given by Mrs. LeFay* to Uncle Andrew* to destroy. Instead, he opens it and uses its dust from another world to make the rings* that allow transportation to other worlds.

dwarfs Three kinds of dwarfs live in Narnia. In Norse mythology there are black and white dwarfs, the former associated with evil. In Narnia there are black dwarfs (like Nikabrik*), red dwarfs (such as Duffle,* Rogin,* Trumpkin* and Bricklethumb*) and dufflepuds* (who were transformed by magic from their earlier form into monopods). Doctor Cornelius, Caspian's tutor, is a half-dwarf. The red dwarfs have the most talent for happiness, enjoying wild dances, opulent feasts and brightly colored garments. In *SC* Trumpkin* is regent to Caspian. In *LWW* the Witch's sleigh is driven by a dwarf, reflecting an alliance between her and some of the dwarfs, probably black ones.

Earthmen In *SC,* gnome creatures who live in the Green Witch's* realm of Underworld—called by them the Shallow Lands.* They originally came from Bism,* deep below the earth's surface. At the time of their slavery to the Witch they all look sad. Physically, they differ greatly from each other—some have tails, and some, round faces; some noses are long and pointed while others are trunk-like or blobbed; some have beards on their faces or horns on their foreheads.

Eastern Ocean (Eastern Sea) In the Chronicles, a great ocean washing the shores of all the countries on the east.

See chapter nine, "The Geography of Narnia."

Edmund, King *See* Pevensie, Edmund.*

efreets In *LWW,* terrifying evil spirits summoned to the Stone Table* for Aslan's execution. The word is a variant of *afreet,* a demon in Islamic stories.

Emeth the Calormene *Emeth* is ancient Hebrew for "truth," and Emeth in *LB* symbolizes what is best in human knowledge unenlightened by Christ. He is a Calormene* who attains to the New Narnia* because he is able to acknowledge Aslan* when the moment of truth arises. Aravis,* whose story is more fully told, is a similar virtuous pagan in *HHB.*

See Paganism.*

Emperor-over-the-sea, -beyond-the-sea In the Chronicles, a metaphorical term for the Father of Aslan,* representing God* the Father of the biblical Trinity. Aslan's Country* lies over the Eastern Ocean,* on the borderland of all created worlds, including this world.

end of Narnia There are two senses of the end of Narnia. The first is geographical—the travelers in *VDT* near the world's end. The second is temporal—the *LB* recounts the eschatological end of Narnia and the beginning of the new Narnia.

England The home of the Pevensies,* the Scrubbs,* Professor Digory Kirke,* Polly Plummer* and Jill Pole* in the Chronicles. The spiritual or inner England, that is, the real England (what Lewis's friend Charles Williams called Logres), is connected, like the real Narnia, to Aslan's Country.* In relation to these spiritual countries, England and Narnia (and other created worlds) are shadowlands.

Erimon In *PC,* a lord of Caspian* IX, executed by the usurping Uncle Miraz* on a trumped-up charge of treason.

Erlian In *LB,* the father of King Tirian,* with whom he is reunited in Aslan's Country,* in the real Narnia.

ettins Foolish, fierce and savage stone giants who, in *SC,* live in the rocks on Ettinsmoor. *Eten* is an old word for "giant." "Eotenas" are mentioned in the Early English poem *Beowulf.*

Ettinsmoor In *SC,* a desolate region of moorland north of Narnia and the Shribble River.* Beyond Ettinsmoor lies the region of giants. Years before the events recounted in the story, Caspian* X had fought the giants and forced them to pay tribute.

Eustace *See* Scrubb, Eustace Clarence.*

Experiment House In *SC,* the experimental school attended by Eustace Scrubb* and Jill Pole.* It partly presents a satire on modern educational methods and is partly based on grim memories of C. S. Lewis's own school experiences.

Farsight In *LB,* the talking eagle who reports the downfall of Narnia to King Tirian.*

Father Christmas In *LWW* Santa Claus arrives when the White Witch's spell of perpetual winter weakens and Christmas comes. He gives sacramental presents to three of the four Pevensie* children, which they use in adventures, to fight, to warn or for healing. Peter is given a shield and sword, Susan is presented with a bow and arrows and a small ivory horn, and Lucy receives a little bottle of healing cordial and a small dagger.

Father Time In *SC* the children discover a sleeping giant in Underland.* He has a snowy beard that covers him to his waist. They are told that he is old Father Time, once a king in Overland. He has sunk into the Deep Realm and there dreams of the happenings in the upper world. He will not wake until the end of the world. Father Time appears again in *LB,* having been given a new name, and helps to end the old Narnia by blowing a last trump on his horn.

fauns Borrowed from classical mythology, they are deities who are human from the waist up, and have the horns, legs and tail of a goat. They play wild music on reed pipes, inducing a sleepy, trancelike state. They are more graceful than dwarfs, but roughly their height. The most famous faun in the Chronicles is Mr. Tumnus.* The first Narnia story originated in a mental picture of a faun carrying parcels and an umbrella through a snowy wood.

Featherstone, Anne In *VDT,* a fellow pupil of Lucy Pevensie. Jealous of Lucy's friendship with Marjorie Preston,* she manipulates Marjorie into pretending that Lucy is not her friend. Lucy magically overhears the conversation, revealing the pitfalls of eavesdropping.

Felimath In *VDT,* one of the Lone Islands, inhabited by sheep. It looks like a low green hill in the ocean. It may be based on Lewis's childhood memory of Rathlin Island, off the holiday resort of Ballycastle, County Antrim.

Felinda In *MN,* a city of the long-dead world of Charn.* It is possible that the name evokes "cruel beauty" (*fel,* cruel, and *linda,* beauty), much like Jadis* herself.

Fenris Ulf In American editions of *LWW* prior to 1994, an enormous wolf and Captain of Jadis's secret police. In the original British editions and in U.S. editions since 1994 he is called Maugrim. He owes his creation to Fenris Wolf, or the Wolf of Fenrir, which is most likely why Lewis changed the name for the U.S. edition. He was the gigantic offspring of Loki and the giantess Angrboda. The wolf was fated to be chained until the doom of the gods, when it would escape and devour Odin. Vidarr would then savagely kill the beast. It is in keeping with the nature of Narnia that Fenris Ulf is a talking wolf. The wolf is a characteristic figure of fairy stories. He is slain by Peter.

fire-berry In *VDT*, a berry that looks like a live coal, brought from the valleys of the sun to renew Ramandu by a bird of morning. The way the fire-berry is laid in his mouth is reminiscent of the coal of fire laid on Isaiah's lips by the seraphim after his vision of God in the temple (Isaiah 6).

fire-flowers In *VDT* these are said to grow in the mountains of the sun. They provide the cordial contained in Lucy's healing flask (given to her by Father Christmas* in *LWW*).

First Council In *MN*, when Narnia is only hours old, this council is called by Aslan* to discuss what to do about the evil introduced by Jadis.*

five black dwarfs In *PC* these are a group of revolutionary dwarfs, opposed to King Miraz,* who live in a cave together. They are allied to Caspian* against the tyrant rather than working to restore the Old Narnia.* Indeed, under the instigation of Nikabrik,* they are willing to call on the help of evil hags* and Wer-wolves.*

Flaming Mountain of Lagour In *LB*, a Calormene* volcano that can erupt with great ferocity.

flask of healing In *LWW*, Lucy's gift from Father Christmas. It is a healing cordial in a beautiful small diamond flask.

Fledge *See* Strawberry.*

Frank the cabby, Frank I In *MN*, a Victorian London cabby. The character perhaps owes something to Diamond's father in *At the Back of the North Wind*, by George MacDonald. Frank is accidently drawn into Narnia as it is being created and, with his cockney wife, Helen, is the first to rule there. His descendant, second son of Frank V, was the first king of Archenland.* All humans in Narnia or its surrounding countries descended either from Frank and Helen or from the Telmarines* who stumbled into its world. Aslan commanded that

Narnia be ruled by Sons of Adam and Daughters of Eve. The name Frank alludes to openness and lack of disguise.

Gale In *LB*, the ninth king of Narnia in descent from King Frank.* He delivers the population of the Lone Islands* of the Eastern Ocean* from a dragon. In gratitude they give the islands over to Narnian sovereignty.

Galma In *VDT*, an island off the coast of Narnia and about a day's sailing northeast of Cair Paravel.* King Caspian* X of Narnia stops here on his great journey across the Eastern Ocean.* Galma's governing duke marks the occasion by a great tournament.

giants In *LWW* the narrator points out that giants of any sort are now extremely rare in England. In Narnia there are many, usually on the side of good or bad. Giants particularly feature in *SC,* with the visit of Eustace Scrubb,* Jill Pole* and Puddleglum* to Harfang.* Not all giants are stupid: in ancient times some had constructed an impressive bridge, and Harfang itself had been built by giants. Named giants include Pire*; Rumblebuffin,* with his honest, ugly face; and Wimbleweather.* The White Witch* has some giant blood in her.

See also ettins.*

gift of speech In *MN* Aslan* confers this gift of selected animals as the highpoint of Narnia's creation. Speech marks the presence of rational thought, making all Narnian talking beasts equal.

See also chapter five, "Literary Features of the Chronicles."

gifts from Father Christmas *See* Father Christmas.*

Ginger the cat In *LB,* an evil and clever cat who joins forces with the perverse Shift,* a talking ape. After meeting Aslan* face to face, he loses the ability to speak. Near the end of his life, Lewis had a ginger tomcat, which he described as "a great Don Juan and a mighty hunter before the Lord."

Girbius In *PC,* a faun.*

Glasswater Creek In *PC,* a coastal inlet that leads in the direction of the hill of the Stone Table.* (Note: C. S. Lewis is not using *creek* in the U.S., Australian or New Zealand sense.)

Glenstorm A centaur* in *PC* who lives in a mountain glen. He is a particularly noble creature with glossy chestnut flanks and a golden red beard, as befits a prophet and stargazer.

Glimfeather A talking owl in *SC* who is as big as a dwarf. In the service of the now elderly King Caspian* X, he takes under his wing Jill Pole* and Eustace

Scrubb.* Glimfeather aids them in their endeavor to find lost Prince Rilian* by carrying them one by one to a parliament of owls and then, with another owl, to Marsh-wiggle* country to the north of Narnia.

Glozelle In *PC,* one of the lords of the usurper Miraz.* He plans the tyrant's defeat by getting him to accept Peter Pevensie's* challenge to a duel.

gnomes In *SC,* the inhabitants of Underworld* and Bism.* These Earthmen* are short, fat, white-faced, goblinlike creatures, but with no malice toward "overlanders," as they call those who live above the world's crust.

gods Spirit beings in Narnia, usually inhabiting rivers and woods, though fauns* are also included in this category. Calormene* deities include Tash,* Azaroth* and Zardeenah.* None of these beings is rival to the unique Aslan,* who created Narnia, its surrounding lands and the cosmos to which it belongs, as well as all other natures or worlds (but under other names and in the form by which he is known in the other worlds).

See also chapter four, "Worldviews and Narnia."

Golden Age of Narnia In *LWW,* the period when Peter Pevensie* was high king in Narnia and his brother and two sisters were king and queens under him (1000-1015 N.T.). The Golden Age begins with the dissolution by Aslan* of the White Witch's one-hundred-year spell of winter upon the land. It is during this celebrated period that Shasta* and Aravis* in *HHB* escape from Calormen.* In *PC* it has come to symbolize Old Narnia,* suppressed by the modernizing tyrant Miraz.*

Golden Tree In *MN,* a tree formed of gold. It grows in the first fecundity of Narnia's new creation from two half-sovereigns dropped by Uncle Andrew.*

Golg A Earthman* in *SC* originally from Bism* but captured by Puddleglum* and the others in Underworld* after the death of its self-styled queen (the Green Witch*). He directs them to the surface, where they reenter Narnia.

Great Council In *PC,* the council held by Caspian* to discuss opposition to the tyrant Miraz.* It is held on the Dancing Lawn.* The discussion is sharply focused when Doctor Cornelius* arrives with the news that Miraz* is marching toward them, having learned about the rebel grouping.

Great Desert In *HHB,* the scorching wilderness between Calormen* and Archenland,* crossed by Shasta,* Aravis,* Bree* and Hwin* in desperate pursuit of freedom to the north.

See also chapter nine, "The Geography of Narnia."

Great Reunion In *LB*, the bringing together of all the characters loyal to Aslan* and Narnia throughout its history. They go on to be united with Mr. and Mrs. Pevensie,* who are now dead as a result of the railway accident* that claimed so many lives. Mr. and Mrs. Pevensie had never been in Narnia.

Great River In *PC*, the river leading to Aslan's How,* for which the children search. It runs its course from Lantern Waste* in the west, across Narnia, into the Eastern Ocean.*

Great Snow Dance In *SC*, an annual dance held on the first moonlit night after snow has fallen. It takes place north of the Great River.* The dancers (dryads,* fauns* and dwarfs*) move to the music of four fiddles, three flutes and a drum. Dancers getting offstep are liable to be hit by well-aimed snowballs.

Great Waterfall In the Chronicles, the source of the Great River on Narnia's western edge. It flows over high cliffs into Caldron Pool.* In *LB* travelers to Aslan's Country* swim up the waterfall and continue westward.

Great Woods In the Chronicles, the huge forest that extends west from the coast around Cair Paravel* to the Stone Table* (later, Aslan's How*) and south to the mountains bordering Archenland. During the period of the Telmarine suppression of Old Narnia* under Miraz* in *PC*, the forest is feared and re-named the Black Woods.*

Greenroof In *PC*, a summer month in Narnia, referring to the freshness of the trees.

Green Witch In *SC*, the witch who tries to dominate Narnia during the reign of King Caspian* X. She appears to the travelers Jill Pole,* Eustace Scrubb* and Puddleglum* as a tall, beautiful young woman wearing a green kirtle. The witch enchants and dominates Caspian's son, Rilian,* in her Under-land.* Eventually she reveals her true nature as she transforms into a green serpent.

See also White Witch.*

Griffle In *LB*, the chief of a band of dwarfs who are convinced that only they themselves are worth believing in and fighting for. This is after being disillusioned by Shift* and his trickery.

Gumpas In *VDT*, the slave-trading and bureaucratic governor of the Lone Islands.* Caspian replaces him with the worthy Lord Bern.*

Gwendolen In *PC*, a pupil in a school in Telmarine-controlled Beruna.* She disrupts her strictly disciplined class when she notices a lion outside (who turns out to be Aslan, freeing the town). She is an example of a virtuous pagan who welcomes Aslan, even though she has not known Old Narnia.* She sheds her uncomfortable school clothes.

Hag In *PC,* an accomplice of the surly dwarf Nikabrik.* She has a nose and a chin that sticks out like nutcrackers, and dirty gray hair.

Hardbiters In *PC,* the family name of three talking badgers called to Caspian's* Great Council.

Harfang In *SC,* the stronghold of wicked giants north of Ettinsmoor.* The children, and even Puddleglum,* are persuaded by the subtlety of the Green Witch* that these giants are friendly. Marsh-wiggles* and man are considered delicacies for a feast.

Harfang stands on a small hill overlooking the ruins of the giant City Ruinous.* Among the crumbling ruined stone, pillars as tall as factory chimneys can be seen in places. From Harfang large sections of pavement can be seen to bear the words "UNDER ME," all that remains of an ancient verse.

Harpha In *LB,* the father of the Calormene* Emeth.*

Hastilude In *HHB,* a dangerous type of spear play, drawn by Lewis from medieval origins.

head teacher In *SC* the head of Experiment House runs a regime, satirized by Lewis, in which bullies end up being praised because of its modern approach to education. Lewis preferred a wide and knowledgeable learning to information-based education, and saw the existence of a government Ministry of Education as disturbingly Orwellian. With the collapse of her approach, the head becomes first an inspector of schools, where she could interfere with other heads, and then a member of Parliament.

hermit of Southern March In *HHB,* a hermit who looks after the wounded Aravis* and the talking horses while Shasta* continues his journey to warn King Lune* of the Calormene* danger. A tall, robed figure with a beard that reaches his knees, the hermit is 109 years of age and has a pool with the properties of a magical mirror. *March* is a variant of *mark,* or boundary—the hermit lives on the southern border of Archenland.*

Hogglestock In *PC,* a talking hedgehog who participates in the Great Council.*

Horn of Narnia Queen Susan's gift from Father Christmas,* which she drops in the Lantern Waste as she returns through the wardrobe. In *PC* the horn has been passed on to Caspian,* who sounds it as a desperate call for help.

house of Professor Kirke This is a rambling country house in the south of England, with a river at the bottom of its garden. It is a long way from a railway
station and a post office. In *LWW* it offers much for the evacuee children, the
Pevensies,* to explore on rainy days. A room of particular interest is empty except for a wardrobe* and a dead bluebottle, a large fly. The house is of historic
interest, attracting many visitors, and strange stories are told about it, even
stranger than the story of the children entering Narnia through the wardrobe.
As a child Digory Kirke had lived there, except for a period when his mother
was ill and he stayed with her in the London home of his aunt and uncle. He
remembers having a pony there. His father eventually inherited the estate from
his great uncle, and hence in time it becomes Digory's. Some time after the adventure with the wardrobe, the house is destroyed. The reason is not revealed—perhaps there was a fire. After this, the professor, suddenly poor,
moves to a small cottage with a spare bedroom. Peter stays there after the war
(according to *VDT,* but Lewis's chronology says 1942) while being coached for
an exam, just as a young C. S. Lewis had stayed at the cottage of W. T. Kirkpatrick while preparing for university entrance.

house of the magician In *VDT,* Coriakin's* house discovered by the voyagers
on the island inhabited by the Monopods.* The two-story house of gray stone
is overgrown by ivy and is reached by a tree-lined avenue that runs through
well-kept lawns. Its paved courtyard has a pump in its center. A passage runs
the length of the house on the upper floor, with seven rooms off it. The last,
entered by Lucy, holds the magician's book along with a library. Another room
is full of various scientific instruments.

House of the Tisroc In *HHB* this is a palace straight out of an Arabian tale. It
stands on the brow of Tashbaan's* dominant hill, which it shares with the
Temple of Tash.* The palace's extensive gardens extend right down to the
river's edge on the northern side of the city island.

Hwin In *HHB,* the talking Narnian mare who plays an important part in the
tale. She helps Aravis* escape an unpleasant marriage. There are many delightful contrasts between her character and that of Bree,* the other talking horse
playing a part in the story. Like Bree, she had been captured and taken to
Calormen* and there had to keep secret her nature. She only speaks at first to
dissuade her mistress, Aravis,* from suicide.

Ilgamuth In *HHB,* one of the lords of Rabadash,* slain by Darrin of Archenland* in the Battle of Anvard.*

Ilkeen In *HHB,* the location in Calormen* of a lake and the beautiful palaces of wealthy Tarkaans, including Ahosta.*

Island of the Monopods In *VDT,* called the Island of the Voices by the seafarers. It is the estate of the magician Coriakin.* The lawns are well kept, like the grounds of Lewis's College in Oxford, Magdalen.* In the center of the Island, approached by an avenue of trees, is the warm stone house of the magician, a long, two-storied building with many windows. The island is inhabited by Monopods,* who, until Lucy* reverses the spell of invisibility, cannot be seen —hence the name "the Island of Voices."

Island of the Star *See* Ramandu's Island.*

Island of Voices In *VDT,* a low-lying island to the west of Deathwater Island* in the Eastern Ocean.* It has lawns and parks that are noticeably well kept. The only important building is a stone house, approached through an avenue of trees, belonging to the island's governor, Coriakin.*

When the voyagers first land on the island, they think it uninhabited. This mistake is understandable because the main inhabitants, the Dufflepuds,* have been made invisible. Their voices, however, can still be heard—hence the origin of the island's name.

Ivy In *LWW,* a servant of Professor Kirke's, along with Betty and Margaret.

Jackle, Edith In *SC,* a tale-bearer and hanger-on to the gang of bullies that terrorize Eustace Scrubb* and Jill Pole* at Experiment House.*

Jadis *See* White Witch.*

Jewel the unicorn In *LB* Jewel, a talking beast, is the dearest friend of Tirian,* last king of Narnia. They save each other's lives in war. Jewel's feelings as he enters the New Narnia remade by Aslan* illustrate C. S. Lewis's constant and special theme of joy.

Jill Pole *See* Pole, Jill.*

Ketterley, Andrew In *MN,* the Victorian uncle of Digory Kirke.* He is the magician to which the title refers, an amateur magician, who forces Digory and his friend Polly Plummer* into the Wood Between the Worlds* by means of magic rings. He is tall, very thin, with a long clean-shaven face, a sharply pointed nose, disturbingly bright eyes and an unruly mop of long gray hair. When he smiles, he shows all his teeth, and the children cannot help noticing his long white fingers. Like his counterpart, Jadis,* he considers himself superior to all rules and animals his mere tools. He is manipulative, playing on Digory's concern for his dying mother, Andrew's sister, and unscrupulous, sending Polly into unknown dangers. Andrew represents the bad scientist, more concerned with power than with truth.

Ketterley, Letitia ("Letty") In *MN,* Digory Kirke's* aunt, who is caring for her sister, Digory's dying mother, and sister also of his Uncle Andrew.* She is unimpressed by Jadis* the Witch, who hurls her across the room.

Kidrash Tarkaan In *HHB,* Aravis's* father, who tries to marry her off to the ugly and aged new Grand Vizier, Ahoshta.* It is claimed in Calormen* that he is a descendant of the god Tash.*

Kirke, Digory In *MN* Digory appears as a boy, then in *LWW* and *LB* as a grown-up. As a boy he and his dying mother lodge with his Uncle Andrew Ketterley* and Aunt Lettie Ketterley* in Victorian London. With his neighbor, Polly Plummer,* he travels to other worlds by means of magical rings and is present at the creation of Narnia by Aslan.* By the beginning of the Second World War he is an elderly professor who owns a country house of historical interest. The Pevensie* children arrive as evacuees and stumble across a way into Narnia through his wardrobe built of wood that grew from a magical Narnian apple. Later, he becomes poor, and, his house destroyed, he is forced to tutor students, including Peter Pevensie, in a small cottage. He perhaps owes something to the professor in T. H. White's *Mrs. Masham's Repose,* admired by Lewis. Digory's surname is an affectionate tribute to Lewis's own tutor, W. T. Kirkpatrick.*

Kirke, Mabel In *MN,* mother of Digory* and younger sister of Andrew Ketterley* and Letitia Ketterley.* She is dying and is being nursed by her sister. (Her husband is forced by his employment to stay in India.) Digory brings an apple for her from the Land of Youth, and she miraculously recovers. Later she and her husband and Digory are able to return to living in the country, and they take Uncle Andrew with them.

Kirke's House, Professor *See* house of Professor Kirke.*

Lady Liln In *HHB,* the beautiful wife of Olvin,* the fair-haired king of Archenland* (around 407 N.T.).

Lady of the Green Kirtle *See* Green Witch.*

Lamb, the In *VDT,* a form Aslan takes in his country (see Aslan's Country*) on the borderlands of all worlds, providing a clue to his identity as redeemer of our world.

lamp post, lantern In *MN* and *LWW* the lamp post stands at the western edge of Narnia, marking a way to the world of humans, according to the White Witch.* The portal between Narnia and our world via the wardrobe is nearby. The place where Digory Kirke,* Polly Plummer* and the others earlier stand and observe as Narnia is created by the song of Aslan* is also close by. In fact, the lamp post originates from a bar of a London lamp post torn off by Jadis, which she still clutches in that other world and hurls at Aslan. It grows like everything grows in the first fecundity of that new creation.

Land of Youth In *MN,* the place west of Narnia* where Digory Kirke* obtains for Aslan* a magic apple from which grows a tree that provides an apple the boy is able to take back to his dying mother. In Celtic mythology the Land of Youth (*Tír-na-nÓg*) is in the realms of heaven.

Lantern Waste In *MN,* the area the children enter in an empty world and see Narnia* created by Aslan. A Victorian London lamp post grows here from a piece of one broken off and brought to Narnia by the White Witch.* In later years children again enter Narnia near here through a wardrobe in *LWW.* Lantern Waste is west of Beaversdam.*

lapsed bear of Stormness In *HHB,* a talking bear that regresses to the behavior of a dumb beast, attacking travelers. Prince Corin* becomes known as "Thunder-Fist" after successfully boxing with the bear and reforming him.

Lasaraleen Tarkheena In *HHB,* a frivolous friend of Aravis,* who helps her to escape from the great Calormen* city of Tashbaan.*

Last Sea In *VDT,* the stretch of ocean between Ramandu's Island and World's End* in which light takes on an intensity that is both physical and spiritual.

LeFay, Mrs. In *MN,* the fairy godmother of Uncle Andrew.* She had passed onto him a box of dust from Atlantis* to destroy, but instead he keeps it. She is probably named after the sinister Morgan Le Fay of Arthurian legend. Like Andrew Ketterley and Jadis,* she saw herself above "ordinary, ignorant people." In Lewis's abandoned "The LeFay Fragment" she also appears, but as Digory's eccentric but benevolent fairy godmother.

Leopard, The In *PC* and *VDT,* Lucy's* favorite Narnian constellation, appearing in the summer sky along with the Ship and the Hammer.

    See astronomy of Narnia.*

Letitia ("Letty") Ketterley *See* Ketterley, Letitia ("Letty").*

Lilith In *LWW,* the maternal progenitor of the White Witch.* She is a figure from Babylonion and Hebrew imagination, in mystical tradition the first wife of Adam, particularly vindictive to babies and children. C. S. Lewis's mentor, George MacDonald, explores the symbolic figure in his fantasy *Lilith* (1895).

Lily Lake *See* Silver Sea.*

Lilygloves In *PC,* a chief mole, a talking animal,* who had helped to plant an orchard at Cair Paravel.* At the time of the events recorded in this book, the orchard has run wild for centuries.

London The setting in Victorian times for part of *MN,* drawing on Lewis's childhood reading about E. Nesbit's fictional Bastable family in London.

Lone Islands A group of islands comprising Felimath,* Doorn* and Avra,* and visited by the travelers in *VDT.* Ancient King Gale of Narnia* had once rid these islands of a dragon and, in gratitude, was given them to be part of Narnia. They lie four hundred leagues to the east of that land in the Eastern Ocean.

Lucy, Queen *See* Pevensie, Lucy.*

Lune, King In *HHB,* the jolly father of Shasta* (Cor) and Corin,* and king of Archenland* during the Golden Age* of Narnia. He rules from the strategic castle at Anvard.* He enjoys dressing in old, comfortable clothes, a quality admired by Lewis, for whom uncomfortable dress is a sign of spiritual restriction.

Macready, Mrs. In *LWW,* Professor Digory Kirke's* formidable housekeeper in his large country house.

maenads These appear in *PC.* In classical mythology they are the female members of Bacchus's* boisterous company.

magic *See* Deep Magic*; Deeper Magic.*

Marjorie Preston *See* Preston, Marjorie.*

Marsh-wiggle In *SC,* long and somewhat froglike creatures who are occupied with most of the watery and fishy work in Narnia. The most famous Marshwiggle is Puddleglum.* His habit of gloomy prognostication is affectionately drawn from C. S. Lewis's groundsman at The Kilns, Fred Paxford.

Master Bowman In *VDT* this sailor in the company on the *Dawn Treader* shoots the dreadful sea serpent.*

Maugrim In *LWW,* an enormous wolf and Captain of Jadis's* secret police. (In American editions of *LWW* before 1994 he is called Fenris Ulf.*) Maugrim owes his creation to Fenris Wolf, or the Wolf of Fenrir, which is perhaps why Lewis changed his name to Fenris Ulf in the American editions. Fenris Wolf was the gigantic offspring of Loki and the giantess Angrboda in northern mythology. Here, the wolf was fated to be chained until the doom of the gods, when it would escape and devour Odin. Vidarr would then savagely kill the beast. It is in keeping with the nature of Narnia that Maugrim is a talking wolf. The wolf is a characteristic evil figure of fairy stories. He is slain by Peter.*

Mavramorn In *VDT,* one of the seven lords for which the voyagers searched. They find him sleeping under a spell on Ramandu's Island.*

mazers Historic drinking bowls made of hardwood, often carved or ornamented with silver. They are fashioned out of mazer wood, that is, wood from gnarly trees. They are employed in *PC* at the feast celebrating the victory of the Old Narnians over the tyranny of Miraz.*

mer-people In *LWW,* inhabitants of the Eastern Ocean* near Narnia's shore, not to be confused with the Sea People* of the Last Sea* encountered in *VDT,* who can only live in water. *Mer* derives from *mere,* an early English word for "sea."

Mezreel In *HHB,* a resort used by the wealthy of Calormen* in the hot summers. It has many attractions, including a lake and notable gardens.

Miraz, King In *PC,* the prince's wicked, modernizing uncle, who had stolen the throne from the boy's father, King Caspian* IX. He was aided and abetted by Queen Prunaprismia* and came to a bad end. Miraz ruthlessly dismisses Caspian's nurse for telling him stories of Old Narnia* and considers stories of Kings Peter and Edmund and the Golden Age* as old wives' tales.

Miraz's castle In *PC,* the stronghold of the usurper Miraz* to Narnia's north, not far from the site of the house of the White Witch,* which had existed ages before, and a mile from Beaversdam.* From its leads can be seen on the one side the battlements and on the other, a steep roof. Below there is an extensive view of the castle garden. From the leads Caspian* and his tutor, Doctor Cornelius,* are able to climb the great central tower of the whole castle, which affords a splendid view of the Narnian sky on a clear night. From there also the Western Mountains* can be glimpsed, as well as the Great River* nearby.

monopods Dwarfs in *VDT* who have been changed into single-footed creatures.

See Dufflepuds.*

Moonwood In *LB,* a hare with such exceptional hearing that it is told that he can sit by Caldron Pool* under the Great Waterfall* and hear what is whispered at Cair Paravel.*

Mount Pire In *HHB,* a mountain in Archenland* created when fair-haired Olvin* fought the two-headed giant, Pire, and turned him into stone. Shasta* uses the twin-peaked mountain as a landmark for finding Archenland.

Muil In *VDT,* the westernmost of the Seven Isles.* It is separated from the isle of Brenn* by a choppy strait.

Mulluguterum In *SC,* the Warden of the Marches of Underland.* He was chief of the Earthmen* in the Underworld realm, the Shallow Lands, of the Green Witch.*

naiads In the Chronicles, water nymphs, presiding over brooks, springs and fountains, taken from classical mythology.

Nain In *PC,* king of Archenland* in the dark time of Miraz* of Narnia.

Narnia *See* chapter nine, "The Geography of Narnia."

Narnia, Chronicles of Seven tales for children by C. S. Lewis. These cover almost half of the twentieth century in our world and over two and a half millennia of Narnian years from its creation to its final days. In chronological order of Narnian time the titles are: *The Magician's Nephew; The Lion, the Witch, and the Wardrobe; The Horse and His Boy; Prince Caspian; The Voyage of the "Dawn Treader"; The Silver Chair* and *The Last Battle.* In reading order, it is probably best to enjoy *The Lion, the Witch, and the Wardrobe* first, as here are set out all the basic "supposals" from which all the stories come.

Narnia, creation of In *MN,* Aslan, the Creator-Lion, brings Narnia into being by his song.

"Narnian Suite" Two poems published in *Poems* (1964) after C. S. Lewis's death. One is a march for "Strings, Kettledrums, and Sixty-three Dwarfs," and the other is a march for "Drum, Trumpet, and Twenty-one Giants." Other poems by Lewis easily fit into a Narnian context because of their medieval or classical subjects, poems like "The Magician and the Dryad," "The Dragon Speaks" (admired by Tolkien) or "Dragon-Slayer." Another poem, "Impenitence," in which Lewis refers affectionately to animals and to talking animals in particular, is almost a defiant defense for the Narnia stories.

Narrowhaven In *VDT,* a town on the island of Doorn,* ruled by Gumpas.* An important feature of the town is its castle, the seat of administration. Under Gumpas's local government, a slave market was allowed. Caspian* and the other voyagers are appalled by the run-down condition of the castle, reflecting the moral rot that had taken place.

Nellie *See* Helen, Queen.*

Nikabrik the dwarf A member of the resistence to the tyrant Miraz* in *PC,* but highly cynical. He prefers the old, "realistic" magic of the witches and turns against Aslan.* His position is a comment on pragmatism in twentieth-century thought.

nine classes *See* classes* of Narnian creatures.

Northern Frontier In the Chronicles, the region where troublesome giants* live. The regions to the north of Narnia represent danger and moral aberration, as do the regions to the south of Archenland. The White Witch lives in the north lands, and Miraz's castle is located in the northern extremity of Narnia. In the south, the Calormenes* represent a constant threat to Narnia's security, even though they have an advanced civilization.

nurse In *PC,* the nurse who tells stories of Old Narnia to Caspian* and is dismissed for this. During the liberation of Narnia from Telmarine* rule, Caspian and his nurse meet again. The nurse owes much to C. S. Lewis's nurse, Lizzie Endicott, who in his boyhood told him myths and folk tales of old Ireland. In Lewis's writings, nurses almost invariably connote the simple goodness of old-time ways.

nymphs In Greek mythology, the female souls or semidivine beings living in rivers, trees and mountains. They are young and beautiful, given to music and dancing, elflike in their long lives and other respects. Nymphs of the trees are called dryads* (or hamadryads); those of lakes, rivers or springs, naiads*; and those of mountains, oreads. In the Chronicles, they dance with fauns, arise from the river at Aslan's roar and participate in royal weddings. As with elves, there is intermarriage with humans: the sons of Frank and Helen, the first king and queen of Narnia, marry nymphs.

Octesian In *VDT,* one of the seven Telmarine* lords sought by the young King Caspian* and his voyagers. He very likely has become the dragon found dying by Eustace Scrubb* on Dragon Island.*

Old Narnia In *PC,* the Narnia of the Golden Age* remembered in secret under the tyranny of the modernizer Miraz* and the rule of the Telmarines.* The spirits of woods and streams are seldom seen, and talking animals are in hiding. The schools banish the true history of Narnia from their dreary curriculum. Caspian,* taught about Old Narnia by his nurse and then his tutor, Doctor Cornelius,* could talk about it for hours.

Olvin In *HHB*, the defeater in 407 N.T. of Pire,* the two-headed giant, who is turned into the twin-peaked Mount Pire.* Olvin is king of Archenland, notable for his fair hair. As a result of his victory he wins the Lady Liln.*

orknies Monsters borrowed from the early English poem *Beowulf* ("Orcneas"). They participate in the horror of the killing of Aslan* on the Stone Table* in *LWW*.

Parliament of Owls In *SC*, a meeting of owls. Jill Pole* and Eustace Scrubb are carried to it on the back of Glimfeather.* Lewis is probably playing with the title of Chaucer's *The Parliament of Fowls*.

Passarids In *PC*, a house of lords under Caspian* IX. When the usurper Miraz* takes over, they are sent to their death to fight giants to the north of Narnia.

Pattertwig In *PC*, a magnificent talking red squirrel, the size of a terrier. He is a loyal Old Narnian* met by the runaway Caspian.* Pattertwig also appears in Lewis's abandoned "The LeFay Fragment,"* his original attempt at what eventually became *MN*.

pavender A beautiful, rainbow-colored fish found in Narnia*; it provides an excellent meal.

Peepiceek In *PC*, one of Reepicheep's* band of talking mice, designated as his successor in *VDT*.

Pennyfather, Adela In *SC*, one of a gang of bullying pupils in Experiment House,* attended by Eustace Scrubb and Jill Pole.*

Peridan In *HHB*, one of the lords and advisers of Queen Susan,* Queen Lucy and King Edmund* in Tashbaan.* Later he leads a charge in battle against the army of Rabadash* the Calormene.*

Peter, High King *See* Pevensie, Peter.*

Pevensie, Edmund Born in 1930, Edmund is the third child of Mr. and Mrs. Pevensie. In *LWW* he is ten when he first enters Narnia, through the magic wardrobe* in Professor Kirke's* house. Edmund turns traitor under the influence of the White Witch* and a hoped-for reward of Turkish Delight, but soon sees his folly (*see* the subhead "Recognition and Undeception" in chapter five). The White Witch asserts her right to take his life, but Aslan* dies in his place according to a Deeper Magic.* Edmund earns the title of Edmund the Just as he rules in Narnia with his brother and sisters during the Golden Age.* In *PC* he returns to Narnia with his siblings, called there to aid Caspian,* the rightful heir to the land. In 1949 he dies in a railway accident and finds himself back in Narnia at the end of time.

Pevensie, Lucy Lucy is often the favorite character with young readers of the Chronicles. She is one of the most vivid characters in the stories and appears more spiritually attuned to Aslan than do others. Aslan evidently has a special affection for her. Born in 1932, she is the youngest in the family, only eight years old when she is the first to enter Narnia through the magic wardrobe in Professor Kirke's* house.

When she is a golden-haired queen during Narnia's Golden Age, she is called, "Lucy the Valiant." Though she is sensitive, trusting and obedient to Aslan, she is also an ordinary human child, at one point getting irritable with the lion. She has a gift of sight, an acute perception of spiritual realities. Yet she is perfectly happy feeding the hens onboard the *Dawn Treader*.* She is also kind to Eustace,* despite his boorishness on the early part of the voyage, before his dragon experience. The focus particularly falls on her on the Island of Voices, as she is called to go upstairs in the magician's house* to try to find the counterspell for invisibility. Reading the magician's book is an adventure of mind for her, resulting in her spiritual growth and increased self-knowledge.

Pevensie, Mr. and Mrs. Mr. Pevensie is a university lecturer, living in London, who at one stage gives a lecture-tour in America, where he and his wife take Susan* with them. Mrs. Pevensie is the sister of Alberta Scrubb, mother of Eustace. It is perhaps she who gives the *Dawn Treader* picture to her sister. By coincidence, Mr. and Mrs. Pevensie are traveling in the same train as many of the Seven Friends of Narnia* and are thus involved in the fatal accident.

Pevensie, Peter Peter, born 1927, is the oldest son of Mr. and Mrs. Pevensie.* He has qualities of leadership that prepare him for the role of high king in Narnia, even though he has lessons to learn. His deed of slaying Maugrim* (Fenris Ulf) in *LWW* wins him renown in Narnia. After two visits in Narnia (recounted in *LWW*, *HHB* and *PC*) Peter prepares for university entrance examinations with Professor Kirke* while his younger brother and sister embark on the voyage in the *Dawn Treader*. When the apparition of King Tirian* appears to him and other Friends of Narnia, Peter and Edmund go to elaborate lengths to dig up the rings* buried long ago by Digory* and Polly* in a London garden. This is so that the youngest of the Friends can use them to travel to help in Narnia's darkest hour. Waiting for the train with Edmund, he is caught up in the fatal accident as it plows into the station. Peter displays the chivalric ideal in his measured decisions, courage and leadership, and is called "Peter the Magnificent" during his reign in the Golden Age* of Narnia.

Pevensie, Susan The black-haired second child of Mr. and Mrs. Pevensie, she twice visits Narnia, once through the portal* of the wardrobe* and once by being directly called into the magical world to help Prince Caspian* and the Old Narnians* against Miraz.* During her reign in the Golden Age* of Narnia she is called "Susan the Gentle." In that period, Rabadash's* passion for her nearly results in invasion by Calormene* forces. Her graceful beauty attracts many suitors. At the end of all the stories Susan, unlike the others who have been in Narnia, is not there. We are told that this is because "She is no longer a friend of Narnia"—she has become too concerned about being "grown-up." As Susan is only twenty-one when she loses her parents and siblings, cousin and friends, in the dreadful railway accident, it would be premature to conclude that Susan would never again remember Narnia and Aslan. As Lewis commented in a letter to a young correspondent worried about Susan's fate: "The books don't tell us what happened to Susan. She is left alive in this world at the end, having by then turned into a rather silly, conceited young woman. But there is plenty of time for her to mend, and perhaps she will get to Aslan's country in the end—in her own way. I think that whatever she had seen in Narnia she *could* (if she was the sort that wanted to) persuade herself, as she grew up, that it was 'all nonsense.'"

Pevensies The four brothers and sisters, evacuees from wartime London, who enter Narnia in *LWW* and become kings and queens there. Peter, as eldest, is the high king during Narnia's Golden Age* (echoes of the biblical Saint Peter). Edmund is for a time a traitor, but repents and is restored by the sacrifice of Aslan* on the Stone Table.* The children return again to Narnia as told in *PC*. After that, however, only the two youngest, Edmund and Lucy, are allowed to return, with their cousin Eustace Scrubb,* in *VDT*. While they are enjoying this adventure, Peter is being tutored by Professor Kirke* for an examination and Susan has gone to America with her parents for Mr. Pevensie's lecture tour.

The Pevensie children, with the exception of Susan, who is no longer a friend of Narnia, return to Narnia after dying in a train crash in the apocalyptic final story, *LB*.

C. S. Lewis learned from other children's writers the potency of having several characters from one family. Drawing particularly on E. Nesbit's innovation in creating her Bastable family, Lewis discovered that a story concerning several children of varied characters and ages would grip the attention of a young reader far more than a tale involving simply one character. With children from the same family, the likelihood of spats and angry clashes would increase.

Phoenix In *MN*, a bird, larger than an eagle, sitting in a tree in the center of Aslan's Garden.* The phoenix is a traditional symbol of rebirth and immortality because of its resurrection from the ashes.

Pire *See* Mount Pire.*

Pittencream In *VDT*, the only sailor left behind at Ramandu's Island* while the *Dawn Treader* proceeds on toward the World's End.* The cowardly sailor eventually deserts the ship on its return voyage and goes to live in Calormen,* where he tells tall stories about his adventures.

Plummer, Polly In *MN*, Digory Kirke's* next-door friend who is drawn with him from Victorian London into other worlds and eventually Narnia.* Polly lives in a row of terraced houses that have back gardens with tall walls and roofs spaces that connect down the row. In later life she is known as Aunt Polly by the Pevensie children and their friends who have been in Narnia, even though she is no relation. Polly is one of the Seven Friends of Narnia* who witness the end of its world.

poesimetres In *VDT*, Coriakin's* instrument for measuring the meter of poetry.

Poggin In *LB*, an independently minded dwarf who sides with King Tirian,* unlike his fellow dwarfs.

Pole, Jill In *SC* and *LB*, a fellow sufferer with Eustace Scrubb* at Experiment House.* She is taken into Narnia with him on two occasions to help in time of need. Jill, like Lucy,* is an important female character in the Chronicles. In terms of the theology underlying the stories, her encounter with Aslan at the stream in *SC* is of great significance. She is entrusted with his instructions, analogous perhaps to Moses' receiving of the Law in the Old Testament. *SC* in fact focuses on her struggles to remember these signs Aslan has given to her in the quest* to find the lost Prince Rilian.*

The sparky relationship between Jill and Eustace, as they are thrown together for the adventures recounted in *SC*, adds reality and depth to the book. They quarrel and make up like real children. Jill grows as a person, from her initial fear in which the idea of adventures was preferable to the reality. By the conclusion of the story, she has developed to the stature of a king or queen of

Narnia, even though she is never crowned, preparing her for her mature involvement in the events of *LB*.

Jill is one of the Seven Friends of Narnia.*

Pomona The Roman goddess of fruit. In *PC* Peter remarks that she placed good spells on the apple orchard at Cair Paravel.*

Preston, Marjorie In *VDT*, Lucy Pevensie's* friend whom she overhears talking about her to another girl through a spell in Coriakin's* book of magic.

Prizzle, Miss In *PC*, the formidable Telmarine* schoolteacher at the girls' school in Beruna.* She scolds Gwendolen* for looking out of the window and claiming to see a lion.

Prunaprismia In *PC*, the red-haired wife of Caspian's* uncle, the usurper Miraz.*

Puddleglum the Marsh-wiggle In *PC*, the companion of Jill Pole* and Eustace Scrubb* in their quest for the lost Prince Rilian.* He is one of C. S. Lewis's most memorable Narnian creations. Puddleglum is delightfully pessimistic, though never cynical or disloyal to Aslan.* He is tall and angular, with webbed hands and feet as befits a marshy existence. His character owed something to Lewis's groundsman at The Kilns, Fred Paxford. The name is inspired by an old translation Lewis found of Euripides' *Hippolytus,* which included the phrase, "Stygian puddle glum" (John Studley's sixteenth-century translation of *"Tacitae Stygis,"* l. 625). Lewis reproduces the phrase in his *English Literature in the Sixteenth Century* (p. 256).

Pug In *VDT*, a pirate encountered on the island of Felimath.* He is involved in slave trading.

Pugrahan In *LB*, the location of the dreaded salt mines in Calormen.*

Puzzle the ass In *LB*, a simple donkey duped by Shift* the ape into dressing in a lion skin and pretending to be Aslan.*

Queen of Underland *See* Green Witch.*

Rabadash, Prince Also called "The Ridiculous." In *HHB*, the vain Calormene* prince who, after being rejected by Queen Susan,* attempts to conquer Archenland* and Narnia during the reign of High King Peter* and the other children. After the battle at Anvard* he is left dangling from a wall-hook. Later Aslan temporarily turns him into a donkey.*

railway accident In *LB*, the accident that takes the lives of the Seven Friends of Narnia.* The train involved is carrying most of the company on it. Their plan is to meet up with Edmund and Peter, who are waiting at a station en route. Eustace Scrubb* and Jill Pole* are on their way back to Experiment House* and have to change at this particular station for the train to their school. Peter* and Edmund Pevensie* are to give them the rings* by which Digory Kirke* and Polly Plummer* had originally arrived in Narnia half a century before. As the youngest in the company, Eustace and Jill are still able to return to Narnia, and they intend to use the rings to get there to provide help in Narnia's hour of need. The train collides with the station platform (presumably after derailing—Eustace mentions a "frightful jerk and a noise," and Peter remembers seeing it "taking the bend far too fast"). By coincidence, Mr. and Mrs. Pevensie are also on the train, on their way to Bristol, leaving Susan as the only surviving family member.

Ram the Great In *HHB* he becomes king of Archenland.* He is the son of Cor (Shasta*) and Aravis.*

Ramandu In *VDT,* a retired star, resplendent in silver clothes, who lives near Aslan's Table* on World's End Island* far across the Eastern Ocean.* The voyagers on the *Dawn Treader** encounter him on their way toward Aslan's Country.* King Caspian* later marries Ramandu's daughter.

Ramandu is undergoing renewal until he once more can return to the stars. The stars of Narnia and its world are made up not of flaming gas but of glimmering people with silver clothes and hair. Ramandu has been brought down to World's End Island when old and fading. The birds each day bring him a fire-berry from the valleys of the sun. These berries are restoring him.

Lewis takes the idea of stars as people (or intelligences) from the imagined world of the Middle Ages.

Ramandu's daughter In *VDT* the voyagers meet Ramandu* and his daughter on World's End Island.* Later King Caspian* marries her. In *SC* we learn that, one day, many years later, while she is sleeping, she is slain by the Green Witch* in the form of a green serpent. It is while Prince Rilian* is seeking his revenge for his mother's murder that he is bewitched by his mother's murderer. Ramandu's daughter owes much to Tolkien's conception of elves, which Lewis was familiar with long before the publication of *The Lord of the Rings* (1954-1955). In simplified form, she is like Lúthien or Arwen, immortal yet marrying a human. Her parentage in the stars is equivalent to Lúthien's mother's status as a Maia, an angelic being.

Ramandu's Island *See* Ramandu.*

Redhaven The main settlement on Brenn,* the second of the Seven Isles.* Its
hospitable inhabitants lavishly feast the crew of the *Dawn Treader.**

Reepicheep the mouse In VDT, a brave and decorous talking mouse of Narnia
who journeys to Aslan's Country.* Following a wood-woman's prophecy when
he was in his cradle, Reepicheep embarks on the journey as a personal quest
motivated by longing for Aslan's country (*see* the discussion of joy in chapter
three). Mice were granted the privilege of becoming talking animals after
gnawing through Aslan's* cords in *LWW.* Reepicheep, the chief of the mice, is
around two feet in height, wears a long crimson feather on his head, and carries a long, sharp sword. In *PC* he is badly wounded, and his proud tail sev-
ered. Lucy* is able to heal him, and Aslan restores his pride. Like King Peter,*
Reepicheep represents the chivalric ideal so central to order in Narnia. Mice,
and talking mice, are frequent subjects in the tradition of children's literature
Lewis draws upon.

Restimar In *VDT* he was one of the seven Telmarine* lords of Caspian* IX. The
usurper Miraz* has sent them away to search for new lands across the vast
Eastern Ocean.* He is found by the voyagers turned to gold in a bewitched
pool on Deathwater Island.*

Revilian In *VDT* he was one of the seven Telmarine* lords of Caspian* IX. The
usurper Miraz* has commanded them to search for new lands across the vast
Eastern Ocean,* expecting their deaths. The travelers discover him sleeping at
Aslan's Table* on World's End Island,* along with two other lords, Argoz* and
Mavramorn.*

Rhince In *VDT,* Drinian's* ship's mate.

Rhindon In *LWW,* the name of the sword given to Peter Pevensie* by Father
Christmas.

Rhoop In *VDT* he is one of the seven Telmarine* lords of Caspian* IX. The
usurper Miraz* has dispatched them to search for new lands across the vast
Eastern Ocean,* hoping thereby to be rid of them. Rhoop is discovered
trapped on the nightmarish Dark Island.* Later in the voyage he is granted
restful sleep at Aslan's Table* on World's End Island.*

Rilian, Prince In *SC,* the son of Caspian* X. The Green Witch* kidnaps Rilian
for ten years. The tale of his daring rescue by Eustace Scrubb,* Jill Pole,* and
Puddleglum* the Marsh-wiggle* is told in *SC.*

rings In *MN,* yellow-colored and green-colored rings made from magical Atlantean* dust by the minor magician and scientist Andrew Ketterley,* uncle of Digory Kirke.* Digory's friend, Polly,* is whisked into another world after being tricked by Uncle Andrew into touching a ring, and Digory uses one ring to follow her and the others to bring her back. This leads to the beginning of all the adventures in other worlds and in Narnia particularly. Nearly fifty years later, the rings are retrieved from the London garden where Polly and Digory have buried them, with the aim of using them once again to travel to Narnia in its hour of greatest need.

Rishda Tarkaan In *LB,* a Calormene* captain who assists Shift the ape* and Ginger the cat* against King Tirian.* His fitting fate is to be carried away by the demon god of Calormen, Tash.*

River Shribble In *SC,* an important Narnian river marking the boundary between the northern marshes and Ettinsmoor.*

river-god In *PC* he is called from the Great River* by Aslan. The modern Telmarine* bridge at Beruna* chains him, and Aslan frees him by destroying it through Bacchus.*

Roonwit In *LB,* a great, golden-bearded centaur. He reads of danger in the stars over Narnia and warns King Tirian.* He is slain by a Calormene* arrow. Centaurs originate in Greek mythology where they are much fiercer and less friendly than in Narnia. The upper half of a centaur's body is human; the remainder is composed of the body and legs of a horse. Roonwit's name may be derived from the word *runwita,* "knower of secrets," found in the Early English poem *Beowulf* (l. 1325).

Ruined City of the Giants *See* City Ruinous.*

Rumblebuffin In *LWW,* the giant who assists in the fight against the White Witch.* In attempting to borrow a handkerchief from Lucy,* he picks her up by mistake! The giant is a member of the respected Buffin family, a family not very clever, but an old family with traditions.

Rush River In *PC* we are informed that the Rush River joins the Great River* at Beruna.*

Rynelf In *VDT,* a wise and experienced sailor on the galleon the *Dawn Treader.**

salamanders In *SC* salamanders dwell in Bism* in the great fire-river. They are small, witty, eloquent and dragonlike.

Sallowpad In *HHB,* an old, wise raven who is adviser to King Edmund,* Queen

Susan* and Queen Lucy.*

satyrs In Greek mythology, fertility gods of the woods and hills. They are grotesque creatures, combining human and bestial features, such as a horse's tail or goat's legs. Satyrs appear throughout the Chronicles. The satyr Wraggle fights against Tirian* in the final battle of Narnia. Another (Silenus,* from classical mythology) accompanies Bacchus.*

Scrubb, Eustace Clarence A cousin of the Pevensie* children, he is drawn into Narnia, along with Lucy and Edmund, in *VDT*. He returns to Narnia on two other occasions with Jill Pole,* a school friend, as recounted in *SC* and *LB*. When we first meet him he is self-centered and spoiled by the modern education he is receiving at Experiment House.* He exemplifies a vice Lewis said he suffered from as a young man, what he called "chronological snobbery." In *VDT*, the focus falls on Eustace for a time when the third-person narrative alternates with quotations from his diaries. Eustace's adventures with the voyagers on the *Dawn Treader* * give him a wider view of life, particularly after his experience of turning into a dragon* on Dragon Island.* This experience, and his undragoning by Aslan,* provide a powerful image of sin, repentance and Christian salvation. Unlike his cousins, Eustace is never a monarch in Narnia, though he is given regal dress (with the other Seven Friends of Narnia*) as the New Narnia unfolds.

Scrubb family The Scrubb family—the parents Alberta and Harold, and their son, Eustace—are "modern" people. Their values are satirized by Lewis (Eustace's preference for books of facts; Alberta's vegetarianism; their use of alternative medicine), but he does not treat them as sinister. Characteristically, the parents send Eustace to boarding school at Experiment House,* representing the worst in modern education. The Scrubbs live in Cambridge. Alberta is the sister of Mrs. Pevensie.*

sea girl In *VDT*, a girl seen herding fish by Lucy* as the ship passes over the clear waters of the Last Sea* before Aslan's Country.* She and Lucy become friends simply by seeing each other, even though their worlds can never touch. *See also* sea people.*

sea people In *VDT*, undersea people seen by Lucy* as the ship passes over the clear waters of the Last Sea* before Aslan's Country.* They ride sea horses, wear no clothes and have bodies the color of old ivory and dark purple hair. Their beautiful submarine land is made up of mountains, hills, forests and parkland. The sea people enjoy hunting, and small fierce fish are used like falcons in our world.

sea serpent In *VDT* this attacks the ship after the voyagers have visited Burnt Island.*

Seven Brothers of the Shuddering Wood In *PC* these are red dwarfs living in the rocks and trees of the mountains of Narnia's southern border with Archenland.* They work in a forge underground, their heavy blows making the ground above tremble. They aid Caspian* in the fight to oust the tyrant Miraz,* providing dwarf-wrought armor and fighters.

Seven Friends of Narnia In *LB* seven of those who have entered Narnia from our world decide to meet up regularly to discuss that magical world and their memories of it. Prince Tirian,* in a dream, sees them assembled, and they see him as a specter (beings from Narnia cannot physically enter our world, with the exception of Aslan, who appears under a different name and form). The friends are: Digory Kirke*; Polly Plummer*; Peter,* Edmund* and Lucy* Pevensie; Eustace Scrubb*; and Jill Pole.* Susan Pevensie* is not part of the company as, at that time, she is no longer a friend of Narnia, because of her immaturity in striving to be "grown-up."

Seven Isles In *VDT,* a group of seven small islands a few days' sailing from the coast of Narnia.* Muil* is the westernmost island, separated from Brenn* by a choppy stretch of water. On Brenn, the town of Redhaven* provides supplies for shipping in the area.

seven lords In *VDT,* Telmarine* lords of Caspian* IX. During his reign as recounted in *PC,* the usurper Miraz* has sent them away to search for new lands in the Eastern Ocean.* Caspian seeks the seven missing lords. The seven are Argoz,* Bern,* Mavramorn,* Octesian,* Restimar,* Revilian* and Rhoop.*

Shadow Lands In *LB,* the name given to this world by Aslan* to mark its contrast to the real, new world of his new country. In this contrast Lewis makes powerful use of Plato, particularly his famous allegory of the cave in *The Republic*.

Shallow Lands *See* Underland.*

Shar In *HHB,* a lord of Archenland who fights valiantly in the battle of Anvard.*

Shasta In *HHB,* a twin son of King Lune* of Archenland. This son was lost in Calormen,* to the south, for many years. There he had the name, Shasta.

208

HHB is a famous Narnian tale of how he returned to Archenland, learned his true identity, and gained his Calormene wife, Aravis.* To them was born Ram the Great, the most notable of all the kings of Archenland. Cor's identical twin was named Corin.* Shasta, in a moment of profound recognition, realizes that Aslan* is behind all stories, including his own and that of Aravis.*

Shift the ape In *LB*, a Narnian* talking animal who deceives many loyal beasts and trees into believing that Aslan* has returned and that Puzzle the ass,* draped in an ill-fitting lion skin, is he. Shift's treachery knows no boundaries, and he forms on alliance with Narnia's traditional enemy, Calormen.*

Shribble River In *SC*, a river flowing from west to east near Ettinsmoor.*

signs, four In *SC*, the signs entrusted to Jill Pole* by Aslan* to lead her and her friend Eustace Scrubb* in their appointed quest* for the lost Prince Rilian,* son of their old friend Caspian.* Jill is instructed to remember and believe the signs, but she has frequent difficulties in doing so.

Silenus In Greek mythology, an elderly drunken satyr* and companion of Bacchus.* In *LWW* and *PC* he accompanies Bacchus* on a donkey and is an expert musician. Enormously overweight, he keeps falling off his steed and constantly calls out for refreshment, which stimulates grapevines to produce lots of fruit. On Tumnus's bookshelf is a learned volume, *The Life and Letters of Silenus.*

Silver Chair In *SC*, the chair in Underland* to which Prince Rilian* is bound each night for the period when his mind starts to clear from the Green Witch's* enchantment that grips him. His freedom from the chair marks the end of his enslavement to the spell.

Silver Sea In *VDT*, the reach of ocean covered with lilylike white flowers found by the voyagers. As they penetrate the dazzlingly bright sea, the voyagers discover its waters becoming gradually more shallow as World's End* is approached. Finally they must leave the *Dawn Treader*★ and use a rowing boat instead. Beyond World's End lies Aslan's Country.*

Silver Tree In *MN*, a tree that springs up from three silver half-crowns and a sixpence that fall onto Narnia's fecund soil on the first day of its creation.

slave trade In *VDT*, slave trading is a strong indicator of the blight that seized Narnia under the tyranny of Miraz* the Telmarine.* Pirates such as Pug* ply their trade in the Lone Islands and sell their captives to Calormen,* where slavery is an accepted part of the economic structure. Slavery returns to Narnia in *LB*, with the alliance between Shift* the ape and the Calormenes.

Slinkey In *LB,* a renegade fox who sides with the Calormenes* and is slain by Eustace.*

Son of Adam In the Chronicles, the name by which male humans are formally addressed. The Narnian throne may only properly be occupied by Sons of Adam and Daughters of Eve.*

Sopespian In *PC,* a lord of the usurper King Miraz* who turns traitor and plans Miraz's death.

Sorlois In *MN,* a city of the long-dead world of Charn.*

Spear-head In *VDT,* Narnia's North Star, brighter than our own pole star.

> *See* astronomy of Narnia.*

speech In Narnia the gift of speech is the mark of rational beings, making all talking animals equal and free by nature. In respect of this rationality, Narnian talking beasts are equal with humans, who have come from outside their world and have no right of domination. Dumb animals, however, may be farmed, husbanded and killed for food, but not exploited and reduced to economic units.

Spivvins In *SC,* a pupil at Experiment House* who is bullied by a gang and whose secret Eustace Scrubb* keeps under torture.

Splendour Hyaline In *HHB* and *PC,* a swan-shaped galleon used by the kings and queens of Narnia. Though richly furnished, she is also able to fight in battle. She has a swan's head at her prow and carved wings going back nearly to her waist. The sails are of silk and great lanterns hang to her stern.

"Spotty" Sorner In *SC,* a member of the gang of bullying pupils in Experiment House.*

Stable Hill In *LB* there is a stable in which Shift* keeps Puzzle* the ass as he pretends to be Aslan.* Later Tash,* the Calormene* demon god, enters the stable, followed by Aslan himself. When the great lion takes over the stable, its inside turns out to be larger than its outside.

stars In the Chronicles, stars are living beings, as in the medieval imagination Lewis draws upon. They are sung into being by Aslan* at the creation of Narnia. Stars featured include Ramandu* and Coriakin.* In his portrayal of stars Lewis may have been influenced by his friend J. R. R. Tolkien, for whom living stars were central to his imagined world in which Middle-earth lay, particularly Earendil.

> *See also* astronomy of Narnia.*

stone knife In *LWW* this was used by the White Witch* to slay Aslan.* Later in the history of Narnia the voyagers in *VDT* discover it kept by Ramandu* at Aslan's Table.*

Stone Table In *LWW,* a table of ancient magic upon which Aslan,* the great lion, is slain by the White Witch* and which is split forever when he returns to life. It is a slab of gray stone supported by four upright stones. The obviously ancient table is covered with engraved lines and figures. A mound called Aslan's How* is eventually built over it. This location plays a significant part in the actions recorded in *PC*. The table has similarities with ancient Celtic flat stones *(cromlechs)*, and represents a transfiguration of the pagan by the Christian.

Stonefoot In *LB,* a giant that Roonwit* summons to battle at the command of King Tirian.*

Stormness Head In *HHB,* a distinctive peak in Narnia's southern mountains. Clouds assembling around the peak signify bad weather, hence the peak's name. The main pass into Narnia from Archenland runs through Stormness Gap nearby.

Strawberry In *MN,* the horse of the London cabby Frank.* The horse is turned into a talking and flying horse by Aslan* and renamed Fledge.*

Sunless Sea In *SC,* the underground sea crossed by Eustace Scrubb,* Jill Pole* and Puddleglum* in their quest for the lost Prince Rilian.*

Susan, Queen *See* Pevensie, Susan.*

Swanwhite In *LB,* a queen of such beauty that if she looked into any pool her reflected face shone out for a year and a day afterwards just like a star in the night sky. In C. S. Lewis's timeline, she lived in Narnia before the days of the ascendancy of the White Witch,* who brought perpetual winter to the land.

Tarva In *PC,* a splendid planet visible in Narnia's night sky. Every two hundred years it passes close to another bright planet, Alambil.* Glenstorm* the centaur* interprets this rare event as a sign to begin the revolt against Telmarine* rule, which has suppressed Old Narnia.*

Tash In *LB,* the demon god of Calormen,* who appears in terrifying form. He has a head of a gigantic vulture, four arms and twenty razor-sharp, long talons. A dreadful smoke surrounding him at times keeps its shape—his shape. The Calormene nobility consider themselves descended from Tash. In the last days, part of the deception of Narnian and Calormene "new theologians," led by Shift,* is to syncretize Tash and Aslan* into a mixture they called "Tashlan."

Tashbaan In *HHB,* the capital of Calormen,* named after the country's deity, Tash.* The city is one of the wonders of the world. It is situated on a river island, with a many-arched bridge leading to it from the southern river bank. The city is gated, with high walls. Within them, buildings are crowded together and climb to the top of a hill. At its summit is displayed the magnificent palace of the Tisroc* and the great temple of Tash,* with its silver-plated dome. From the city hill, it is possible for visitors to see the masts of ships at anchor at the river's mouth. To the south of Tashbaan a range of low wooded hills is visible.

Tashlan In *LB,* a merging of Tash* and Aslan* to deny the latter's uniqueness as creator of Narnia and the other lands. This "new theology" is spearheaded by Shift* the talking ape (a satire by C. S. Lewis on modernist theology of his time).

Tehishbaan In *LB,* a Calormene* town lying west of the Great Desert.* Emeth* comes from here.

Telmar, Land of This lies to the far west of Narnia. Pirates who accidentally stumbled into the region from a South Sea island in our world populated it.

    See also Telmarines.*

Telmarines Descendants of pirates who accidently stumbled into the land of Telmar* after entering a magical cave in a South Sea island. They have become a proud and fierce nation. After a famine, the Telmarines, led by King Caspian* the First, crossed the Western mountains and conquered the peaceful land of Narnia, long after the reign of High King Peter* and the other Pevensie* children. They have silenced the talking animals and trees, driven away dwarfs* and fauns,* and even tried to cover up the memory of such things. Prince Caspian learns of the "Old Narnia," as it is then called in secret, from his nurse* and then his tutor, Doctor Cornelius.

    See also chapter eight, "The History of Narnia."

Terebinthia In *VDT,* an island visited by the *Dawn Treader* before Eustace,* Edmund* and Lucy* joined the voyage. It lies off the coast of Narnia, beyond Galma.* The island, a haunt of pirates, has been plagued by a terrible illness, and its main town is in quarantine. In *SC,* King Caspian* seeks Aslan* there. A terebinth is a type of tree found in Europe and the Middle East.

three sleepers In *VDT,* three of the seven missing lords sought by Caspian*: Argoz,* Revilian* and Mavramorn.* The voyagers find them sleeping an enchanted sleep at Aslan's Table* on the island of Ramandu.*

Time Narnia, being another world, has a time that only occasionally touches time in our world. This is when people enter Narnia through portals (such as the wardrobe*) or by being called into it. No matter how long someone is in Narnia, no time has passed when they return. Thus the events described in the Chronicles span just under fifty years of our time (A.D. 1900-1949), but 2555 years of Narnian time pass.

Time, Father In *SC* a giant sleeping man with a noble face and a flowing beard is discovered by Eustace,* Jill* and Puddleglum.* He is sleeping until the end of the world. In *LB* he is awakened by Aslan's* roar. He sounds a vast horn that signals the end of time in Narnia, after which the stars* fall from the sky.

Tirian, King In *LB,* the final king of Narnia,* who, along with his dear friend, Jewel* the Unicorn, makes a heroic last stand against the Calormenes* and other forces of darkness. Eustace Scrubb* and Jill Pole* come to help him in answer to his prayer to Aslan.*

Tisroc In *HHB* and *LB,* the Calormene* sovereign.

Tombs of the Ancient Kings In *HHB,* tombs north of the great city of Tashbaan,* capital of Calormen.* They are reputed to be haunted and look like giant beehives. Shasta* spends the night there. He has agreed to rendezvous at the tombs with Aravis,* and the two Narnian* talking horses Bree* and Hwin.*

Tree-people In the Chronicles, tree spirits, or dryads,* taken from classical mythology. The life of a tree-person is tied up with the life of the tree with which it is associated. If the tree dies, he or she dies. The spirits are embodied in trees a little like the Ents in Tolkien's *The Lord of the Rings.*

Trufflehunter In *PC,* a badger and loyal Old Narnian* who helps Caspian* against the tyrant King Miraz.*

Trumpkin the dwarf In *PC* the Pevensie* children rescue Trumpkin, a red dwarf,* from some of the men of King Miraz.* He is a loyal Old Narnian* and leads the children to Prince Caspian's* hideout in Aslan's How.* Trumpkin is referred to as the D.L.F. (the "Dear Little Friend"). By the time of the events in *VDT* he is Caspian's Regent and is later, in *SC,* an aged lord chancellor. He is the most fully drawn dwarf in the Chronicles and has an important narrative role, filling out the back story about Caspian. He is also an affectionate allusion to the "Great Knock," C. S. Lewis's nickname for his old tutor, W. T. Kirkpatrick. He is an honest skeptic.

Tumnus, Mr. In *LWW,* a faun first encountered by Lucy Pevensie* as she steps through the wardrobe* into the land of Narnia.* For not handing Lucy over to the White Witch,* Tumnus is punished by being turned to stone. He is later restored by Aslan,* the great lion. In *HHB,* set in the same period, Mr. Tumnus is with the visiting Narnian party in Tashbaan,* the capital of Calormen.*

C. S. Lewis tells us that the story of *LWW,* and thus the entire Chronicles, began with Mr. Tumnus: "The Lion all began with a picture of a Faun carrying an umbrella and parcels in a snowy wood. This picture had been in my mind since I was about sixteen. Then one day, when I was about forty, I said to my-self: 'Let's try to make a story about it.' "

Mr. Tumnus represents a pagan element in Narnia, a wildness in nature. His name may also be intended to suggest a shortened form of the word *autumn,* the idea of which evoked "sweet desire" in Lewis as a child. Mr. Tumnus is near the portal between our world and Narnia when Lucy comes across him, and he functions initially as a guide. (Portals between worlds are discussed in chapter five, "Literary Features of the Chronicles.")

Tumnus's Cave In *LWW,* a cave in an unusually large, reddish rock, in which a cheerful wood fire burns. Further light is provided by an oil lamp. It is dry and clean, with a carpet on the floor and two chairs, one for Mr. Tumnus "and one for a friend." There is a table, a dresser and a mantelpiece over the fire, with a portrait of an old faun hanging above it. In a corner is a door, probably leading to a bedroom and, on another wall, a shelf of books, one of which is called *Is Man a Myth?* The cave is later ransacked and despoiled by Maugrim* after he arrests Mr. Tumnus.

Turkish Delight In *LWW,* a favorite confection of Edmund Pevensie.* The White Witch* uses Turkish Delight to take Edmund into her power.

Underland In *SC,* the Green Witch's* realm, where she keeps Prince Rilian* in enchanted imprisonment. Underland* is known by the even deeper world of Bism* as the Shallow Lands. Gnomes, or Earthmen,* under the Green Witch's rule have been forced to dig tunnels to be used in an invasion of Narnia. Eustace Scrubb* and Jill Pole,* with the lugubrious help of Puddleglum* the Marsh-wiggle,* enter Underland and rescue Prince Rilian after his undeception. With the death of the Green Witch, Underland is destroyed, but not before the party escapes and the gnomes joyfully return to Bism.

Utter East *See* Aslan's Country.*

Uvilas A great Telmarine lord in the reign of Caspian* IX, who is murdered at Miraz's instigation during a hunting party. The event, recorded in *PC,* is made to seem like an accident with arrows.

War of Deliverance A name used in *LB* for the liberating battle against the tyrant Miraz* by the Old Narnians,* led by Caspian,* the proper monarch. In *PC* he calls on help from outside the world by sounding the horn* given to Susan Pevensie* long before by Father Christmas.* In answer, the Pevensie* children are called into Narnia and aid Caspian. While the brothers fight, Susan and Lucy accompany Aslan on a joyful and wild romp of dance and celebration that is as essential as fighting to restore the Old Narnia.

Warden of the Marches of Underland In *SC,* the watcher of the borders of Underland* who accosts Eustace Scrubb,* Jill Pole* and Puddleglum* the Marsh-wiggle when they tumble down into the dark world below Narnia. The Warden is accompanied by a hundred armed Earthmen,* all dull with the spell cast upon underworld creatures by the Green Witch.*

wardrobe In *LWW,* a wardrobe that has been made out of a tree that grew from a magic apple brought from Narnia by Digory Kirke.* It stands in an empty room in his rambling country house. The wardrobe provides a portal into Narnia. Lewis was inspired by wardrobes in stories of two authors he admired, George MacDonald and E. Nesbit. In *Phantastes,* Anodos enters a mysterious wardrobe in a spare chamber; from there he is transported into Fairy Land, where he is inflicted with a baleful shadow he cannot lose. In E. Nesbit's short story "The Aunt and Amabel," Amabel finds her way into a magical world through a "Bigwardrobeinaspareroom."

water rat In *LB* Tirian* and Jewel* come across a water rat on a raft on the river carrying logs destined for Calormen.* Thus Tirian learns that something is gravely wrong in Narnia.

Wer-wolf A human being who can turn into a wolf (possibly from early English "wer", man). C. S. Lewis does not explain how such changeling humans arrived in Narnia. In *LWW* the White Witch* calls Wer-wolves into battle, and in *PC* Nikabrik has a sinister friend with a dull, gray voice who turns out to be a Wer-wolf.

Western Wild In *MN,* a region of high hills and broken mountain ranges to the far west of Narnia. Digory Kirke* and Polly Plummer* travel there on the back of Fledge,* the flying horse, in their quest for the magic apple.

white stag In *LWW,* a creature of extraordinary beauty that, while being pursued in a hunt, leads the Pevensie* children, now long-established kings and queens in Narnia, back to the Lantern Waste,* where they return to England via the back of the wardrobe.* It is said that the stag granted wishes if caught.

White Witch Another name for Jadis, the destroyer of the exhausted world of Charn,* visited by Digory Kirke* and Polly Plummer* in *MN.* Through foolish curiosity, and despite Polly's reservations, Digory rings a bell that awakens her. Jadis is drawn with them first back to Edwardian London and then to Narnia, just as it is being created. As the Narnian ages flow on, she grows in power and puts the land under a curse of perpetual winter but never Christmas. Finally, in *LWW,* she is slain by Aslan.* Jadis is the progenitor of a line of witches, including the Green Witch* who tries in *SC* to dominate Narnia during the time of King Caspian* X.

The White Witch owes something to "The Snow Queen," the short story by Hans Christian Anderson, particularly where Little Kay meets the Snow Queen on her sledge. In *MN* there are many parallels between Jadis and Andrew Ketterley.* Jadis, for instance, has a superior attitude to ordinary people, thinking she is above all moral rules. In *PC* the Hag* calls her the "White Lady," and Nikabrik* also sees her positively, because of her alliance with dwarfs.

White Witch's House *See* Castle of the White Witch.*

wild fresney In *LB,* a wild herb looking like wood sorrel but with a better flavor, especially if seasoned with a little butter and pepper.

Wimbleweather In *PC,* a giant,* and one of the loyal Old Narnians.* He is a marshall in the combat between Peter Pevensie* and the usurper King Miraz.* Like most giants, he is not at all clever, at one stage muffing a strategic battle move. His tears of misery after that occasion soak some sleeping talking mice in Caspian's* hideout in Aslan's How.*

Winding Arrow In *HHB,* a river marking the northern fringe of the Great Desert* and border of Calormen. It flows eastward to the sea.

Winterblott, Edith In *SC,* one of the gang of bullying pupils in Experiment House.*

Wood Between the Worlds In *MN,* a quiet and rich woodland where the trees seem alive and nothing can unrule its peace. It contains many pools, which lead to other worlds. First Polly Plummer* and then Digory Kirke* arrive here after touching a ring* made by Uncle Andrew* from magical dust. After the dissolution of Charn,* its particular pool disappears. There is a pool, however, to enter a world of Nothing in which Narnia is created by the song of Aslan.*

wooses In *LWW,* haunting spirits summoned to the execution of Aslan* by the White Witch.* Lewis probably derived their name from *wodwos* in *Sir Gawain and the Green Knight* (l. 721), perhaps via Tolkien's *woses* (wild men of the woods).

Word, Deplorable *See* Deplorable Word.*

World's End In *VDT,* a vast, flat plain of short green grass that at its horizon seems to intersect with a bright blue sky, almost as with a glasslike wall. Here, on the boundary of all worlds near Aslan's Country,* Edmund,* Lucy* and Eustace meet a lamb,* or rather they meet Aslan as a lamb rather than a lion.

World's End Island In *VDT,* an island encountered by the voyagers. It is so far to the east of Narnia, across the Eastern Ocean,* that it is close to Aslan's Country.* The island is carpeted with a fine, springy turf, sprinkled with a plant like heather. On it there is a roofless wide space paved with smooth stones and surrounded by gray pillars. A long table is to be found on this space, covered with a crimson cloth and known as Aslan's Table* because he placed it there. The table is stocked with food each day by flocks of great white birds. As they swoop toward the island, the birds sing an unknown human language.

Ramandu,* an elderly star, and his beautiful daughter live here. Three of the missing seven lords* lie asleep at Aslan's Table.

Wraggle In *LB,* a satyr* who traitorously fights against Tirian's loyal Narnians and who is fatally wounded by one of Jill Pole's* arrows.

Zalindreh In *HHB,* the location of a Calormene* battle in which Bree* had valiantly fought as a warhorse.

Zardeenah In *HHB,* a Calormene* moon goddess, known as Lady of the Night, to whose service all maidens are pledged until they marry.

A Brief Chronology
of C. S. Lewis

1862: Birth of Florence (Flora) Augusta Hamilton, mother of C. S. Lewis, in Queenstown, County Cork, in the south of Ireland.

1863: Birth of Albert J. Lewis, father of C. S. Lewis, in County Cork, in the south of Ireland.

1892, January 3: J. R. R. Tolkien, friend of C. S. Lewis, born in South Africa of British parents.

1895, June 16: Birth of C. S. Lewis's brother, Warren Hamilton Lewis, in Belfast.

1898, November 29: Clive Staples Lewis born in Belfast.

1901, January 22: Queen Victoria dies.

1905: Lewis family moves to their new home, "Little Lea," on the outskirts of Belfast.

1908, February 15: Flora Lewis has major surgery for cancer.

1908, August 23: Flora Lewis dies of cancer, on her husband's birthday.

1908, September: Lewis is sent to Wynyard School in Watford, near London, where his brother already attends.

1910, autumn: Lewis attends Campbell College near his Belfast home for half a term.

1911: Lewis is sent to Malvern, England, to study. During this time at Malvern he abandons his childhood Christian faith.

1914, February: Warren enters the Royal Military Academy at Sandhurst.

1914, April: Lewis becomes acquainted with Arthur Greeves.

1914, August 4: Britain declares war on Germany.

1914, September 19: Lewis commences private study with W. T. Kirkpatrick, "The Great Knock," in Great Bookham Surrey. Lewis remains with him until April 1917.

1916, December: Lewis sits for a classical scholarship and is elected to University College, Oxford.

1917, April 26 until September: Lewis studies at University College, Oxford. He meets "Paddy" Moore.

1917, November: Lewis reaches the front lines in France.

1918, April 15: Lewis is wounded in battle. The same month "Paddy" Moore is killed in another part of the battle.

1918, November 11: End of World War One.

1919-1923: Lewis resumes his studies at University College, Oxford, where he receives a First Class in Honour Moderations (Greek and Latin literature) in 1920, a First Class in Greats (philosophy and ancient history) in 1922 and a First Class in English in 1923.

1919, March: Lewis's *Spirits in Bondage* is published by Heinemann under the name Clive Hamilton.

1920: Lewis establishes a house in Oxford for Mrs. Moore and her daughter, Maureen. Lewis lives with the Moores from June 1921.

1921: Death of W. T. Kirkpatrick, "The Great Knock."

1924, October: Lewis begins teaching philosophy at University College, standing in for E. F. Carritt for one year.

1925, May 20: Lewis elected a Fellow of Magdalen College, Oxford, where he serves as tutor in English language and literature for twenty-nine years until leaving for Magdalene College, Cambridge, in 1954.

1926, May 11: The first recorded meeting between Tolkien and Lewis.

1928, May 2: Albert Lewis retires with an annual pension from his position as Belfast Corporation County Solicitor.

1929: Lewis becomes a theist.

1929, September: Albert Lewis dies of cancer in Belfast.

1930, May: Warren Lewis decides to edit and arrange the Lewis family papers.

1930, October: Mrs. Moore, Lewis and his brother purchase "The Kilns" near Oxford.

1931: Tolkien's reformed English School syllabus is accepted, backed by C. S. Lewis, bringing together "Lang." and "Lit."

1931, September 19-20: After a long night of conversation on Addison's Walk in Oxford with Tolkien and Hugo Dyson, Lewis becomes convinced of the truth of Christian faith.

1931, September 28: Lewis returns to Christian faith while riding to Whipsnade Zoo in the sidecar of his brother's motorbike.

1933, May 25: Lewis's *The Pilgrim's Regress* published. The autumn term marks the beginning of Lewis's convening of a circle of friends dubbed the Inklings.

1936: Publication of Lewis's *The Allegory of Love*.

1939, September 2: Evacuee children arrive at The Kilns. Around this time Lewis begins a story, soon abandoned, about some evacuees who stay with an old Professor.

1939, September 4: Warren Lewis recalled to active service the day after Britain declares war on Germany.

1939, September 7: Charles Williams moves with the London branch of Oxford University Press to Oxford.

1940: Lewis begins lecturing on Christianity for the Royal Air Force, which he continues to do until 1941.

1940, October 14: Lewis's *The Problem of Pain* is published. It is dedicated to the Inklings.

1941 August 6: Lewis broadcasts the first of twenty-five talks on BBC radio.

1942: Lewis publishes *The Screwtape Letters*.

1945: Germany surrenders on May 8, Japan on September 2, ending World War Two.

1945, May 15: Death of Charles Williams.

1947: Lewis publishes *Miracles* (later revised).

1950, January 10: Lewis receives a letter from a thirty-four-year-old American writer, Helen Joy Davidman Gresham.

1950: Publication of *LWW.*

1951, January 12: Mrs. Moore dies. Since the previous April, she had been confined to a nursing home in Oxford. Publication of *PC* (subtitled, *The Return to Narnia*).

1952: Publication of Lewis's *Mere Christianity*.

1952, September: Lewis meets Joy Davidman for the first time. Publication of *VDT.*

1953: Publication of *SC.*

1954: Lewis accepts the Chair of Medieval and Renaissance Literature at Cambridge. He gives his inaugural lecture, *De Description Temporum*, on his fifty-sixth birthday. Lewis publishes *English Literature in the Sixteenth Century, Excluding Drama* and *HHB.*

1955: Publication of Lewis's *Surprised by Joy: The Shape of My Early Life* and *MN.*

1956, April 23: Lewis enters into a civil marriage with Joy Davidman at the Oxford Registry Office. Later in the year Lewis publishes *LB,* which is awarded the Carnegie Medal, a prestigious award for children's books. His *Till We Have Faces* is also published this year.

1957, March 21: Lewis's ecclesiastical marriage with Joy Davidman while she is hospitalized.

1957, September: Joy Davidman's health is improving; by December 10 she is walking again.

1957: Death of Lewis's Ulster friend, Jane McNeill.

1959, October: X-ray shows return of Joy's cancer.

1960, July 13: Joy dies, at the age of forty-five, not long after the couple's return from a vacation in Greece.

1963, June 15: Lewis admitted to Acland Nursing Home following a heart attack and almost dies.

1963, September: Warren returns to The Kilns after having been in Ireland for several months.

1963, November 22: Lewis dies, at home, one week before his sixty-fifth birthday.

1964: Publication of *Letters to Malcolm: Chiefly on Prayer,* prepared for publication by Lewis before his death.

1966: Warren Lewis publishes *Letters of C. S. Lewis.* Death of Arthur Greeves.

1973, April 9: Warren Lewis dies, still mourning his beloved brother.

1973, September 2: Tolkien dies in Bournemouth.

1975: Death of H. V. D. "Hugo" Dyson.

1997, Febuary 15: Death of Maureen Moore (Dame Maureen Dunbar of Hempriggs, Baroness).

1997, December 14: Owen Barfield dies, just short of his hundredth birthday.

1998: Conferences are held worldwide to commemorate the centenary of Lewis's birth.

N O T E S

Preface

Page 10   The Chronicles "must be judged": Humphrey Carpenter and Marie Prichard, *The Oxford Companion to Children's Literature* (Oxford: Oxford University Press, 1984), p. 370.

Page 11   "The imaginative man in me": *Letters of C. S. Lewis,* 2nd ed., ed. Walter Hooper (London: Bles, 1988), p. 444.

Page 12   "He possessed to an extraordinary degree": Rachel Trickett, "Uncrowned King of Oxford," in *We Remember C. S. Lewis: Essays & Memoirs,* ed. David Graham (Nashville: Broadman & Holman, 2001), p. 64.

Page 12   Rosamund Bott's recollections: Unpublished e-mail to the author from Rosamund Bott.

Page 13   "We need a place": Katherine Paterson, *Bridge to Terabithia* (New York: Crowell, 1977), pp. 38-40.

Page 13   "I did experiment, sometimes": Francis Spufford, *The Child That Books Built: A Life in Reading* (New York: Metropolitan, 2002), p. 107.

Page 14   "A world haunted by the supernatural": Austin Farrer, "The Christian Apologist," in *Light on C. S. Lewis,* ed. Jocelyn Gibb (London: Bles, 1965), p. 34. Farrer's comment is about Lewis's *The Problem of Pain.*

Chapter One: The Life of C. S. Lewis

Page 21   "The castle of Cair Paravel": *LWW,* chap. 17.

Page 22   "It flashed upon his mind": *MN,* chap. 7.

Page 23   "Chivalrous mice and rabbits": C. S. Lewis, *Surprised by Joy* (London: Bles, 1955), chap. 1

Page 25   "The Sailor: A Study": *Boxen: The Imaginary World of the Young C. S. Lewis,* ed. Walter Hooper (London: Collins, 1985), p. 192.

Page 25   List of his writings: *Memoirs of the Lewis Family, 1850-1930,* ed. Warren Lewis (unpublished collection), 3:230. Archived at the Wade Center, Wheaton, Illinois.

Page 26   "Jacks told us his tales": Unpublished letter to Clyde S. Kilby from Claire Lewis Clapperton, August 20, 1979, quoted in C. S. Lewis, *C. S. Lewis: Letters to Children,* ed. Lyle W. Dorsett and Marjorie Lamp Mead (New York; London: Collins, 1985), p. 13.

Page 26   "[Lucy's] not being silly at all": *LWW,* chap. 3.

Page 27   "Digory . . . went softly into his mother's room": *MN,* chap. 15.

Page 27   "We were coming, my brother and I": Lewis, *Surprised by Joy,* chap. 1.

Page 27   "All settled happiness": Ibid.

Page 29   "The fact is he should never": "Memoir," in *Letters of C. S. Lewis,* ed. W. H. Lewis (London: Bles, 1966), p. 5.

Page 29   "Susan . . . had never dreamed": *LWW,* chap. 5.

Page 30   "Of course it is hopeless for me to try to describe it": *Letters of C. S. Lewis,* p. 27.

Page 31   "My external surroundings are beautiful": Ibid., p. 104.

Page 34   Without Lewis's encouragement over many years: For a full account of the friendship and the mutual influence of the friends, see my *J. R. R. Tolkien and C. S. Lewis: The Story of Their Friendship* (Stroud: Sutton, 2003); published in U.S.A. as *Tolkien and*

C. S. Lewis: The Gift of Friendship (New York: HiddenSpring, 2003).

Page 34   "It must have seemed clear to him": A. N. Wilson, *C. S. Lewis: A Biography* (London: Collins, 1990), p. 119.

Page 34   "Friendship with Lewis compensates for much": Ibid.

Page 34   "Nor harm in him": C. S. Lewis, *All My Road Before Me*, ed. Walter Hooper (San Diego: Harcourt Brace Jovanovich, 1991), p. 393.

Page 36   "A man who gives the impression": *Brothers and Friends: The Diaries of Major Warren Hamilton Lewis*, ed. Clyde S. Kilby and Marjorie Lamp Mead (San Francisco, Calif.: Harper & Row, 1982), p. 112.

Page 36   Tolkien's argument: See Tolkien, "On Fairy Stories" and "Mythopoeia," in *Tree and Leaf*, 2nd ed. (London: Unwin Paperbacks, 1988).

Page 36   "The heart of Christianity is a myth": C. S. Lewis, "Myth Became Fact," in *Essay Collection and Other Short Pieces*, ed. Lesley Walmsley (London: HarperCollins, 2000), p. 141. The piece first appeared in a journal in 1944. Italics in original.

Page 37   "Art has been verified": J. R. R. Tolkien, "On Fairy Stories," in *Tree and Leaf*, 2nd ed. (New York: Houghton Mifflin, 1989), p. 66.

Page 38   "She was living in the story as if it was real": *VDT,* chap. 10.

Page 38   "I never had the experience of looking for God": *Christian Reflections*, ed. Walter Hooper (London: Bles, 1967), p. 169.

Page 39   "The very first tear he made": *VDT,* chap. 7.

Page 40   "You will be both grieved and amused": *Letters of C. S. Lewis*, p. 167.

Page 41   " 'It isn't Narnia, you know,' sobbed Lucy": *VDT,* chap. 16.

Page 42   "The cut and parry of prolonged, fierce, masculine argument": C. S. Lewis, ed., *Essays Presented to Charles Williams* (London: Oxford University Press, 1947), p. ix.

Page 43   "His thin form in his blue suit": *Brothers and Friends: The Diaries of Major Warren Hamilton Lewis*, ed. Clyde S. Kilby and Marjorie Lamp Mead (San Francisco: Harper & Row, 1982), p. 207.

Page 43   "This book is about four children": Quoted in R. L. Green and Walter Hooper, *C. S. Lewis: A Biography,* 3rd ed. (London: Collins, 2002), p. 303.

Page 44   "Some people think": C. S. Lewis, *Essay Collection and Other Short Pieces*, p. 527.

Page 45   "With his pen and with his voice": Walter Hooper, *C. S. Lewis: A Companion and Guide* (London: HarperCollins, 1996), p. 43-44.

Page 45   "It really won't do, you know!": R. L. Green and Walter Hooper, *C. S. Lewis: A Biography,* rev. ed. (London: Collins, 2002), p. 307.

Page 45   "It is sad": *Letters of J. R. R. Tolkien*, ed. Humphrey Carpenter (London: George Allen and Unwin, 1981), letter 265, November 11, 1964.

Page 46   "Aslan came bounding into it": C. S. Lewis, "It All Began with a Picture . . . ," in *Of This and Other Worlds,* ed. Walter Hooper (London: Collins Fount, 1962), p. 79.

Page 46   "The only life he had ever known": Walter Hooper, *Past Watchful Dragons* (London: Collins Fount, 1980), p. 69. The entire "LeFay Fragment" is reproduced in this book.

Page 47   "It seems the best of the lot": Green and Hooper, *C. S. Lewis: A Biography,* pp. 313-14.

Page 48   " 'Hush!' said Doctor Cornelius": *PC,* chap. 4.

Page 49   "Her mind was lithe and quick": Lewis, *A Grief Observed*, p. 8.

Page 49   "I never expected to have": Jocelyn Gibb, ed., *Light on C. S. Lewis* (London: Bles, 1965), p. 63.

Page 49   "A whole dimension to his nature": W. H. Lewis, "Memoir," in *Letters of C. S. Lewis,* p. 23.

Page 49   "For those few years": Lewis, *A Grief Observed*, p. 10.

Page 50   "The wonderful recovery": C. S. Lewis, *Letters to an American Lady*, ed. Clyde S. Kilby (Grand Rapids: Eerdmans, 1967), p. 88.

Page 51   "Then Aslan turned to them": *LB,* chap. 16.

Page 51   "There was a Shakespearean calendar": W. H. Lewis, "Memoir," in *Letters of C. S. Lewis,* ed. W. H. Lewis (London: Bles, 1966), p. 3.

Chapter Two: The Background to the Chronicles of Narnia

Page 54   " 'In my opinion,' Lewis wrote, 'such deliberate organization'": C. S. Lewis, *A Preface to Paradise Lost* (London: Oxford University Press, 1942), p. viii.

Page 55   Archetypes: Adapted from *Dictionary of Biblical Imagery,* ed. Leland Ryken, James C. Wilhoit and Tremper Longman III (Downers Grove, Ill.; Leicester: InterVarsity Press, 1998), p. xix.

Page 56   "It's all in Plato": *LB,* chap. 15.

Page 57   "love for myth and marvel": Tom Martin, ed., *Reading the Classics with C. S. Lewis* (Grand Rapids: Baker Academic, 2000), p. 92.

Page 58   Literary scholar Doris Myers believes: Doris Myers, "Spenser," in *Reading the Classics with C. S. Lewis,* ed. Thomas L. Martin (Grand Rapids: Baker Academic; Carlisle, U.K.: Paternoster, 2000), pp. 98-99.

Page 59   "baptised his imagination": *Surprised by Joy,* chap. 11.

Page 59   "Every age has its own outlook": C. S. Lewis, "On the Reading of Old Books," in *Essay Collection and Other Short Pieces* pp. 439-40.

Chapter Three: Aslan, Narnia and Orthodoxy

Page 62   "Every other miracle prepares for this": C. S. Lewis, *Miracles: A Preliminary Study* (London: Bles, 1947), p. 131.

Page 63   In a letter to the child Anne: Quoted in Walter Hooper, *C. S. Lewis: A Companion and Guide* (London: HarperCollins, 1996), p. 426.

Page 67   "I think the lion": C. S. Lewis, *The Problem of Pain* (London: Bles, 1940), p. 131.

Page 67   "The Seer of Revelation is shown Christ as a Lamb": Walter Hooper, *Past Watchful Dragons,* p. 106.

Page 68   "The sound, deep and throbbing": *PC,* chap. 11.

Page 69   According to Warren Lewis: The Malory and Tennyson sources are usefully quoted in Hooper, *C. S. Lewis: A Companion and Guide,* pp. 441-42.

Page 70   "All the beauty withers": *Letters of C. S. Lewis,* rev. ed., ed. Walter Hooper (London: Bles, 1988), pp. 408-9.

Page 70   "But do you really mean, sir": *LWW,* chap. 5.

Page 71   "In space and time there is no such thing": C. S. Lewis (with E. M. W. Tillyard), *The Personal Heresy: A Controversy* (London: Oxford University Press, 1939), chap. 5.

Page 71   " 'In our world,' said Eustace": *VDT,* chap. 14.

Page 72   "The evil reality": *Miracles: A Preliminary Study* (London: Bles, 1947), p. 179.

Page 72   "real universe, the divine,": Preface to *George MacDonald: An Anthology,* edited by C. S. Lewis.

Page 72   "The familiar is in itself group for affection": *Letters of C. S. Lewis,* rev. ed., p. 409.

Page 73   "The happiness which it presents to us": C. S. Lewis, *Of This and Other Worlds,* ed. Walter Hooper (London: Collins Fount, 1982), p. 38.

Page 73   "We were talking about cats and dogs": C. S. Lewis, *Letters to an American Lady*, ed.

Clyde S. Kilby (Grand Rapids: Eerdmans, 1967), p. 40.

Page 74 "The settled happiness and security": C. S. Lewis, *The Problem of Pain* (London: Bles, Centenary Press, 1940), chap. 7.

Page 74 "Lewis's concept of nature is threefold": Kathryn Lindskoog, *The Lion of Judah in Never-Never Land: God, Man and Nature in C. S. Lewis's Narnia Tales* (Grand Rapids: Eerdmans, 1973), pp. 128-29.

Page 76 "The sense that in this universe": C. S. Lewis, *The Weight of Glory,* Little Books on Religion 189 (London: SPCK, 1942), chap. 1.

Page 76 "Perhaps it has sometimes happened to you": *LWW,* chap. 7.

Page 77 "Edmund and Eustace would never talk about it": *VDT,* chap. 16.

Page 77 *Sehnsucht:* Rudolf Otto, *The Idea of the Holy: An Inquiry into the Idea of the Divine and Its Relation to the Rational,* trans. John W. Harvey (London: Oxford University Press, 1936). Also explored by Corbin S. Carnell, in his book *Bright Shadows of Reality* (Grand Rapids: Eerdmans, 1974), pp. 14-15.

Page 78 "To construct plausible": *Of This and Other Worlds*, pp. 35-36.

Page 78 "the secret signature of each soul": *Problem of Pain*, chap. 10.

Page 78 "There are times when I think we do not desire heaven": Lewis, *Problem of Pain,* chap. 10.

Page 79 "To awaken a desire for love": Corbin S. Carnell, *Bright Shadows of Reality* (Grand Rapids: Eerdmans, 1974), p. 161.

Page 79 "Beyond comparison, the most beautiful noise": *MN,* chap. 8.

Page 80 "This is the land": *LB*, chap. 15.

Chapter Four: Worldviews and Narnia

Page 83 "That's all nonsense, for babies": *PC,* chap. 4.

Page 83 "What is this sun that you speak of?": *SC,* chap. 12.

Page 84 "Do *you* believe in Aslan?": *PC,* chap. 6.

Page 85 Lewis regarded Plato as a pagan: *Letters of C. S. Lewis*, ed. W. H. Lewis (London: Bles, 1966), p. 167.

Page 87 "I say, Lu—": *PC,* chap. 11.

Page 87 "We must not be nervous": "Myth Became Fact," in *Essay Collection and Other Short Pieces,* ed. Lesley Walmsley (London: HarperCollins, 2000), p. 142. See also "Second Meanings," in *Reflections on the Psalms* (London: Bles, 1958), chap. 10.

Page 88 "Instantly I was uplifted": C. S. Lewis, *Surprised by Joy: The Shape of My Early Life* (London: Bles, 1955), chap. 1.

Page 88 "For my part I believe": C. S. Lewis, *Letters: C. S. Lewis and Don Giovanni Calabria: A Study in Friendship,* edited by and with an introduction by Martin Moynihan (Glasgow: Collins, 1988), p. 89.

Page 89 Lewis placing the highest value: See Maria Kuteeva, "C. S. Lewis's Chronicles of Narnia: Their Origins in Mythology, Literature and Scholarship," M.Phil. thesis, University of Manchester, 1995, p. 32.

Page 91 "Child, if you will, it is mythology": C. S. Lewis, *The Pilgrim's Regress: An Allegorical Apology for Christianity, Reason and Romanticism* (London: Dent, 1933), pp. 219-20.

Chapter Five: Literary Features of the Chronicles

Page 92 "Any amount of theology": *Letters of C. S. Lewis*, ed. W. H. Lewis (London: Bles, 1966), p. 167.

Page 93   "A romantic theologian does not mean": C. S. Lewis, Preface to *Essays Presented to Charles Williams*, ed. C. S. Lewis (London: Oxford University Press, 1947), p. vi.

Page 93   Lewis particularly worked out: *Letters of C. S. Lewis*, p. 260.

Page 94   "To say that the real life of men": C. S. Lewis, "Tolkien's *The Lord of the Rings*," in *Of This and Other Worlds: Essays and Stories*, ed. Walter Hooper (London: Collins, 1982), p. 120.

Page 95   "The child enjoys his cold meat": Ibid.

Page 95   Fantasy generalizing and adding to life: C. S. Lewis, "Sometimes Fairy Stories May Say Best What Needs to Be Said," in *Of This and Other Worlds*, ed. Walter Hooper (London: Collins, 1982), p. 74.

Page 96   "By an allegory I mean a composition": *Letters of C. S. Lewis*, p. 283.

Page 96   "You've got it exactly right": C. S. Lewis, *Letters to Children*, ed. Lyle W. Dorsett and Marjorie Lamp Mead (New York; London: Collins, 1985), September 11, 1958.

Page 97   "I'm hunger. I'm thirst": *PC*, chap. 12.

Page 97   "I think that many confuse": Foreword to *Lord of the Rings*, 2nd ed. (London: n.p., 1966).

Page 97   "story out of which ever varying meanings will grow": *Letters of C. S. Lewis*, p. 271, dated September 22, 1956.

Page 98   Fantasy and Christian fantasy: See J. R. R. Tolkien, "On Fairy Stories," in *The Monsters and the Critics and Other Essays* (London: Allen & Unwin, 1983); C. S. Lewis, *Of This and Other Worlds*, ed. Walter Hooper (London: Collins Fount, 1982); Colin Duriez, *Tolkien and C. S. Lewis: The Gift of Friendship* (Stroud, U.K./New York: Sutton/HiddenSpring, 2003); Colin Manlove, *Christian Fantasy: From 1200 to the Present* (Basingstoke; London: MacMillan, 1992); Derek Brewer, *Symbolic Stories: Traditional Narratives of the Family Drama in English Literature* (Cambridge: Brewer; Totowa, N.J.: Rowman & Littlefield, 1980).

Page 99   By this he meant that fantasy, like myth: "Sometimes Fairy Stories May Say Best What's to be Said," in *Of This and Other Worlds*, p. 74.

Page 100   "What you see and hear depends": *MN*, chap. 10.

Page 100   "Does anyone believe": "On Stories," in *Of This and Other Worlds*, p. 37.

Page 101   "It could be argued that, if fantasy has a purpose": John Clute and John Grant, *The Encyclopedia of Fantasy* (London: Orbit, 1997), p. 750.

Page 101   "The creatures came rushing on": *LB*, chap. 14.

Page 102   Recognition in story: For an insightful discussion, see John Clute, "Recognition," in *Encyclopedia of Fantasy*, ed. John Clute and John Grant (Orbit: London, 1997), p. 804.

Page 105   "We do not want merely to see beauty": *Essay Collection and Other Short Pieces*, p. 104.

Page 106   What the narrator knows: There remains the tantalizing question of how the narrator knew of what had happened to the Friends of Narnia after their deaths in the accident. Obviously he could not have quizzed them as he had done some of the protagonists after their returns from Narnia in earlier adventures.

Page 106   "If one could run without getting tired": *LB*, chap. 16.

Page 106   "As He spoke, [Aslan] no longer looked to them": *LB*, chap. 16.

Page 107   "When the Pevensie children had returned to Narnia": *VDT*, chap. 1.

Page 107   "The author's voice in the Narnia books": Francis Spufford, *The Child That Books Built: A Life in Reading* (New York: Metropolitan, 2002), pp. 101-2.

Page 107   "Inner consistency of reality": J. R. R. Tolkien, "On Fairy-Stories," in *Tree and Leaf*,

2nd ed. (London: Unwin Paperbacks, 1988), p. 45.

Page 108   "The realm or state where faeries have their being": Ibid., p. 14.

Chapter Six: Themes, Concepts and Images in Narnia

Page 113   "She was flogging the horse": *MN*, chap. 7.

Page 115   "does not despise real woods": C. S. Lewis, *Of This and Other Worlds*, ed. Walter Hooper (London: Collins Fount, 1982), p. 65.

Page 115   "in that sense only a taste": J. R. R. Tolkien, "On Fairy-Stories," in *Tree and Leaf*, 2nd ed. (London: Unwin Paperbacks, 1988), p. 53.

Page 116   "Barfield . . . made short work": C. S. Lewis, *Surprised by Joy* (London: Bles, 1955), chap. 13.

Page 117   "Human life means to me": C. S. Lewis, *Rehabilitations and Other Essays* (London: Oxford University Press, 1938), p. 83.

Page 118   "Michael Ward has argued": Michael Ward, "Planet Narnia," *The Times Literary Supplement*, April 23, 2003. Ward is elaborating and defending this thesis in a forthcoming Ph.D.

Page 120   "The tree of life my soul hath seen": From *Divine Hymns or Spiritual Songs*, compiled by Joshua Smith (New Hampshire, 1784).

Chapter Seven: An Overview of the Chronicles of Narnia

Page 123   "a faun carrying an umbrella": C. S. Lewis, *Of This and Other Worlds*, ed. Walter Hooper (London: Collins Fount, 1982), p. 79.

Chapter Nine: The Geography of Narnia

Page 138   "I still remember from one occasion": Cosslet Quinn, quoted by Frank Kastor, *Search* 21, no. 1 (Spring 1998): 179. Kastor, of Wichita State University, finds parallels between the geography and landscapes of Narnia and those of the Ulster that Lewis knew as a boy. In a quotation from *MN*, he adds his comments in brackets to demonstrate some of them.

> All Narnia, many-coloured with lawns and rocks and heather and different sorts of trees, lay spread out below them; the river winding through it like a ribbon of quicksilver [the River Lagan]. They could already see over the tops of the low hills which lay northward on their right [Hills of Antrim]; beyond those hills, a great moorland sloped gently up and up to the horizon. On their left [southward] the mountains were much higher [mountains of Mourne], but every now and then there was a gap when you could see, between steep pine woods, a glimpse of the southern lands that lay beyond them [now The Republic of Ireland] looking blue and far away.

Kastor adds that their destination is the garden, with the magic apple tree, which lies west of Narnia at the end of the blue lake (Lough Neagh), in the mountains of the Western Wild (Northwestern Ireland).

Chapter Ten: Other Writings of C. S. Lewis in a Narnian Context

Page 141   "to combine my two chief literary pleasures": C. S. Lewis, *Surprised by Joy* (London: Bles, 1955), chap. 1

Page 143   "We can no longer dismiss": C. S. Lewis, *The Discarded Image* (Cambridge: Cambridge University Press, 1964), p. 222.

Page 144 "Illustrates well enough": C. S. Lewis, *English Literature in the Sixteenth Century Excluding Drama*, vol. 3 of *The Oxford History of English Literature* (Oxford: Clarendon, 1954), pp. 558.

Page 144 "I regret that the brutes cannot write books": C. S. Lewis, *An Experiment in Criticism* (Cambridge: Cambridge University Press, 1961), pp. 140-41.

Page 146 "an attempt to convince people": *Letters of C. S. Lewis,* ed. W. H. Lewis (London: Bles, 1966), p. 193.

Page 151 The *Mappa Mundi:* See J. I. Packer, "Living Truth for a Dying World: The Message of C. S. Lewis," in *The J. I. Packer Collection,* ed. Alister McGrath (Downers Grove, Ill.: InterVarsity Press, 1999), p. 273.

Page 151 The attacks on the soul: Quotations from C. S. Lewis, preface to *The Pilgrim's Regress*, 3rd ed. (London: Bles, 1943).

Page 151 "With both the 'North' and the 'South'": Ibid.

Page 153 "Casting all these things": C. S. Lewis, *Of This and Other Worlds,* ed. Walter Hooper (London: Collins Fount, 1982), p. 73.

Page 154 "On the one side a many-islanded sea of poetry and myth": C. S. Lewis, *Surprised by Joy* (London: Bles, 1955), chap. 11

Chapter Eleven: A Who's Who of the Making of Narnia

Page 156 Barfield's "intellectual epiphany": "Owen Barfield," *The New York Times Obituary,* December 19, 1997.

Page 156 "What impressed me particularly": Ibid.

Page 158 "A Scot of genius": G. K. Chesterton, *The Victorian Age in Literature* (1913; reprint, Oxford: Oxford University Press, 1946), p. 94.

Page 162 "To me, George MacDonald's": W. H. Auden, afterword to *The Golden Key: George MacDonald* (New York: Farrar, Straus and Giroux, 1967).

Page 163 "It sometimes happens that the town child": Humphrey Carpenter and Mari Prichard, *The Oxford Companion to Children's Literature* (Oxford: Oxford University Press, 1984), p. 420.

Page 163 "Came through *Squirrel Nutkin*": C. S. Lewis, *Surprised by Joy* (London: Bles, 1955), chap. 1.

Page 164 The friendship of Lewis and Tolkien: See Colin Duriez, *Tolkien and C. S. Lewis: The Gift of Friendship* (New York: HiddenSpring, 2003).

Chapter Twelve: The A-Z of Narnia

Page 187 Ginger the cat: Mentioned in C. S. Lewis, Letters to an American Lady, ed. Clyde S. Kilby (Grand Rapids: Eerdmans, 1967), October 2, 1962, p. 107.

Page 201 "The books don't tell us what happened to Susan": C. S. Lewis, *Letters to Children,* ed. Lyle W. Dorsett and Marjorie Lamp Mead (New York; London: Collins, 1985), January 22, 1957. p. 67.

Page 202 The Pevensie children and E. Nesbit: See "Deconstructing C. S. Lewis," in *Behind the Veil of Familiarity: C. S. Lewis (1898-1998),* ed. Margarita Carretero González and Encarnación Hidalgo Tenorio (Bern: Lang, 2001), pp. 237-50.

BIBLIOGRAPHY

WRITINGS OF C. S. LEWIS IN ORDER OF FIRST PUBLICATION

Spirits in Bondage: A Cycle of Lyrics. London: Heinemann, 1919. (This book has now entered the public domain; the text can be obtained from Internet sources.)

Dymer. London: Dent, 1926.

The Pilgrim's Regress: An Allegorical Apology for Christianity, Reason and Romanticism. London: Dent, 1933; 3rd ed., London: Bles, 1943.

The Allegory of Love: A Study in Medieval Tradition. Oxford: Clarendon, 1936.

Out of the Silent Planet. London: Lane, 1938.

Rehabilitations and Other Essays. London: Oxford University Press, 1938.

The Personal Heresy: A Controversy (with E. M. W. Tillyard). London: Oxford University Press, 1939.

The Problem of Pain. London: Bles, Centenary Press, 1940.

Broadcast Talks. London: Bles, 1942.

A Preface to Paradise Lost. London: Oxford University Press, 1942.

The Screwtape Letters. London: Bles, 1942. Reprinted with an additional letter as *The Screwtape Letters and Screwtape Proposes a Toast.* London: Bles, 1961. Further new material in *The Screwtape Letters with Screwtape Proposes a Toast.* New York: Macmillan, 1982.

The Weight of Glory. Little Books on Religion 189. London: SPCK, 1942.

The Abolition of Man: Reflections on Education with Special Reference to the Teaching of English in the Upper Forms of Schools. Riddell Memorial Lectures, 15th series. London: Oxford University Press, 1943.

Christian Behaviour: A Further Series of Broadcast Talks. London: Bles, 1943.

Perelandra. London: Lane, 1943. Reprinted in paperback as *Voyage to Venus.* London: Pan Books, 1953.

Beyond Personality: The Christian Idea of God. London: Bles, Centenary Press, 1944.

That Hideous Strength: A Modern Fairy Tale for Grown Ups. London: Lane, 1945.

A version abridged by the author was published as *The Tortured Planet* (New York: Avon, 1946) and as *That Hideous Strength* (London: Pan Books, 1955).

George MacDonald: Anthology. Compiled by and with an introduction by C. S. Lewis. London: Bles, 1946.

The Great Divorce: A Dream. London: Bles, Centenary Press, 1946. Originally published as a series in *The Guardian.* Bles inaccurately dated the book as 1945.

Essays Presented to Charles Williams. Edited by and with an introduction by C. S. Lewis. London: Oxford University Press, 1947.

Miracles: A Preliminary Study. London: Bles, 1947. Reprinted, with an expanded version of chapter 3, Collins Fontana Books: London, 1960.

Arthurian Torso: Containing the Posthumous fragment of the Figure of Arthur by Charles Williams and A Commentary on the Arthurian Poems of Charles Williams by C. S. Lewis. London: Oxford University Press, 1948.

Transposition and Other Addresses. London: Bles, 1949. Published in the United States as *The Weight of Glory and Other Addresses* (New York: Macmillan, 1949).

The Lion, the Witch, and the Wardrobe. London: Bles, 1950.

Prince Caspian: The Return to Narnia. London: Bles, 1951.

Mere Christianity. London: Bles, 1952. A revised and expanded version of *Broadcast Talks, Christian Behaviour* and *Beyond Personality.*

The Voyage of the "Dawn Treader." London: Bles, 1952.

The Silver Chair. London: Bles, 1953.

English Literature in the Sixteenth Century Excluding Drama. Vol. 3 of *The Oxford History of English Literature.* Oxford: Clarendon, 1954. In 1990 the series was renumbered and Lewis's volume was reissued as volume 4, *Poetry and Prose in the Sixteenth Century.*

The Horse and His Boy. London: Bles, 1954.

The Magician's Nephew. London: Bodley Head, 1955.

Surprised by Joy: The Shape of My Early Life. London: Bles, 1955.

The Last Battle. London: Bodley Head, 1956.

Till We Have Faces: A Myth Retold. London: Bles, 1956.

Reflections on the Psalms. London: Bles, 1958.

The Four Loves. London: Bles, 1960.

Studies in Words. Cambridge: Cambridge University Press, 1960.

The World's Last Night and Other Essays. New York: Harcourt, Brace, 1960.

An Experiment in Criticism. Cambridge: Cambridge University Press, 1961.

A Grief Observed (published under the pseudonym N. W. Clerk). London: Faber & Faber, 1961.

They Asked for a Paper: Papers and Addresses. London: Bles, 1962.

POSTHUMOUS WRITINGS AND COLLECTIONS

The Discarded Image: An Introduction to Medieval and Renaissance Literature. Cambridge: Cambridge University Press, 1964.

Letters to Malcolm: Chiefly on Prayer. London: Bles, 1964.

Poems. Edited by Walter Hooper. London: Bles, 1964.

Letters of C. S. Lewis. Edited, with a memoir, by W. H. Lewis. London: Bles, 1966. Revised edition edited by Walter Hooper (London: Bles, 1988).

Of Other Worlds: Essays and Stories. Edited by Walter Hooper. London: Bles, 1966.

Studies in Medieval and Renaissance Literature. Edited by Walter Hooper. Cambridge: Cambridge University Press, 1966.

Christian Reflections. Edited by Walter Hooper. London: Bles, 1967.

Letters to an American Lady. Edited by Clyde S. Kilby. Grand Rapids: Eerdmans, 1967; London: Hodder & Stoughton, 1969.

Spenser's Images of Life. Edited by Alistair Fowler. Cambridge: Cambridge University Press, 1967.

A Mind Awake: An Anthology of C. S. Lewis. Edited by Clyde S. Kilby. London: Bles, 1968.

Narrative Poems. Edited and with a preface by Walter Hooper. London: Bles, 1969.

Selected Literary Essays. Edited and with a preface by Walter Hooper. Cambridge: Cambridge University Press, 1969.

God in the Dock: Essays on Theology and Ethics. Edited and with a preface by Walter Hooper. Grand Rapids: Eerdmans, 1970. A paperback edition of part of it was published as *God in the Dock: Essays on Theology* (London: Collins Fontana, 1979) and as *Undeceptions: Essays on Theology and Ethics* (London: Bles, 1971).

Fern Seeds and Elephants and Other Essays on Christianity. Edited and with a preface by Walter Hooper. London: Collins Fontana, 1975.

The Dark Tower and Other Stories. Edited and with a preface by Walter Hooper. London: Collins, 1977.

The Joyful Christian: Readings from C. S. Lewis. Edited by William Griffin. New York: Macmillan, 1977.

They Stand Together: The Letters of C. S. Lewis to Arthur Greeves (1914-1963). Edited by Walter Hooper. London: Collins, 1979.

Of This and Other Worlds. Edited by Walter Hooper. London: Collins Fount, 1982.

The Business of Heaven: Daily Readings from C. S. Lewis. Edited by Walter Hooper. London: Collins Fount, 1984.

Boxen: The Imaginary World of the Young C. S. Lewis. Edited by Walter Hooper. London: Collins, 1985.

First and Second Things: Essays on Theology and Ethics. Edited and with a preface by Walter Hooper. Glasgow: Collins Fount, 1985.

Letters to Children. Edited by Lyle W. Dorsett and Marjorie Lamp Mead. New York; London: Collins, 1985.

Present Concerns. Edited by Walter Hooper. London: Collins Fount, 1986.

Timeless at Heart. Edited by Walter Hooper. London: Collins Fount, 1987.

Letters: C. S. Lewis and Don Giovanni Calabria: A Study in Friendship. Edited by and with an introduction by Martin Moynihan. Glasgow: Collins, 1988 (includes Latin text). First issued as *The Latin Letters of C. S. Lewis* (paperback edition Westchester, Ill.: Crossway Books, 1987 [without Latin text]).

The Collected Poems of C. S. Lewis. Edited by Walter Hooper. London: HarperCollins, 1994.

The Collected Letters. Vol. 1, *Family Letters 1905-1931.* Edited by Walter Hooper. HarperCollins: London, 2000.

Essay Collection and Other Short Pieces. Edited by Lesley Walmsley. London: HarperCollins, 2000.

C. S. Lewis: Collected Letters. Vol. 2, *Books, Broadcasts and the War 1931-1949.* Edited by Walter Hooper. London: HarperCollins, 2004.

SELECTED WRITINGS RELEVANT TO C. S. LEWIS AND NARNIA

Adey, Lionel. *C. S. Lewis: Writer, Dreamer and Mentor.* Grand Rapids; Cambridge: Eerdmans, 1998.

————. *C. S. Lewis's "Great War" with Owen Barfield*. Victoria: University of Victoria Press, 1978.

Arnott, Anne. *The Secret Country of C. S. Lewis*. London: Hodder, 1974.

Brewer, Derek. *Symbolic Stories: Traditional Narratives of the Family Drama in English Literature*. Cambridge: Brewer; Totowa, N.J.: Rowman & Littlefield, 1980.

Burson, Scott, and Jerry Walls. *C. S. Lewis and Francis Schaeffer*. Downers Grove, Ill.: InterVarsity Press, 1998.

Carnell, Corbin S. *Bright Shadows of Reality*. Grand Rapids: Eerdmans, 1974.

Carpenter, Humphrey. *The Inklings: C. S. Lewis, J. R. R. Tolkien, Charles Williams and Their Friends*. London: Allen and Unwin, 1978; Boston: Houghton Mifflin, 1979.

Carpenter, Humphrey, and Marie Prichard. *The Oxford Companion to Children's Literature*. Oxford: Oxford University Press, 1984.

Chesterton, G. K. *Orthodoxy*. London: The Bodley Head, 1908.

————. *The Victorian Age in Literature*. London; New York: Oxford University Press, 1966.

Christopher, Joe R. *C. S. Lewis*. Boston: Hall, 1987.

Clute, John, and John Grant. *The Encyclopedia of Fantasy*. London: Orbit, 1997.

Cobley, Paul. *Narrative*. London: Routledge, 2001.

Como, James T., ed. *C. S. Lewis at the Breakfast Table and Other Reminiscences*. New York: Macmillan, 1979.

Cunningham, Richard B. *C. S. Lewis, Defender of the Faith*. Philadelphia: Westminster, 1967.

Dorsett, Lyle. *Joy and C. S. Lewis*. London: HarperCollins, 1988.

Downing, C. David. *Planets in Peril: A Critical Study of C. S. Lewis's Ransom Trilogy*. Amherst: University of Massachusetts Press, 1992.

Downing, C. David. *The Most Reluctant Convert: C. S. Lewis's Journey to Faith*. Downers Grove, Ill.; Leicester: InterVarsity Press, 2002.

Duncan, John Ryan. *The Magic Never Ends: The Life and Work of C. S. Lewis*. Nashville: W Publishing; Milton Keynes: Authentic, 2002.

Duriez, Colin. *The C. S. Lewis Encyclopedia*. Wheaton, Ill.: Crossway; London: SPCK, 2000.

————. "C. S. Lewis' Theology of Fantasy." In *The Pilgrim's Guide*. Edited by David Mills. Grand Rapids: Eerdmans, 1998.

————. "C. S. Lewis' Theology of Fantasy." In *Behind the Veil of Familiarity: C. S.*

Lewis (1898-1998). Edited by Margarita Carretero González and Encarnación Hidalgo Tenorio. Bern: Lang, 2001.

————. *J. R. R. Tolkien and C. S. Lewis: The Story of Their Friendship*. Stroud: Sutton, 2003. Published in U.S.A. as *Tolkien and C. S. Lewis: The Gift of Friendship*. Mahwah, N.J.: HiddenSpring, 2003.

————. *Tolkien and The Lord of the Rings*. London: Azure; Mahwah, N.J.: HiddenSpring; Wellington, New Zealand: Garside, 2001.

Edwards, Bruce L. *A Rhetoric of Reading: C. S. Lewis's Defense of Western Literacy*. Salt Lake City: Brigham Young University Press, 1986.

Edwards, Bruce L., ed. *The Taste of the Pineapple: Essays on C. S. Lewis as Reader, Critic, and Imaginative Writer*. Bowling Green, Ohio: Bowling Green State University Popular Press, 1988.

Filmer, Kath. *The Fiction of C. S. Lewis: Mask and Mirror*. New York: Macmillan, 1993.

Ford, Paul F. *Companion to Narnia*. San Francisco: Harper & Row, 1994.

Fuller, Edmund. *Books with Men Behind Them*. New York: Random House, 1962.

Gibb, Jocelyn, ed. *Light on C. S. Lewis*. London: Bles, 1965.

Goffar, Janine. *C. S. Lewis Index: Rumours from the Sculptor's Shop*. Riverside, Calif.: La Sierra University Press, 1995; Carlisle: Solway, 1997.

Graham, David, ed. *We Remember C. S. Lewis: Essays & Memoirs*. Nashville: Broadman & Holman, 2001.

Green, R. L., and Walter Hooper. *C. S. Lewis: A Biography*. London: Collins, 1974, 2002.

Gresham, Douglas. *Lenten Lands: My Childhood with Joy Davidman and C. S. Lewis*. London: Collins, 1989.

Griffin, William. *Clive Staples Lewis: A Dramatic Life*. San Francisco: Harper & Row, 1986. Published in the U.K. as *C. S. Lewis: The Authentic voice*. (Tring: Lion, 1988).

Harris, Richard. *C. S. Lewis: The Man and His God*. London: Collins Fount, 1987.

Holbrook, David. *The Skeleton in the Wardrobe: C. S. Lewis's Fiction, A Phenomenonological Study*. Lewisburg: Bucknell University Press; London: Associated University Press, 1991.

Holmer, Paul L. *C. S. Lewis: The Shape of His Faith and Thought*. New York: Harper & Row, 1976; London: Sheldon, 1977.

Hooper, Walter, ed. *All My Road Before Me: The Diary of C. S. Lewis, 1922-1927*.

San Diego: Harcourt Brace Jovanovich, 1991.

Hooper, Walter. *C. S. Lewis: A Companion and Guide.* London: HarperCollins, 1996.

———. *Past Watchful Dragons.* London: Collins Fount, 1980.

Howard, Thomas. *The Achievement of C. S. Lewis: A Reading of His Fiction.* Wheaton, Ill.: Shaw, 1980.

Huttar, Charles A., ed. *Imagination and the Spirit: Essays in Literature and the Christian Faith.* Grand Rapids: Eerdmans, 1971.

Keefe, Carolyn, ed. *C. S. Lewis: Speaker and Teacher.* London: Hodder, 1974.

Kilby, Clyde S. *The Christian World of C. S. Lewis.* Grand Rapids: Eerdmans, 1965.

———. *Images of Salvation in the Fiction of C. S. Lewis.* Wheaton, Ill.: Shaw, 1978.

Kilby, Clyde S., and Douglas Gilbert. *C. S. Lewis: Images of His World.* Grand Rapids: Eerdmans, 1973.

Kilby, Clyde S., and Marjorie Lamp Mead, eds. *Brothers and Friends: The Diaries of Major Warren Hamilton Lewis.* San Francisco: Harper and Row, 1982.

Kort, Wesley A. *C. S. Lewis: Then and Now.* New York: Oxford University Press, 2001.

Knight, Gareth. *The Magical World of the Inklings.* Longmead, Dorsett: Elements Books, 1990.

Kuteeva, Maria. "C. S. Lewis's Chronicles of Narnia: Their Origins in Mythology, Literature and Scholarship." M.Phil. thesis, University of Manchester, 1995.

Lindskoog, Kathryn. *C. S. Lewis: Mere Christian.* Glendale, Calif.: Gospel Light, 1973.

———. *The Lion of Judah in Never-Never Land: God, Man and Nature in C. S. Lewis's Narnia Tales.* Grand Rapids: Eerdmans, 1973.

Lochhead, Marion. *Renaissance of Wonder: The Fantasy Worlds of C. S. Lewis, J. R. R. Tolkien, George MacDonald, E. Nesbit and Others.* Edinburgh: Canongate, 1973; San Francisco: Harper & Row, 1977.

Manlove, C. N. *C. S. Lewis: His Literary Achievement.* New York: St. Martin's, 1987.

———. *Christian Fantasy: From 1200 to the Present.* Basingstoke; London: Macmillian, 1992.

Martin, Thomas L., ed. *Reading the Classics with C. S. Lewis.* Grand Rapids: Baker Academic; Carlisle, U.K.: Paternoster, 2000.

Menuge, Angus, ed. *Lightbearer in the Shadowlands: The Evangelistic Vision of C. S. Lewis*. Wheaton, Ill.: Crossway, 1997.

Mills, David, ed. *The Pilgrim's Guide: C. S. Lewis and the Art of Witness*. Grand Rapids: Eerdmans, 1998.

Myers, Doris. *C. S. Lewis in Context*. Kent, Ohio: Kent State University Press, 1994.

Nicholi, Armand M. *The Question of God: C. S. Lewis and Sigmund Freud Debate God, Love, Sex, and the Meaning of Life*. New York: Simon & Schuster, Free Press, 2002.

Otto, Rudolf. *The Idea of the Holy: An Inquiry into the Idea of the Divine and Its Relation to the Rational*. Translated by John W. Harvey. London: Oxford University Press, 1936.

Payne, Leanne. *Real Presence: The Holy Spirit in the Works of C. S. Lewis*. Eastbourne: Monarch, 1989.

Paterson, Katherine. *Bridge to Terabithia*. Illustrated by Donna Diamond. New York: Crowell, 1977.

Phillips, Justin. *C. S. Lewis at the BBC*. London: HarperCollins, 2002.

Purtill, Richard L. *C. S. Lewis's Case for the Christian Faith*. San Francisco: Harper & Row, 1982.

Purtill, Richard L. *Lord of the Elves and Eldils: Fantasy and Philosophy in C. S. Lewis and J. R. R. Tolkien*. Grand Rapids: Zondervan, 1974.

Reilly, Robert J. *Romantic Religion: A Study of Barfield, Lewis, Williams and Tolkien*. Athens: University of Georgia Press, 1971.

Ryken, Leland, James C. Wilhoit and Tremper Longman III, eds. *Dictionary of Biblical Imagery*. Downers Grove, Ill.; Leicester: InterVarsity Press, 1998.

Sammons, Martha A. *A Guide Through Narnia*. London: Hodder & Stoughton, 1979.

Sayer, George. *Jack: C. S. Lewis and His Times*. London: Macmillan, 1988.

Schakel, Peter J. *Reading with the Heart: The Way into Narnia*. Grand Rapids: Eerdmans, 1979.

————. *Reason and Imagination in C. S. Lewis: A Study of 'Till We Have Faces.'* Exeter: Paternoster, 1984.

Schmidt, Donald R., and Gary D. Hettinga, eds. *British Children's Writers*. Vol. 160 of *Dictionary of Literary Biography*. Detroit: Bruccoli Clark Layman, 1996.

Schofield, Stephen, ed. *In Search of C. S. Lewis*. New Jersey: Bridge, 1984.

Schultz, Jeffrey D., and John G. West Jr., eds. *The C. S. Lewis Readers' Encyclopedia*. Grand Rapids: Zondervan, 1998.

Sibley, Brian. *The Land of Narnia*. Illustrated by Pauline Baynes. London: Collins, 1989.

—————. *Shadowlands*. London: Hodder, 1985.

Spufford, Francis. *The Child That Books Built: A Life in Reading*. New York: Metropolitan Books, 2002.

Stone, Elaine Murray. *C. S. Lewis: Creator of Narnia*. New York: Paulist, 2001.

Tolkien, J. R. R. *Letters of J. R. R. Tolkien*. Edited by Humphrey Carpenter. London: George Allen and Unwin, 1981.

Tolkien, J. R. R. *Tree and Leaf*. 2nd ed. London: Unwin Paperbacks, 1988.

Urang, Gunnar. *Shadows of Heaven: Religion and Fantasy in the Writing of C. S. Lewis, Charles Williams and J. R. R. Tolkien*. London: SCM Press, 1970; Philadelphia: United Church Press, 1971.

Walker, Andrew, and James Patrick, eds. *A Christian for All Christians: Essays in Honour of C. S. Lewis*. London: Hodder, 1990.

Walsh, Chad. *C. S. Lewis: Apostle to the Skeptics*. New York: Macmillan, 1949.

—————. *The Literary Legacy of C. S. Lewis*. New York: Harcourt Brace Jovanovich, 1979.

Watson, George, ed. *Critical Essays on C. S. Lewis*. Aldershot, U.K.: Scolar, 1992.

White, William L. *The Image of Man in C. S. Lewis*. London: Hodder, 1970.

Wilson, A. N. *C. S. Lewis: A Biography*. London: Collins, 1990.

Index

For beings, places, things and events in Narnia see "The A-Z of Narnia," pages 165-217.